21st Century Beach Houses

Published in Australia in 2010 by
The Images Publishing Group Pty Ltd
ABN 89 059 734 431
6 Bastow Place, Mulgrave, Victoria 3170, Australia
Tel: +61 3 9561 5544 Fax: +61 3 9561 4860
books@imagespublishing.com
www.imagespublishing.com

Copyright © The Images Publishing Group Pty Ltd 2010
The Images Publishing Group Reference Number: 897

All rights reserved. Apart from any fair dealing for the purposes of private study, research, criticism or review as permitted under the Copyright Act, no part of this publication may be reproduced, stored in a retrieval system or transmitted in any form by any means, electronic, mechanical, photocopying, recording or otherwise, without the written permission of the publisher.

National Library of Australia Cataloguing-in-Publication entry:

Title:	21st century beach houses.
ISBN:	9781864703757 (hbk.)
Subjects:	Vacation homes.
	Seaside architecture.
Dewey Number:	728.72

Coordinating editor: Andrew Hall

Designed by The Graphic Image Studio Pty Ltd, Mulgrave, Australia
www.tgis.com.au

Pre-publishing services by United Graphic Pte Ltd, Singapore

Printed on 140 gsm GE Matt Art paper by Everbest Printing Co. Ltd.,
in Hong Kong/China

IMAGES has included on its website a page for special notices in relation to this and our other publications. Please visit www.imagespublishing.com.

21st Century Beach Houses

Andrew Hall

Contents

8   23 Breeze
R&D Architects

12   Acqua House
Middap Ditchfield Architects

16   Albarella House
Gabbiani & Associati

20   Albatross Residence
BGD Architects

24   Anglesea House
Andrew Maynard Architects

28   Anglesea Beach House
Emma Mitchell Architects

32   Back Beach House
watson architecture + design

36   Bay Residence
Stelle Architects

40   Bayview Beach Residence
Hammer Architects

44   Blairgowrie Residence
Leon Meyer Architects

48   Brighton House
SJB Architects

52   Cape Schanck House
Wolveridge Architects

56   Cloudy Bay House
1 + 2 Architecture

60   Compass Rose
Obie G. Bowman

64   The Cottage
Paul Uhlmann Architects

68   Elma Bay Residence
Helliwell + Smith: Blue Sky Architecture

72   Emu Bay House
Max Pritchard Architect

76   Freshwater House
Chenchow Little Pty Ltd

80   Greenant House
Middap Ditchfield Architects

84   Hermosa Beach House
KAA Design Group

88   Ingoldsby House
Seeley Architects

92   Island Beach House
Architects Ink

96   JZ House
Bernardes Jacobsen Arquitetura

100   Kenny House
Godward Guthrie Architecture

104   Le Fevre House
Longhi Architects

108   Martin House
Techne Architects

112   Metamorphosis
Ulloa Davet + Ding

116   Mount Eliza House
Graham Jones Design

120   Northwood House
Cullinan Ivanov Partnership

124   Ocean House
Olson Kundig Architects

128   Ocean View House
Bromley Caldari Architects

132   Ocean Weekender
Graham Jones Design

136   Onetangi House
Stevens Lawson Architects Ltd

140	Palmasola Girvin Associates and Manolo Mestre	
144	Parmela Residence Paul Uhlmann Architects	
148	Peloponnese House Alexandros N. Tombazis and Associates Architects Ltd	
152	Peregian Beach House Middap Ditchfield Architects	
156	Phillip Island Beach House Pleysier Perkins	
160	Portrane Residence Damien Murtagh Architects	
164	Point Dume Residence Griffin Enright Architects	
168	Raumati Beach House Herriot + Melhuish: Architecture Ltd	
172	Rubinsztein House Rolf Ockert Design	
176	St George's Basin House Brian van der Plaat Design	
180	Sandhill House Max Pritchard Architect	
184	Seola Beach House Eggleston Farkas Architects	
188	She Oak Beach House Base Architecture	
192	Sorrento House F2 Architecture	
196	Southampton Beach House Alexander Gorlin Architects	
200	Spotted Gum Beach House Jolson	
204	Stonington House Estes/Twombly Architects	
208	Sunrise Beach House Wilson Architecture	
212	Sunshine Beach Residence Bark Design Architects	
216	Tigh na Dobhran studioKAP	
220	Treehouse Jackson Clements Burrows Pty Ltd Architects	
224	Truro Residence ZeroEnergy Design	
228	Tuckeroo Residence Paul Uhlmann Architects	
232	Villa Shambhala RAD Architecture, Inc.	
236	Villa Surgawi Graham Jones Design/Manguning Architects	
240	Waimarama House Herriot + Melhuish: Architecture Ltd	
244	Wallace Marshall House Arthouse Architecture Ltd.	
248	Wamberal Beach House Virginia Kerridge Architect	
252	Whale Beach House Cullen Feng	
256	Zeidler House Ehrlich Architects	
261	Index of Architects	

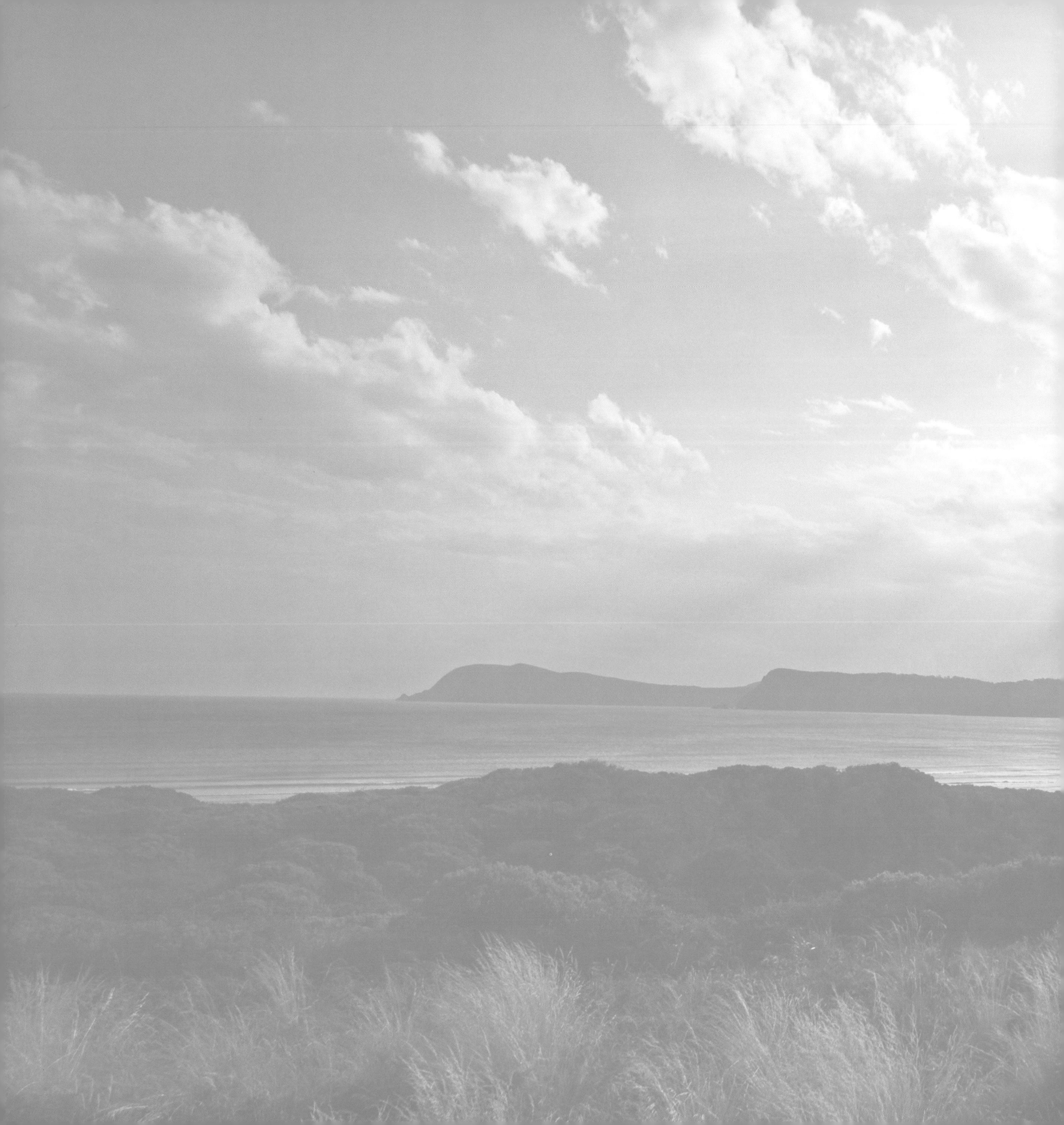

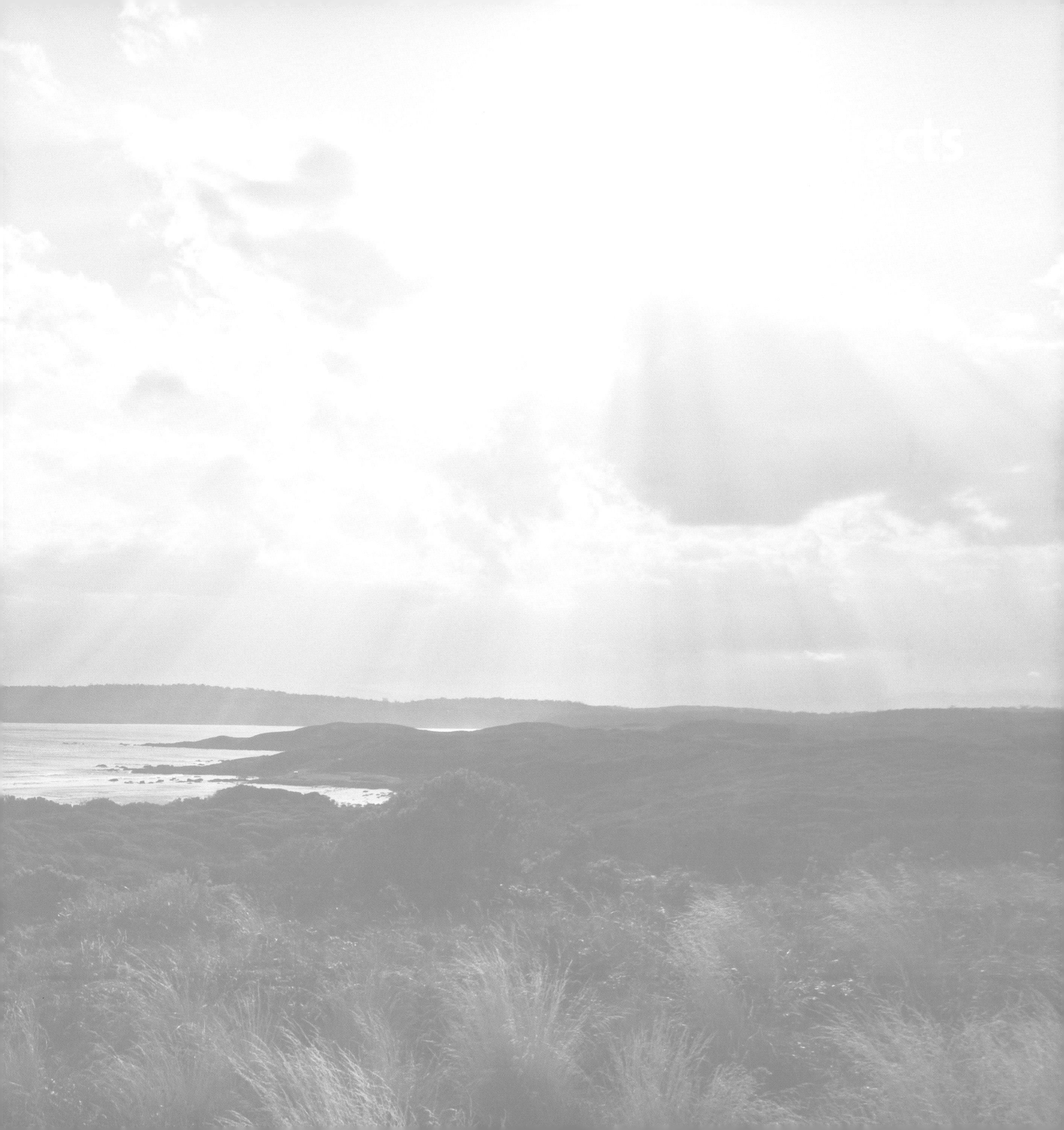

23 Breeze

Venice, California, USA
R&D Architects, David Reddy AIA and Betty Duffy

Located on the appropriately named Venice Walk, this 3,000-square-foot house consciously reflects and reacts toward its site. The first floor and roof function as hybrid public–private spaces that allow the inhabitants to connect with the vibrant energy of Venice Beach while still enjoying privacy from the street. On the second floor, the design utilizes a mirrored plan to create two double-height volumes that open public spaces to abundant light, sea air, and coastal views.

One of these volumes faces the beach and boardwalk, while the other fronts the gritty urban fabric of the city. The private bedrooms located on the third floor are cool, quiet retreats from the buzz and heat that radiate from the beach below. A final unifying element is the cement panel façade, which provides a colorful canvas created by artist Nancy Monk that energizes the architectural form and simultaneously offers public art to the community. Green and environmentally conscious features of the house include solar radiant floors, photovoltaic energy panels, and renewable and recyclable materials used throughout.

Photography by Benny Chan – Fotoworks

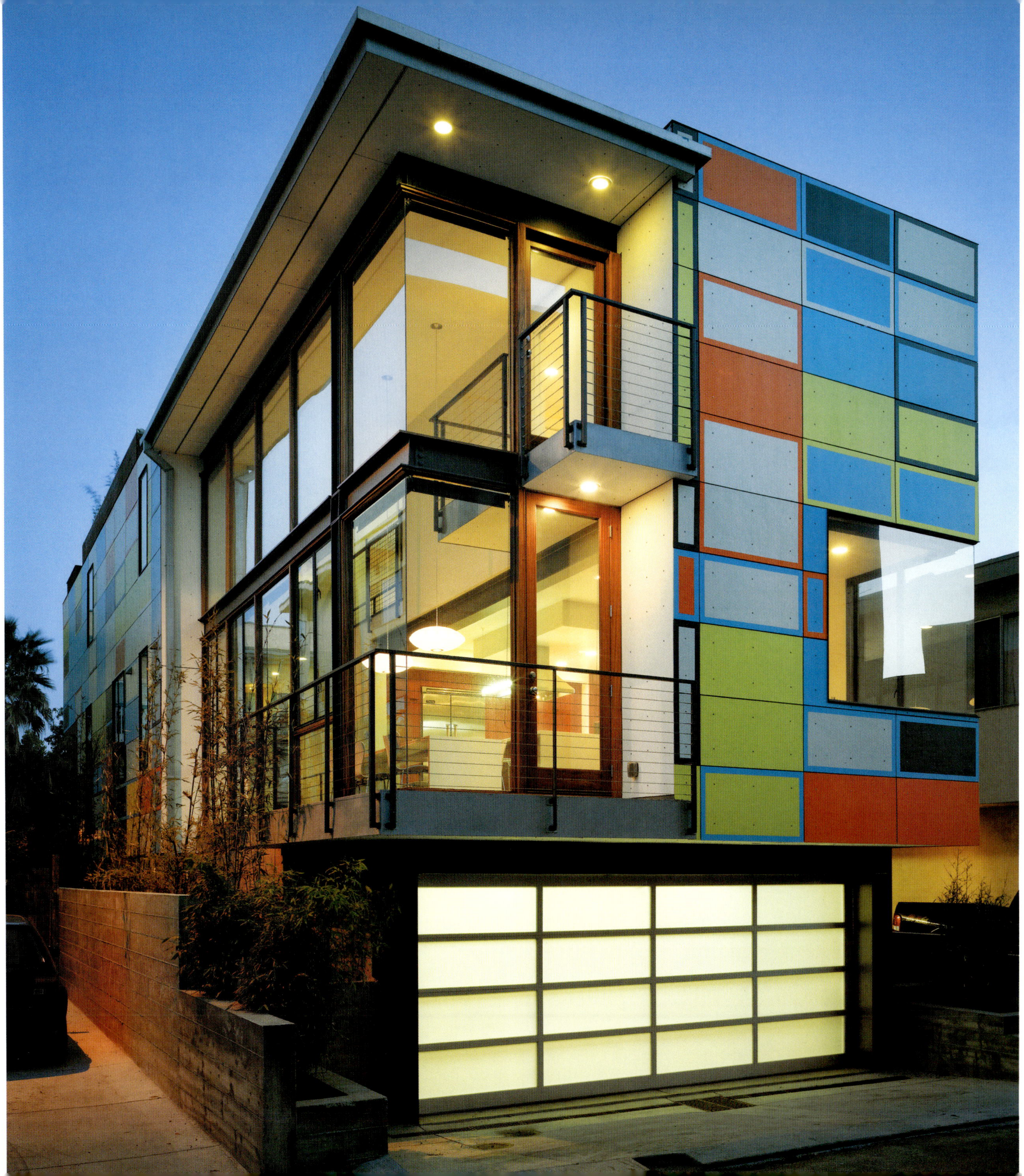

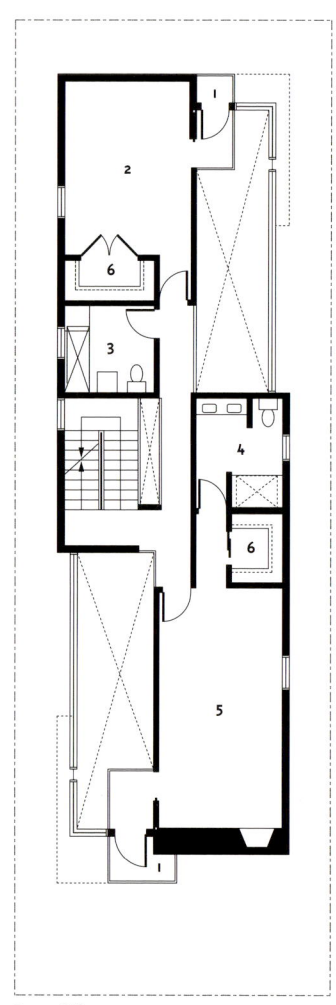

Second floor

1. Balcony
2. Bedroom
3. Bathroom
4. Master bathroom
5. Master bedroom
6. Closet

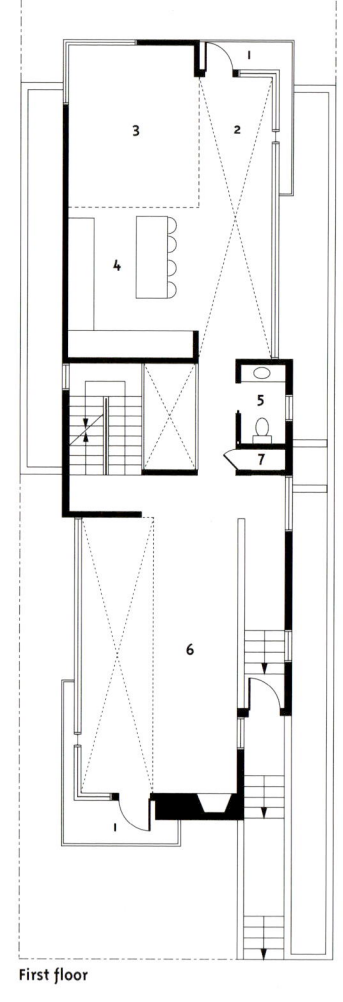

First floor

1. Balcony
2. Dining
3. Family
4. Kitchen
5. Bathroom
6. Living
7. Closet

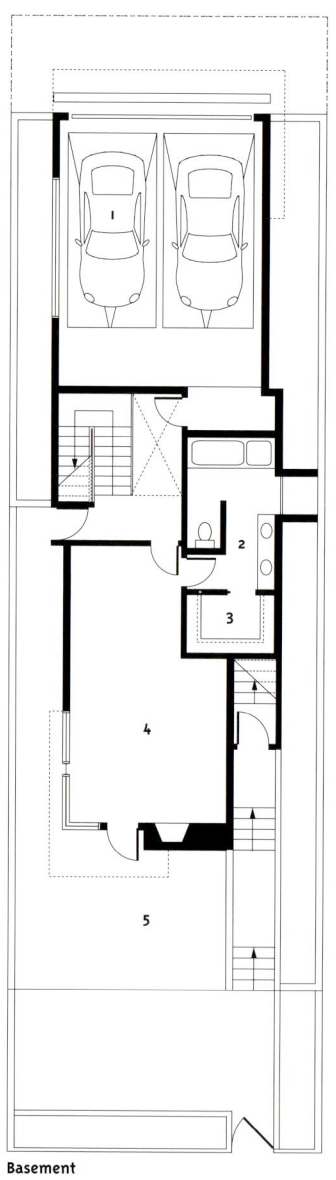

Basement

1. Garage
2. Bathroom
3. Closet
4. Bed
5. Garden

23 Breeze

Acqua House

Agnes Water, Queensland, Australia
Middap Ditchfield Architects

The core idea for this house was to establish a central veranda living space that included a swimming pool and focused on a north-facing landscaped courtyard providing views through the building to the ocean. The owner placed strong emphasis on being able to relax and enjoy this vacation house with young children, which led to the house being single level with easy surveillance/visual connection to the major internal and external spaces.

The site's ridge-top location is characterized by an almost-level area that drops away to a steep slope facing the ocean. Accordingly, the house is located within this level area to avoid disturbing the ground and ensure that the building connects closely to the site. The structure is lightweight and features pad footings to ensure minimum site excavation. The roof form is broken with a central high-level roof that links to lower roof sections and helps reduce building bulk.

As the site is in a relatively remote location with limited building resources, an early decision was made to design a lightweight building, with carpentry as the major trade and featuring prefabricated structural componentry. The house is located in a cyclone-prone area and the central steel portal frame structure was developed with the structural engineer to meet tie-down and bracing requirements but also to allow maximum uninterrupted glazing and transparency to the main living/kitchen wing.

Photography by Aperture Photography

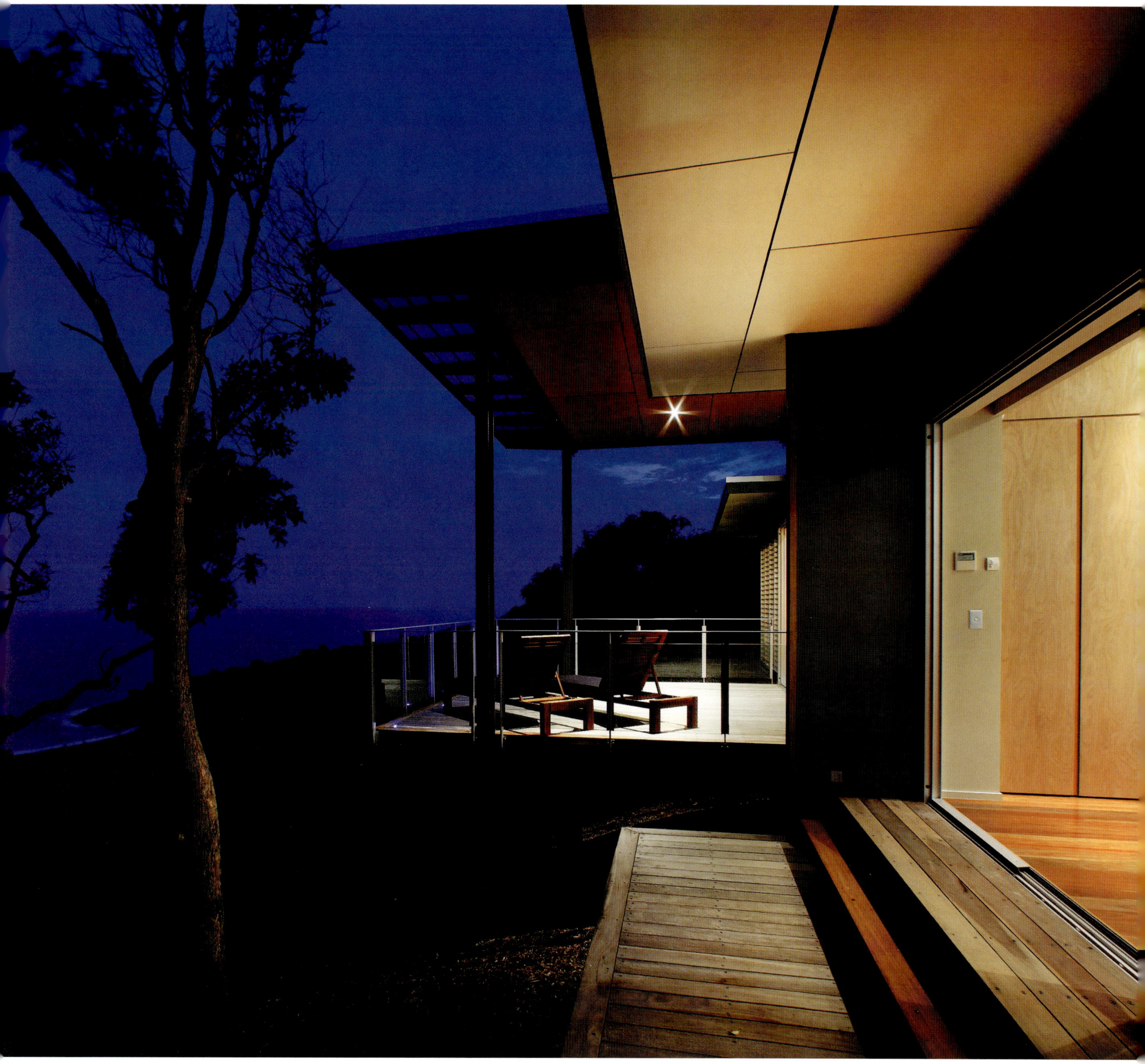

1 Entry
2 Deck
3 Living
4 Kitchen
5 Master bedroom
6 Bedroom
7 Office
8 Ensuite
9 WC
10 Bathroom
11 Laundry
12 Garage
13 Store
14 Effluent tanks
15 Driveway
16 Pool
17 Water feature
18 Barbecue

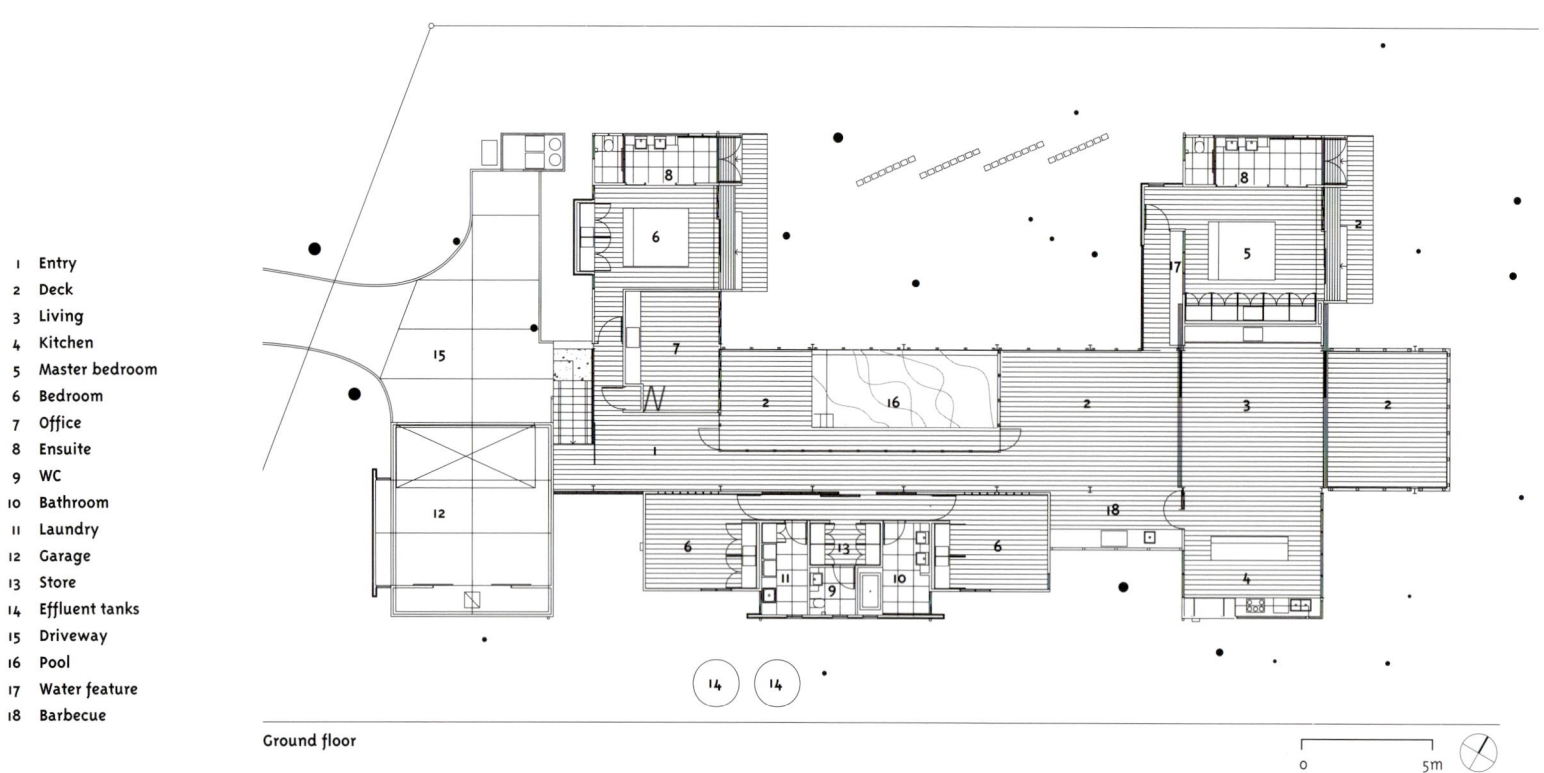

Ground floor

15

Acqua House

Albarella House

Albarella Island, Venice, Italy
Gabbiani & Associati

This holiday house is on Albarella Island, a small privately owned island south of the Venetian Lagoon, between Venice and Ravenna. The island, connected to the mainland by a private causeway, comprises hotels, private villas, a sports center, and beach and golf clubs.

Taking advantage of the double waterfront site, the house is split into three interconnected volumes. Seamless integration between indoors and outdoors is achieved through wide glass walls, and continuity of flooring and finishing materials. Each of the three volumes connects with its surrounds through a different approach, depending on its orientation, the type of landscape it overlooks, and its function.

The western volume, which connects with the nature reserve, houses the living quarters on a single floor composed almost entirely of glass walls. The double-height entrance volume acts as a type of hinge between the other two. The two-story eastern volume, the furthest from the water, contains the sleeping quarters and bathrooms. The curved roof forms integrate gracefully into the landscape, recalling the shape of the sand dunes on the Adriatic coast.

Photography by Arnaldo Dal Bosco and Gabbiani & Associati

17

18

Albarella House

Albatross Residence

Gold Coast, Queensland, Australia
BGD Architects

Situated on an exclusive residential street, this house successfully achieves its own oasis by capturing beachfront vista and access while maintaining a private yet expansive pool and entertaining core. It is designed to accommodate a growing family, multiple guests, and frequent entertaining. The interiors were designed by Edge Design and Interiors.

Entry to the residence is via a recycled timber colonnade and gatehouse that grants covered access to both wings of the house. A glazed hallway wraps the central courtyard on both the ground and first floor, allowing scenic circulation past the main amenities and providing aesthetic flow through the timber stair. Louvered glazing has been utilized throughout the home to control ventilation by natural breezes.

The internal and external palette of finishes, including natural timbers and stone, creates a tropical, modern, and comfortable ambience. External finishes of recycled timber, natural stone, and copper were chosen to allow the property to further develop character over time. Tall mature trees matching the scale of the house are intentionally located about the property to frame the beachfront, main entrance, and internal courtyard. Lighting of the landscape at night creates drama within the timber battens and palm fronds, backed by the ambient aqua glow of the swimming pool.

Photography by Remco Jansen

21

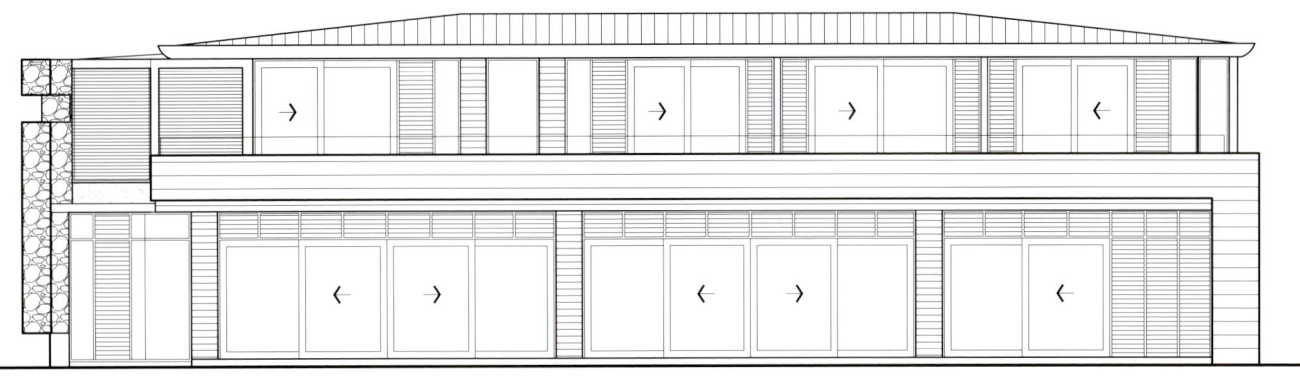

22

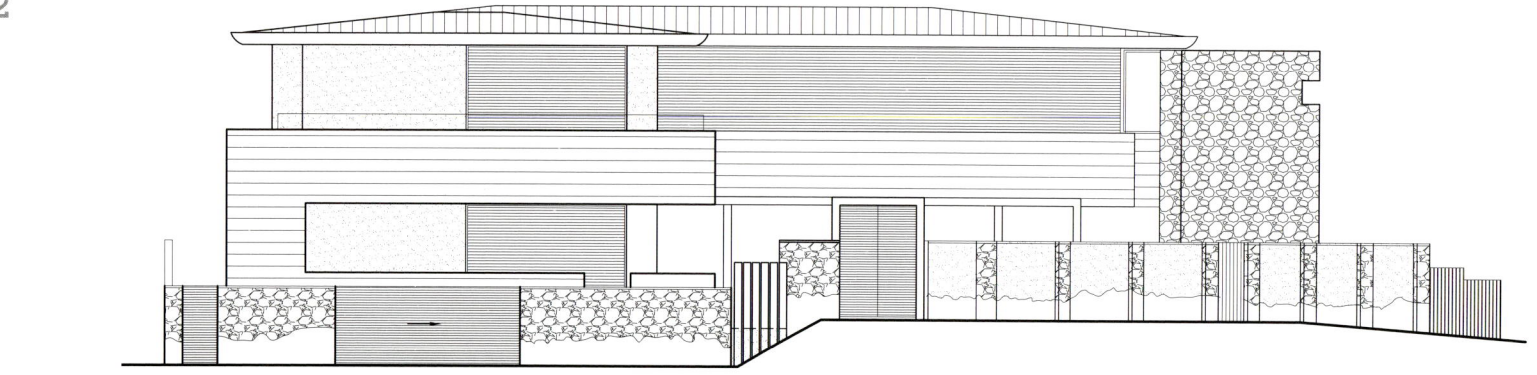

Albatross Residence

Anglesea House

Anglesea, Victoria, Australia
Andrew Maynard Architects

This beach house addition and renovation is a celebration of the iconic Australian beach shack. Conceived as a multi-generational vacation home, the project has versatile spaces that allow simultaneous use by a large extended family. The northern addition replaces an old timber deck that previously divided the two stories. The trafficable roof of this addition is now extruded down to the earth, creating a 10-foot-thick deck and grounding the entire house to the site. This "thick deck" was then carved out to allow the space within to become habitable areas. The spaces to the north can be opened up entirely to the surrounding bush block. Sliding windows above the daybed are concealed within the structure when open, and full-height glazed doors to the north and west allow sun to penetrate deep into the interior.

Other, carefully located "timber boxes" appear on the southern and eastern edges of the existing structure. The southern addition is glass roofed and contains a walled shower, while the eastern structure nestles under the existing carport, providing external storage space and a children's bunk retreat.

A spotted gum deck surrounds the new footprint. The grainy, soft brown tone of the hardwood allows the additions to melt into the surrounding eucalypts and tussock grass. Throughout the day, the addition's timber façades produce a harmonious connection with its surroundings, while at night the internal lights amplify the bold color scheme, giving the structure an almost synthetic and rendered appearance.

Photography by Peter Bennetts

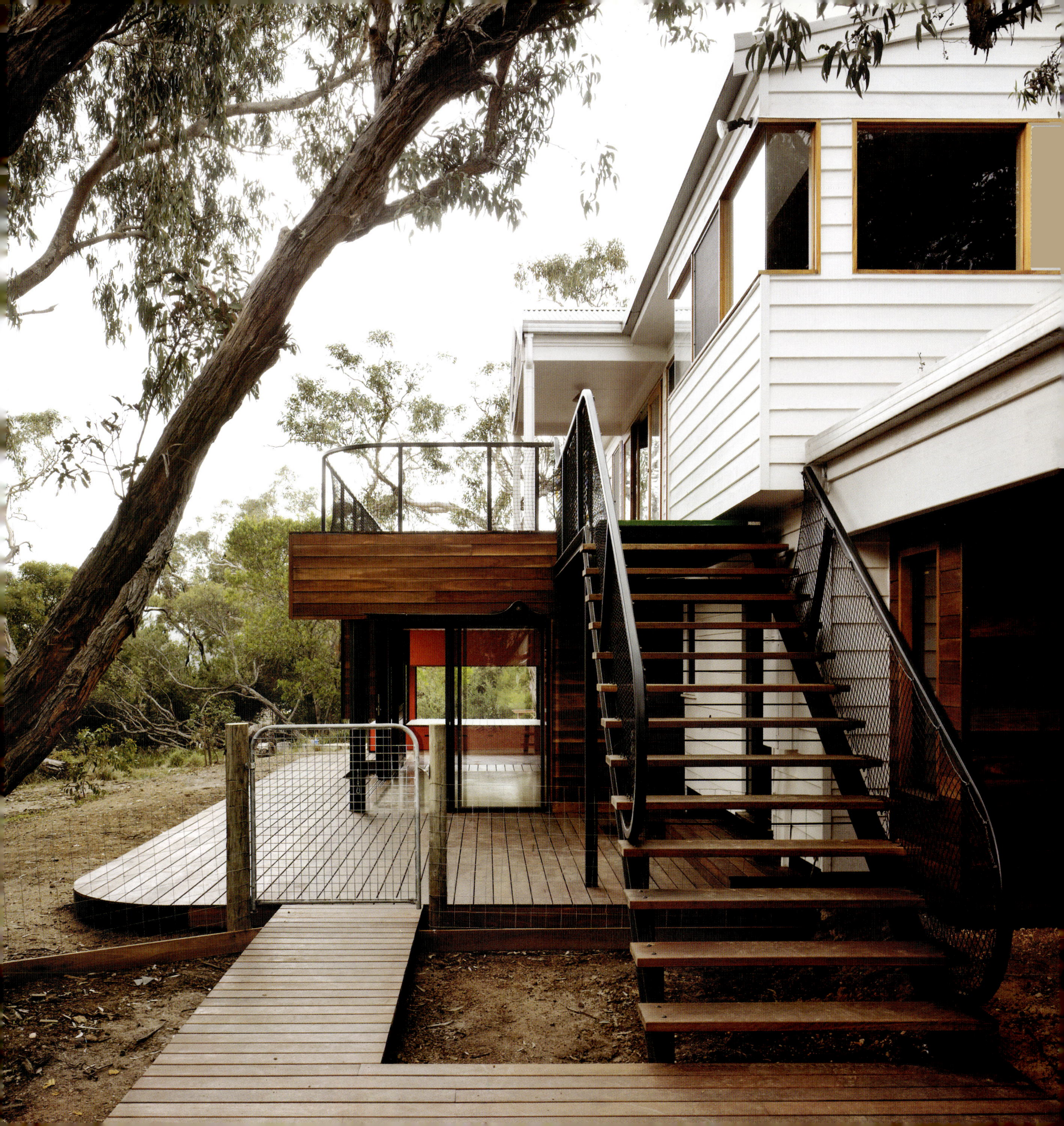

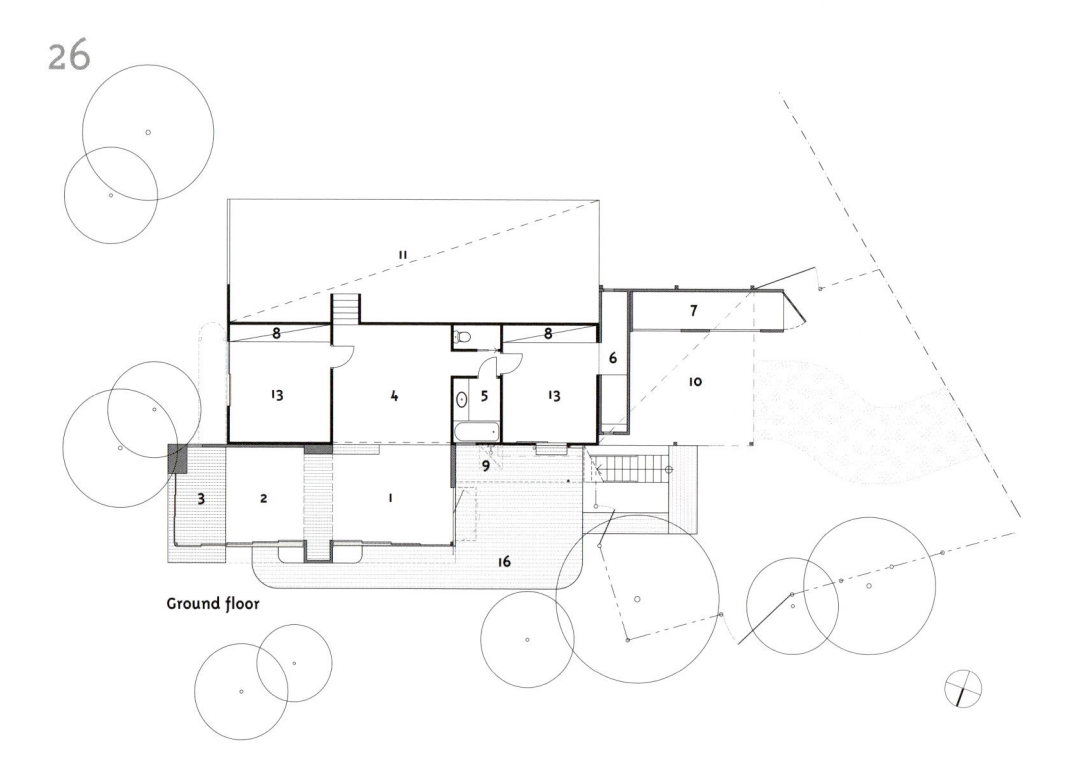

Ground floor

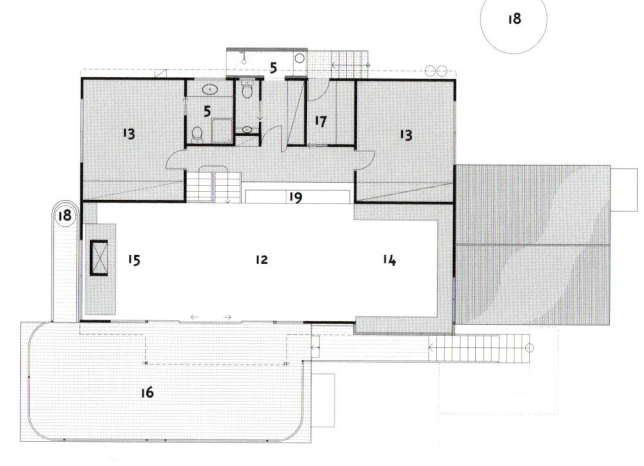

First floor

1	Games room	8	Closet	15	Fireplace
2	Bedroom	9	Surf shower	16	Deck
3	Daybed	10	Existing car port	17	Laundry
4	Family	11	Subfloor of existing building	18	Water tank
5	Bathroom	12	Existing living	19	Joinery
6	Bunk box	13	Existing bedroom		
7	Storage	14	Existing kitchen		

Anglesea House

Anglesea Beach House

Anglesea, Victoria, Australia
Emma Mitchell Architects

Intended as a vacation house that can be used the whole year round, the building needed to accommodate a large extended family as comfortably as a single couple. An important element of the design brief was to free up an additional ground floor bedroom and rumpus room so that the owners' teenage sons could have their own living spaces separate from the adult areas on the floor above.

To maximize opportunities for social gatherings and entertaining, a large dining table was incorporated in the kitchen design. Areas of built-in seating, the sun room, and the east deck all provide overflow spaces and alternate seating areas for times when the house is filled with people. The first floor areas are filled with an abundance of natural light and the living and dining spaces frame views over moonah trees and the beach dunes, ensuring a strong connection between interior and exterior

A covered entry for this house, designed with timber battens, references nearby tracks leading through a dense area of mature moonah trees to the beach. The house features a simple palette of materials, including pegboard wall panels, polycarbonate sliding screens, laminate, and blackbutt and cedar windows and doorframes. Cement sheet cladding with grayed timber battens is used, which complements the surrounding older style beach houses and moonah trees.

Photography by Dianna Snape

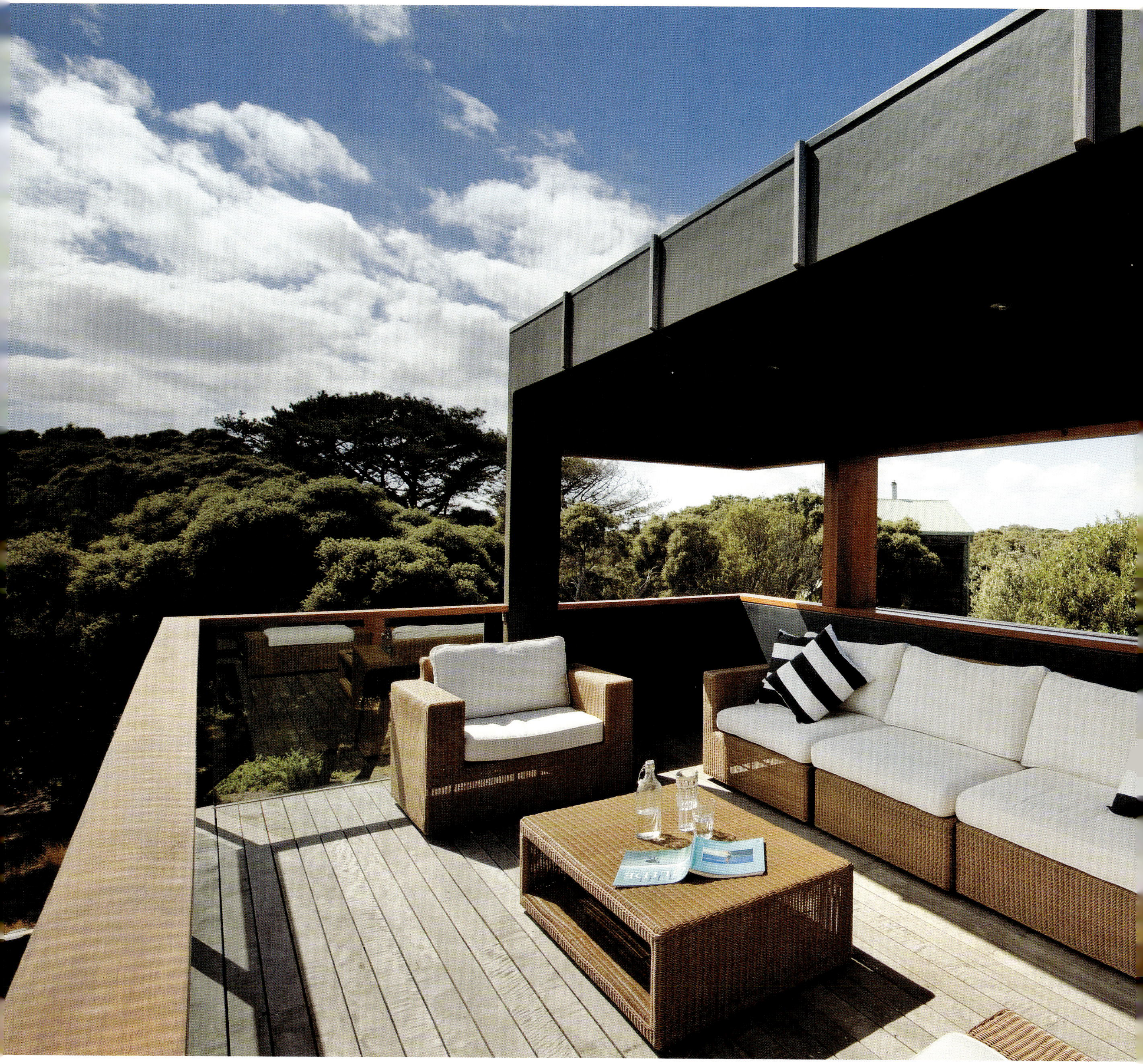

Ground floor

First floor

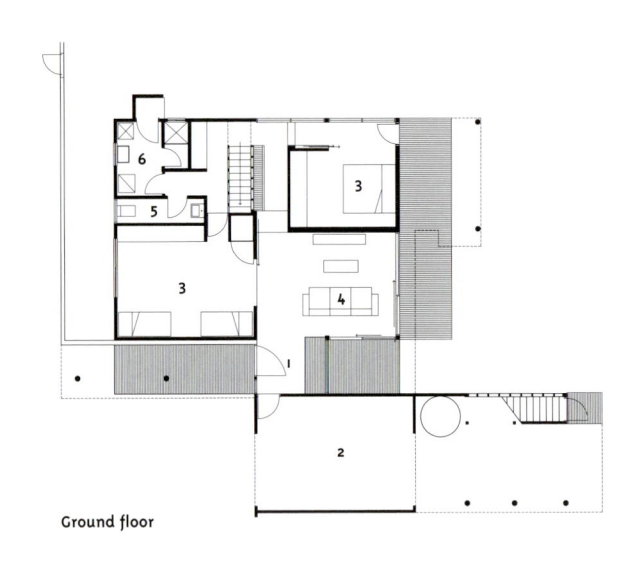

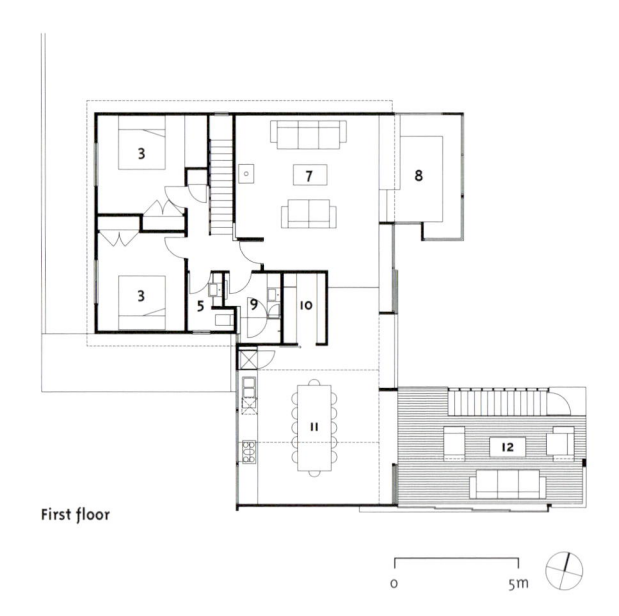

0 5m

1. Entry
2. Garage
3. Bedroom
4. Rumpus
5. WC
6. Laundry
7. Living
8. Sunroom
9. Bathroom
10. Pantry
11. Kitchen/dining
12. Deck

Anglesea Beach House

Back Beach House

Portsea, Victoria, Australia
watson architecture + design

This split-level house on a 23,000-square-foot block of land comprises a master bedroom and ensuite, two large bedrooms with a shared central bathroom, and a large open-plan living, dining, and kitchen area that opens fully to large north- and west-facing decks. Below the living areas are an underground parking space, laundry, and storage areas.

The design brief was to create an informal ambience to ensure that it would be as comfortable and easy to maintain by one person as it would by ten. The owner also requested that there should be distinct private and communal areas and wanted openable communal areas to blur the threshold between interior and exterior. The architect's response was to explore the idea of private and communal living by having these functions in two totally separated zones. This was achieved by placing the areas in separate pavilions linked by a series of exterior timber decks. All the floors, decking, and timber cladding in the house is recycled timber that was once used as the seating for a large sports stadium, and massive laminated jarrah wall columns are recycled timbers that 50 years ago comprised the roof beams in a warehouse in Perth.

Photography by Earl Carter

33

Ground floor

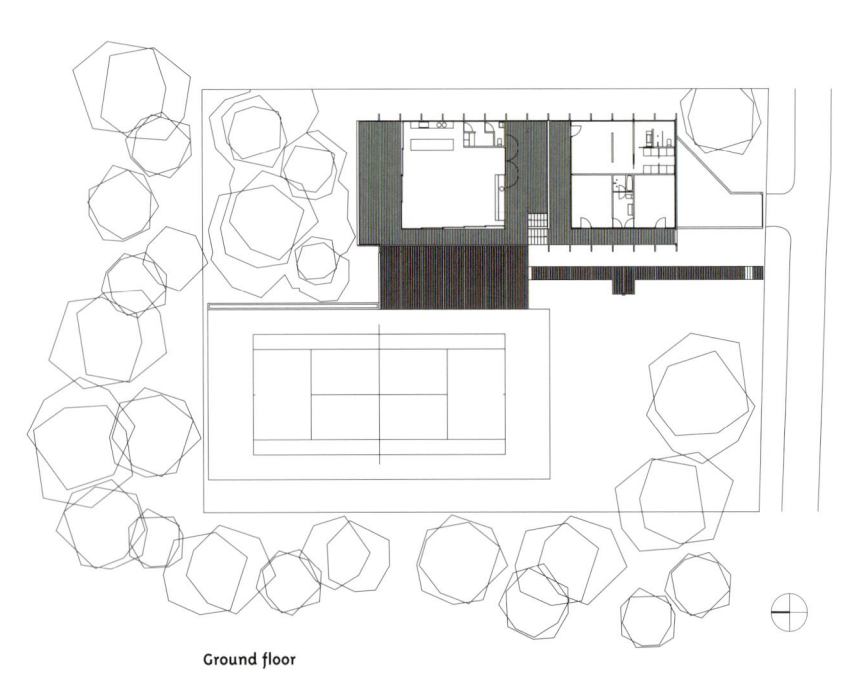

Back Beach House

Bay Residence

Eastern Long Island, New York, USA
Stelle Architects

This waterfront property unfolds in a sequence of views—both revealed and concealed—and was conceptualized as a kind of Kabuki shadow play that starts at the driveway and snakes down the entire length of the 5-acre lot. A narrow wooden boardwalk leads from the parking area up to and under the house, continues through a thicket of brambles, and ends at the beach. All plant materials used in the project were native species and have been orchestrated for maximum effect, and sand has been sculpted into wind-blown mounds surrounding the house. The main level is a 90-foot slab of glass and steel raised to gain water views and summer breezes. Specially fabricated screens of horizontal teak lattice break up the expanse of glass and serve as brise soleils, blocking the sun along the south side and providing privacy. A staircase is subtly concealed behind another wall of lattice and leads up to the main living area.

Inside, the house is furnished with Spartan restraint, ensuring that the views of water and wild sunsets are the real decoration. The central living area has been geared for entertaining with freestanding kitchen islands and a seating area clustered around a fireplace. A master bedroom suite lies to the east while guest rooms and a bathroom are located to the west. The central living area extends out towards a terrace with a swimming pool that spills over the edge of a retaining wall to form a gently splashing waterfall. In a protected corner beneath the house is a terrace with an open-air fireplace that provides shelter on rainy, blustery days.

Photography by Jeff Heatley

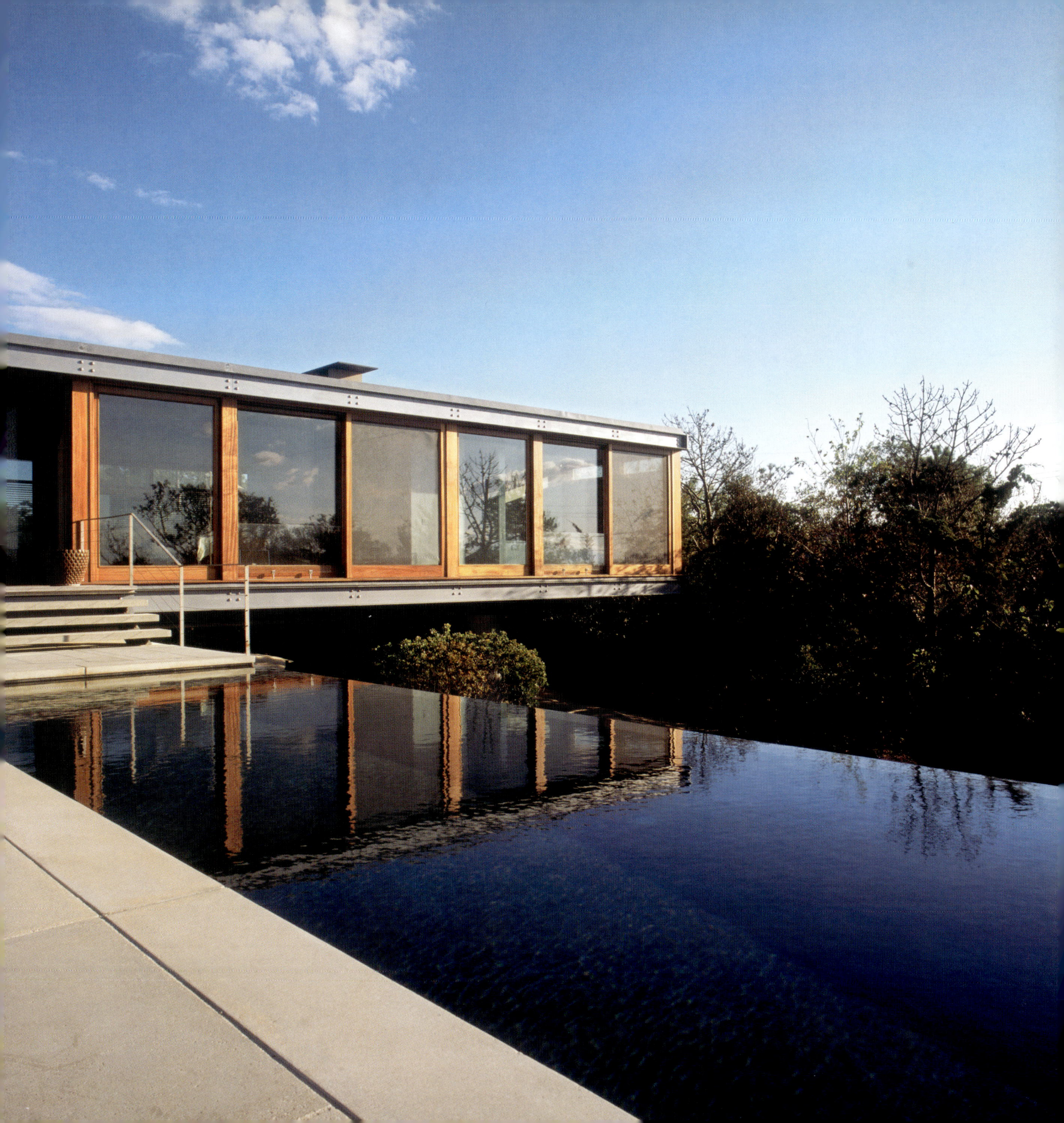

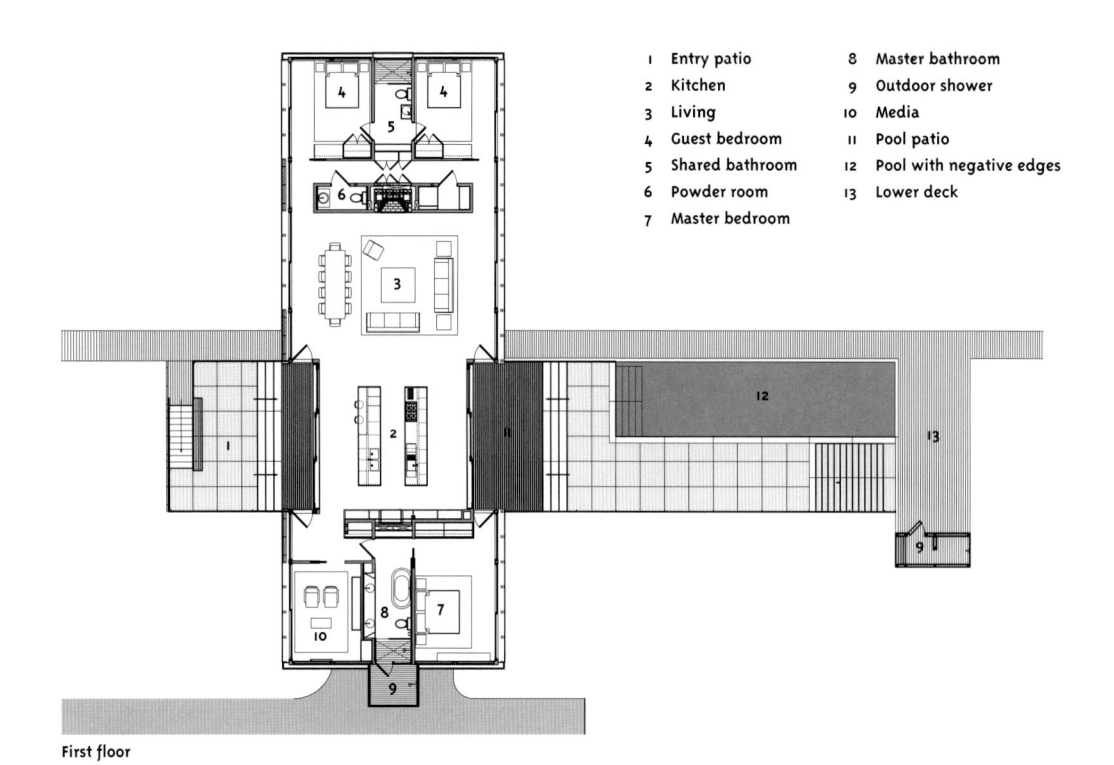

1	Entry patio	8	Master bathroom
2	Kitchen	9	Outdoor shower
3	Living	10	Media
4	Guest bedroom	11	Pool patio
5	Shared bathroom	12	Pool with negative edges
6	Powder room	13	Lower deck
7	Master bedroom		

First floor

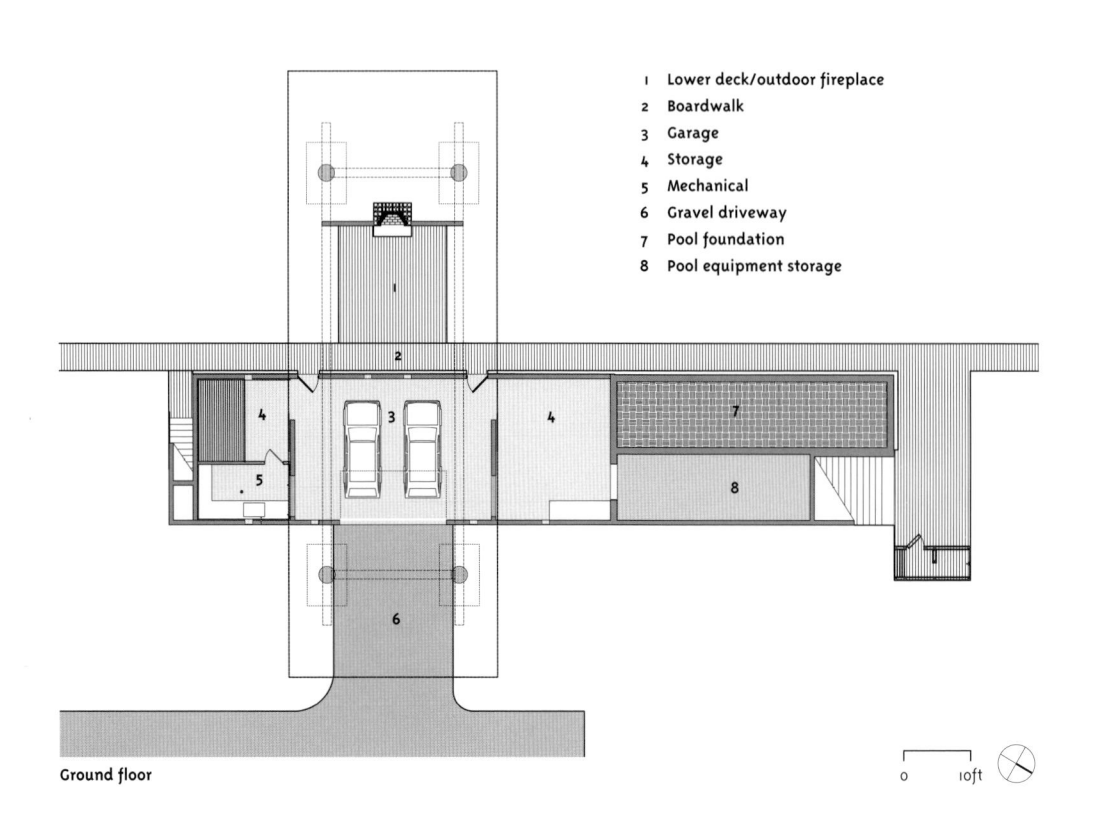

1	Lower deck/outdoor fireplace
2	Boardwalk
3	Garage
4	Storage
5	Mechanical
6	Gravel driveway
7	Pool foundation
8	Pool equipment storage

Ground floor

0   10ft

Bay Residence

Bayview Beach Residence

Wellfleet, Massachusetts, USA
Hammer Architects

This five-bedroom home is located on a coastal dune overlooking Cape Cod Bay. The design consists of comprehensive renovations and additions to a single-story 1960s modern house. The existing 30-square-foot footprint and foundation could only be altered on the non water-facing side, as the original structure was built within a 100-foot environmental conservation easement area.

The first floor was renovated to provide a living room, family room, dining room wing, and screened porch. The lower level includes a suite of three children's bedrooms and a playroom. Additional space was accommodated in the new second story, which comprises a master bedroom suite with its own private deck, guest bedroom, and home office. The smaller square addition on the front side accommodates the new interior stair and entry. An outdoor stair from the bluff was constructed to access a private beach.

The sunscreen structure shades the double-height living space and reduces heat gain, thereby eliminating the need for air-conditioning and significantly reducing energy consumption. Operable windows, sliding doors, and skylights permit natural ventilation by prevailing sea breezes, cooling the house.

Photography by Bill Lyons

41

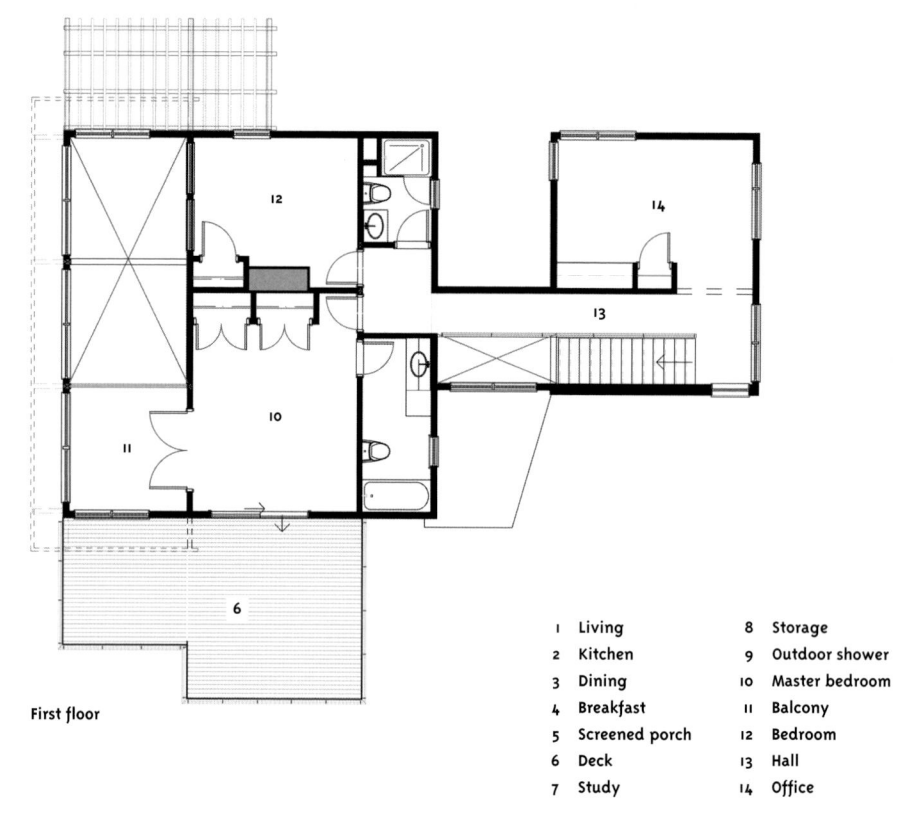

First floor

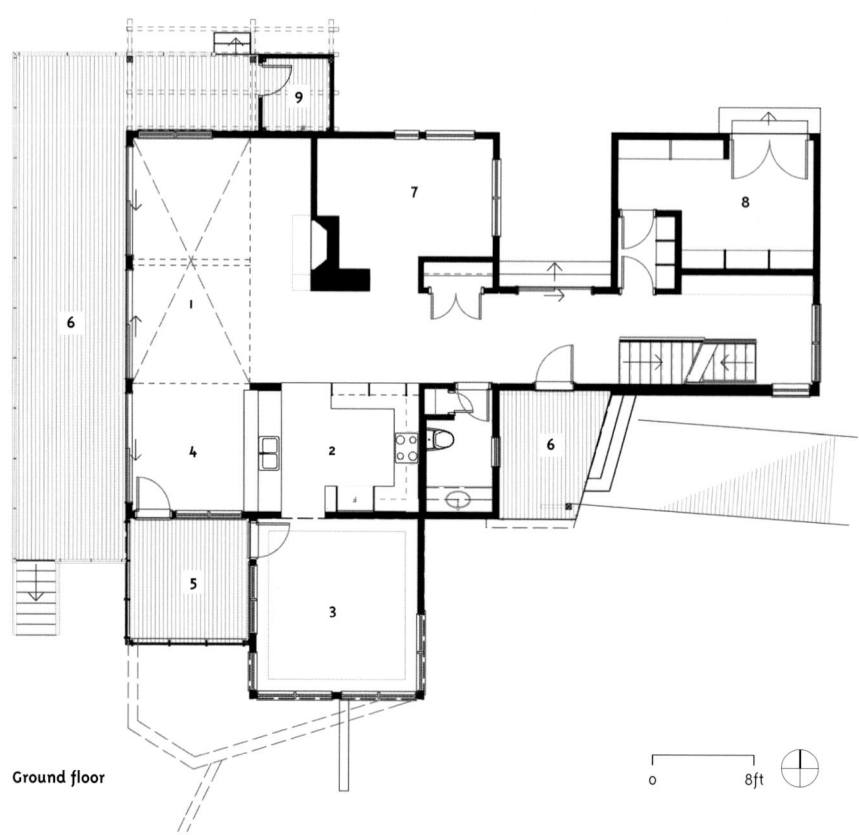

Ground floor

1	Living	8	Storage
2	Kitchen	9	Outdoor shower
3	Dining	10	Master bedroom
4	Breakfast	11	Balcony
5	Screened porch	12	Bedroom
6	Deck	13	Hall
7	Study	14	Office

0 8ft

Bayview Beach Residence

Blairgowrie Residence

Blairgowrie, Victoria, Australia
Leon Meyer Architects

The site of this two-story house was substantial enough to allow a resort-style complex of buildings that can accommodate a busy family's need for a recreational lifestyle. A drive-through boatshed with a car parking area is located at the front of the property, which is connected to a mid-level entry point of the house via a covered timber walkway through the bush. The house, which was built by Inform Design and Construction, is connected by a deck to the freestanding guest pavilion and the tennis court, and at another level links—via a covered external dining and barbeque area—to an elevated swimming pool. Adult and children's activity and sleeping areas are separated to ensure comfort and privacy, but are linked with a pivotal stairwell and a soaring, stone blade wall adjacent to the entry. The spacious kitchen links via a servery to the barbeque area, and the living areas open up and connect seamlessly with the various outdoor activity areas.

The building form draws on a simple, strong, and stark geometric shape that contrasts with the rolling landscape of the dunes and coastal bush habitat. This form is then diffused and articulated by the skeletal nature of the attached balconies, pergola, and sunshading elements. The composition further explores the interplay between forms and materials with the use of dark-stained plywood cladding and chunky timber battens, which contrast with the sharp industrial nature of galvanized steel framing for the balcony and pergola. The use of commercial aluminum windows and expansive areas of glass further reinforce this contradiction.

Photography by Andrew Lecky

45

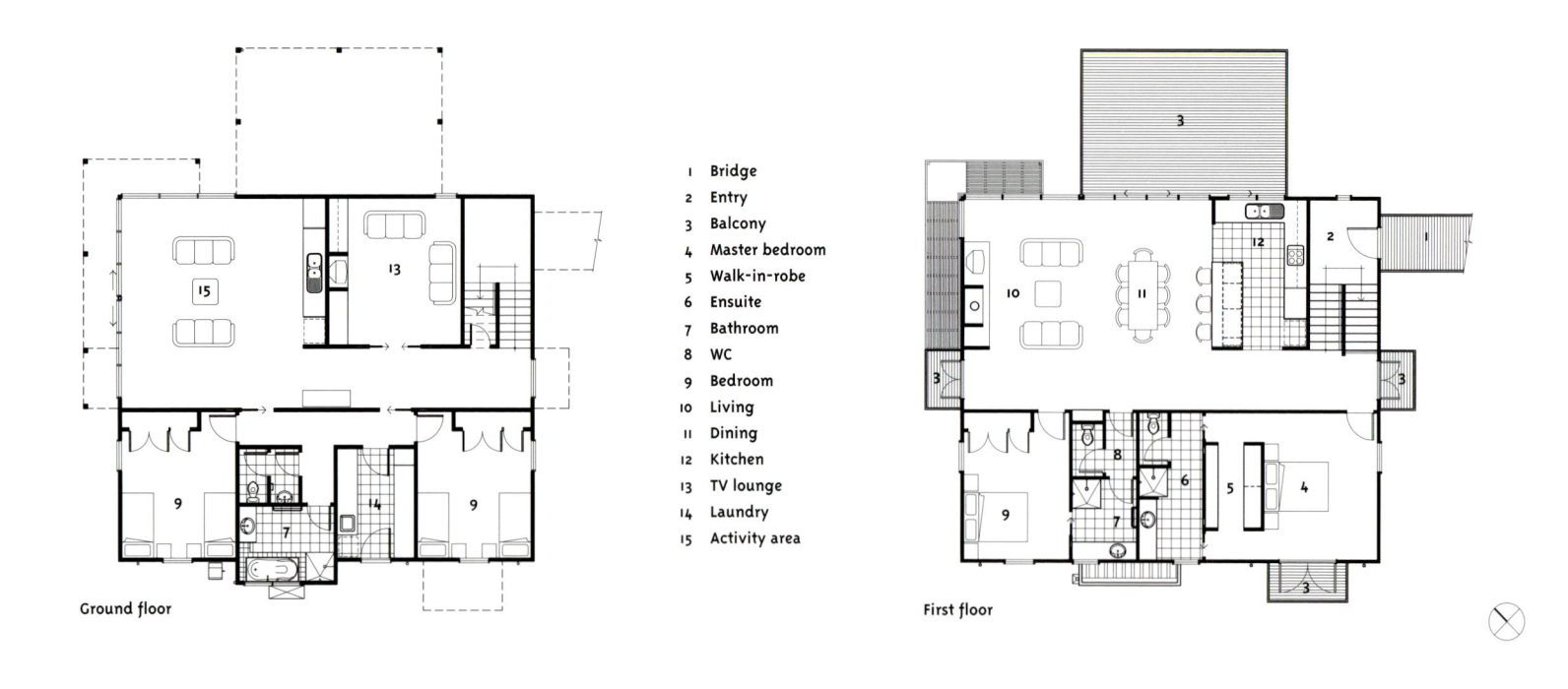

1   Bridge
2   Entry
3   Balcony
4   Master bedroom
5   Walk-in-robe
6   Ensuite
7   Bathroom
8   WC
9   Bedroom
10 Living
11 Dining
12 Kitchen
13 TV lounge
14 Laundry
15 Activity area

Ground floor

First floor

Blairgowrie Residence

Brighton House

Brighton, Victoria, Australia
SJB Architects

"One goes through the opening in a protective wall and comes to an inward looking environment of gardens and buildings. One feels protected and safe in calm surroundings." Guilford Bell

This adaptive re-use of a 1972 Guilford Bell Residence seeks to creatively transform the original house into a contemporary family home, while celebrating the strength, order and purity of Bell's original design.

The original house was superbly located by Bell to provide a generous northern exposure to all habitable rooms. Bell's signature motif of the perimeter colonnade became the primary external expression of the home. New additions were designed to be set back above the white colonnade. The eastern additions are pivoted around the central spiral stair and the new bedroom wing cantilevers parallel to the southern site boundary to create a sheltered arrival point.

Beyond the main entry door the central spiral stair rises dramatically within the foyer and opposite is an indoor–outdoor room with direct views over the garden and pool toward the horizon line. The views are framed by the original arched colonnade in whitewashed masonry, and the interface between the indoor and outdoor space is blurred.

The architects have approached this project in a boldly creative yet respectful manner, with innovative solutions to address the client's brief, while maintaining a level of humility and care in executing these solutions that will not only preserve the grandeur of Bell's 1972 proposition, but to do so in a contemporary manner suitable for an Australian family home.

Photography by Tony Miller

0   6m

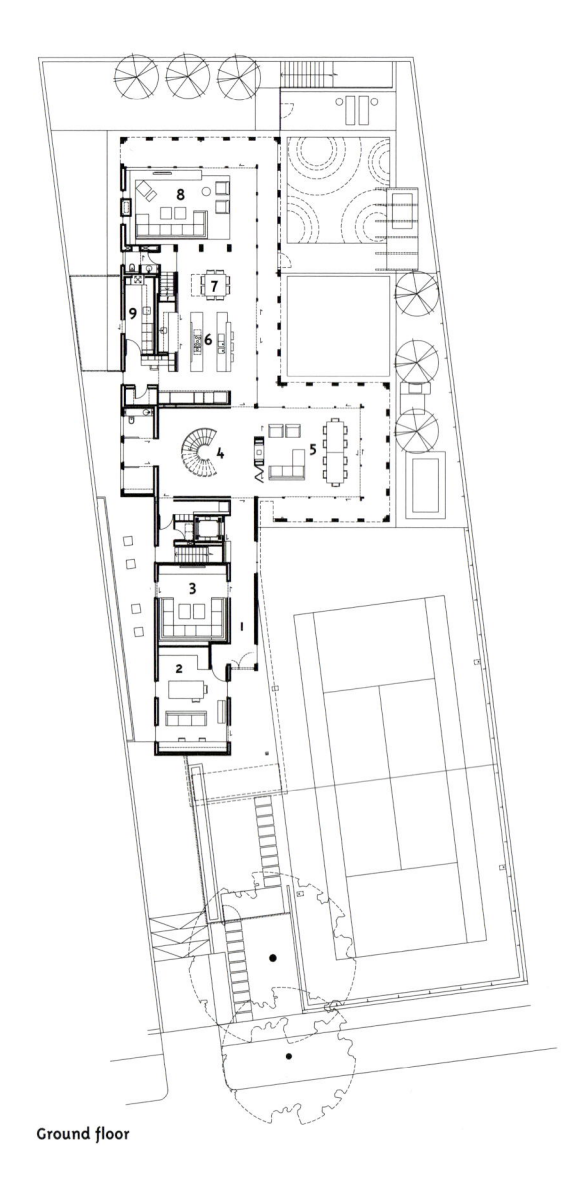

Ground floor

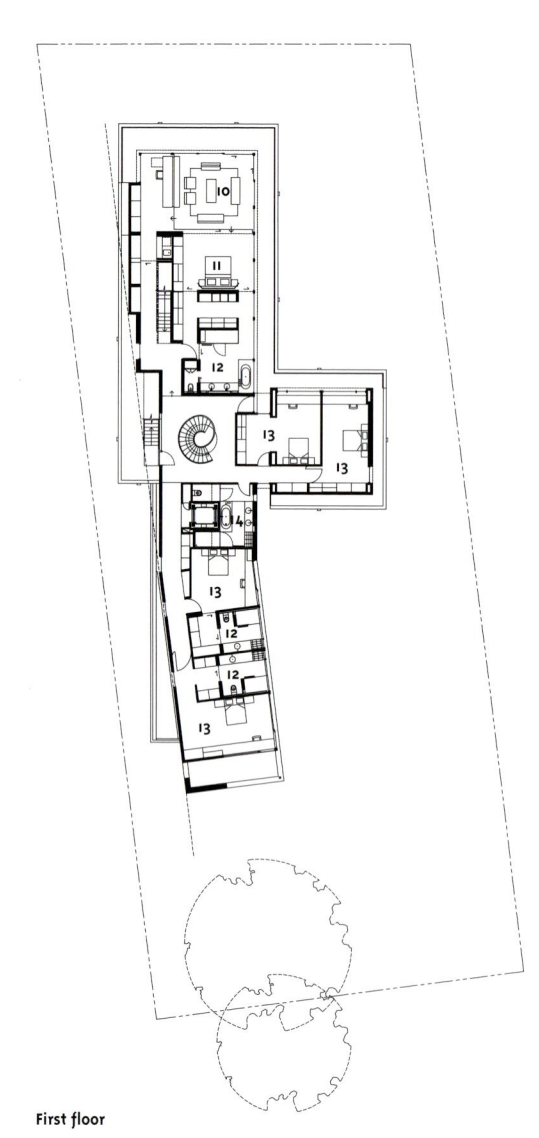

First floor

1	Entry hall	8	Living
2	Rumpus	9	Laundry
3	Media	10	Parents' retreat/study
4	Gallery	11	Master bedroom
5	Indoor/outdoor room	12	Ensuite
6	Kitchen	13	Bedroom
7	Dining	14	Bathroom

Brighton House

Cape Schanck House

Cape Schanck, Victoria, Australia
Wolveridge Architects

The architect designed this stunning, contemporary beach house to rest comfortably as an object in the rugged, coastal landscape. Set along a steep contour, the house is sited between an open and exposed street nature strip and an existing tennis court, with the building itself functioning as a retaining wall against the sloping site. A heavy concrete panel wall fronts the street, and the entry is marked by a dark-stained plywood box that punctures the front façade. In the context of its bushland setting, the concrete picks out the silver of the tea-trees and shimmers when soaked by rain.

To ensure privacy, windows and other openings are not visible from the street, and the front façade is intentionally cold and uninviting, not unlike the region's prevailing conditions. While the house purposefully turns its back on the public aspect, beyond the entry it unfolds as a light-filled, north-facing, and deceptively spacious building. Comprising a master bedroom, living areas, and connecting decks at the upper level, there is also space to park two cars and a golf cart. As the land falls away, further bedrooms and a large rumpus at the lower level have a greater connection with the site.

The west elevation incorporates 10-foot overhangs and the north-facing façade also features generous overhangs. The building is clad in materials typical to southern Australian coastal environments—stained, rough-sawn cedar cladding, naturally finished concrete panels, and sections of compressed sheet as a feature. The house has a four-star energy rating and includes insulated concrete panels, double-glazing, water tanks, and upgraded insulation.

Photography by Derek Swalwell Photography

53

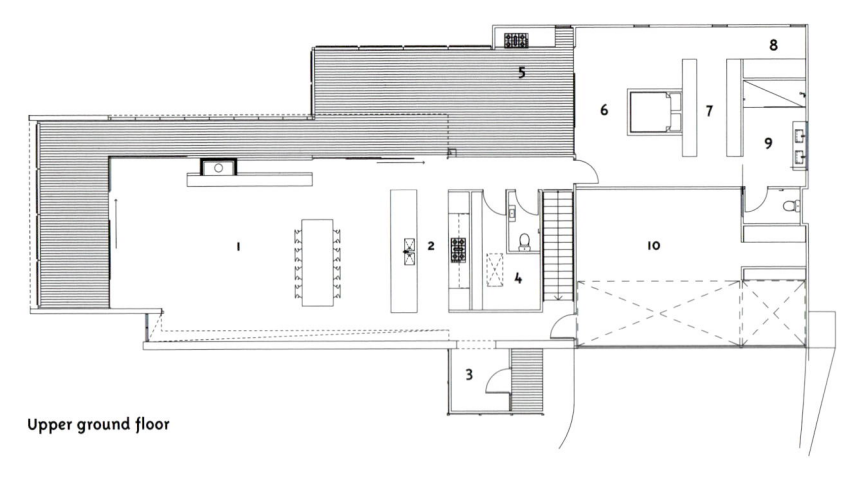

Upper ground floor

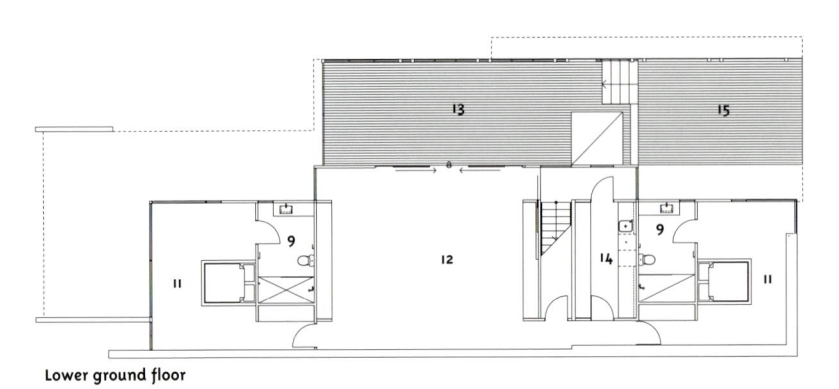

Lower ground floor

1	Lounge/dining	9	Ensuite
2	Kitchen	10	Garage
3	Entry	11	Bedroom
4	Pantry	12	Lounge/pool room
5	Barbecue	13	Deck
6	Master bedroom	14	Laundry
7	Robe	15	Undercroft play area
8	Study		

0   5m

Cape Schanck House

Cloudy Bay House

Cloudy Bay, Tasmania, Australia
1 + 2 Architecture

Located at the southern end of Bruny Island, this three-bedroom house was designed as a vacation home for its American owners. The 82-acre beachfront site comprises a combination of farmland and heath-covered coastal dune.

A primary objective for the architect was to create an appropriate intervention that minimized impact on native flora and the natural landscape while regenerating the landscape by removing weeds and pine tree remnants and reintroducing native species. The architect has balanced the conflicting objectives of achieving views to the landscape and ocean beyond while minimizing the imposition of the house in views back to the site from key public external view points.

Conceptually, the house comprises two primary zones interlinked in a conventional "bi-nuclear" plan. The two zones are conceived as an inversion of each other in terms of function and form—an open-plan, lightweight, transparent structure forms the living zone and a heavier, enclosed, protective structure organizes the sleeping zone. The two areas straddle a series of timber and concrete external decks strategically positioned in relation to adjacent internal areas, sun, specific views, and shelter from prevailing winds.

Materials were chosen for their environmental qualities, fitness for purpose, and appropriateness to the site and its context. An example is the use of macrocarpa cladding. This timber, harvested from redundant farm windbreaks, has excellent durability and has been left untreated, allowing a natural patina to develop.

Photography by Jonathan Wherrett

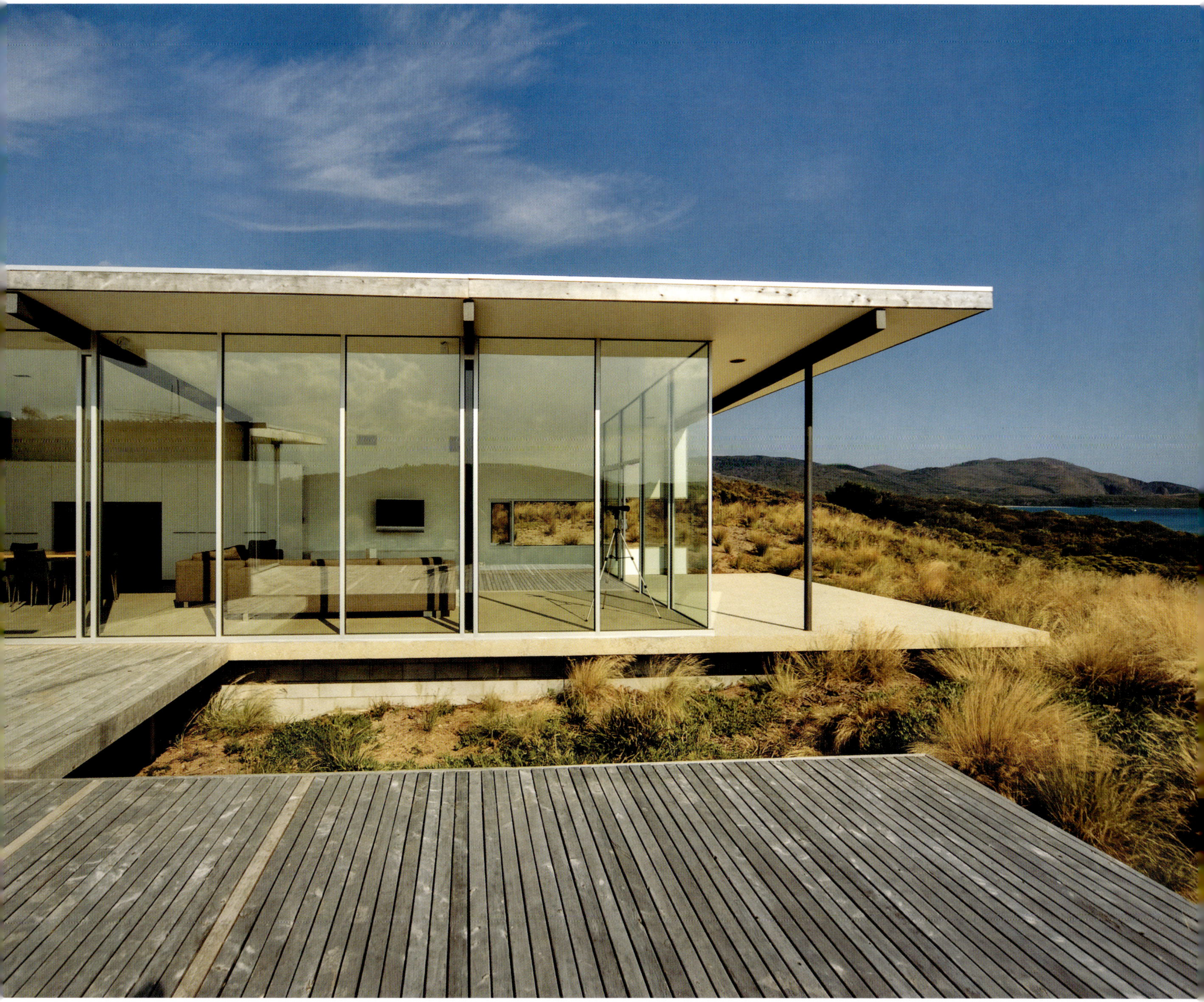

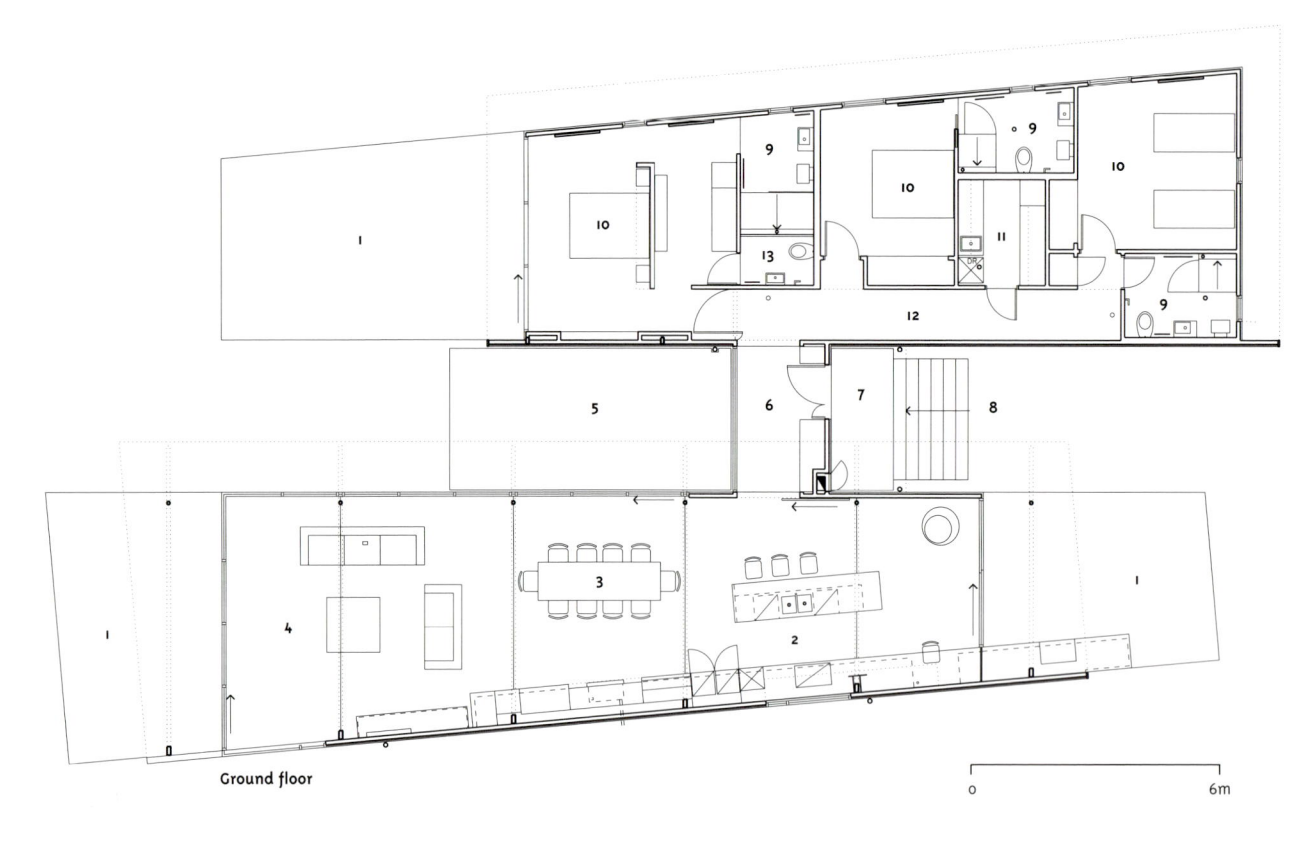

1 Deck
2 Kitchen
3 Dining
4 Living
5 Court yard
6 Entry
7 Porch
8 Stairs
9 Bathroom
10 Bedroom
11 Laundry
12 Passage
13 WC

Ground floor

0 6m

Cloudy Bay House

Compass Rose

California, USA
Obie G. Bowman

Located on a bluff-top lot with primary coastal views to the north and secondary coastal views to the south, this three-bedroom house includes an office, library, two-car garage, darkroom, and courtyard for a total of 2,500 square feet of heated space. The heavy timber-framed house bridges over the west side of a wind-protected courtyard to allow ocean views from the first-floor bedrooms and sitting room on the east side. A long corner solarium captures panoramic coastal views and sunlight while extending the living, dining, and kitchen areas toward the ocean. Natural ventilation and cooling are provided via an array of automated air intake vents and thermal exhaust chimneys.

The exterior walls comprise columns fixed to the foundation with horizontal girts bolted to them. Vertical decking spans between the girts with shear plywood, insulation, building paper, and redwood siding fastened to the exterior. The roof construction is similar—although thicker decking is used—and the end result is a wooden interior highly expressive of its structure and construction. All interior timber is Douglas fir, except for the floors, which are red ash. Floors on grade are exposed concrete or sun-dried Mexican pavers and the interior walls are painted gypsum wallboard.

Photography by Tom Rider

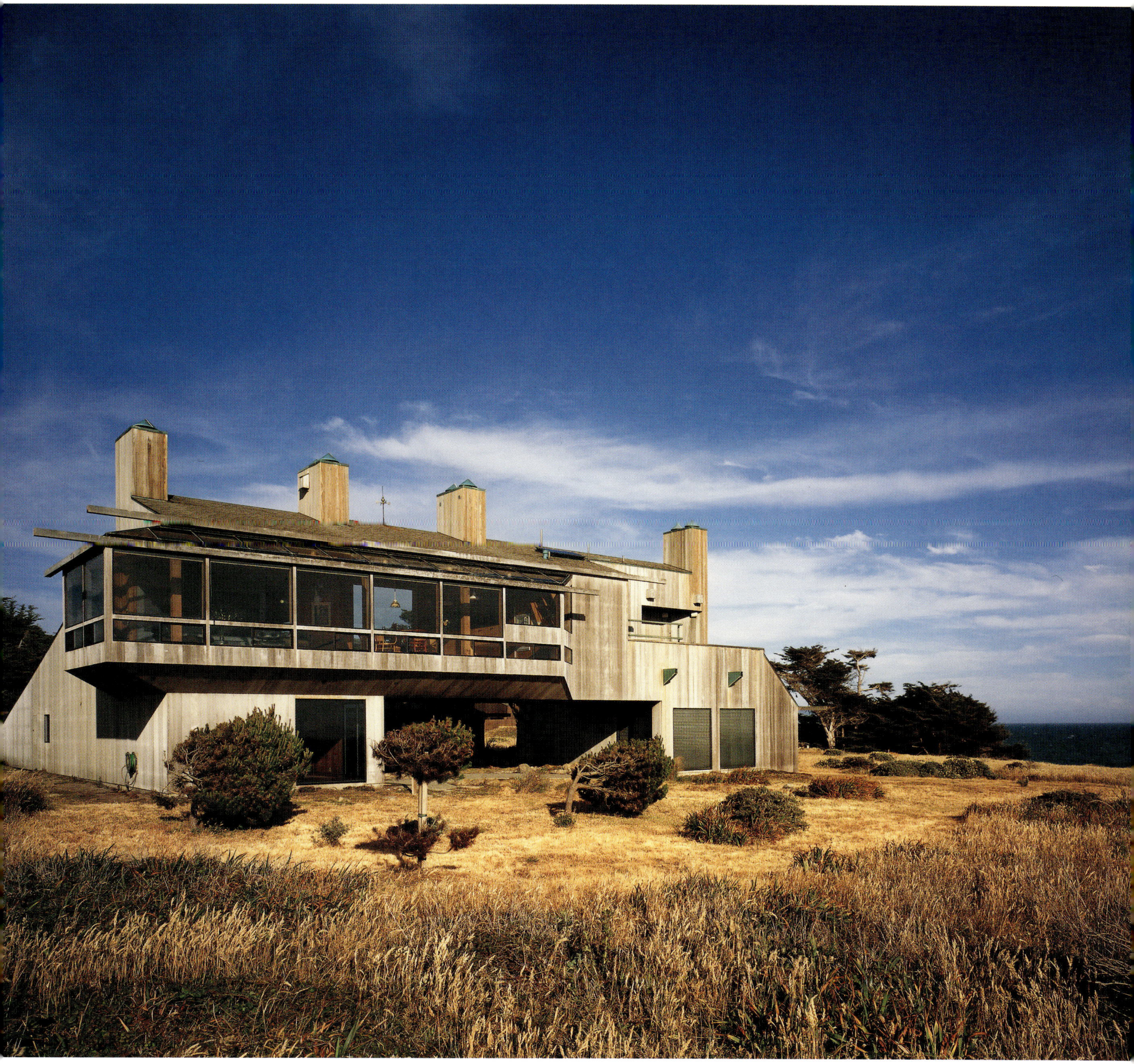

62

Compass Rose

The Cottage

Gold Coast, Queensland, Australia
Paul Uhlmann Architects

This beachfront house was designed as a weekend getaway for a busy city couple and their small children. The narrow site faces the ocean toward the east and is surrounded by dense residential development and medium-rise apartments. The design features a raised ground-floor living area that takes advantage of the diagonal beach views at this height. The central void area was incorporated to allow afternoon light to penetrate the east-facing living spaces.

The main living area has sliding doors that open back to allow the internal spaces to interact directly with the external terrace that runs down to the beach. Aluminum shutters were used on the side of the terraces to provide a degree of protection from unwanted breezes and weather. Painted timber cladding and battens were used extensively to provide a residential texture, quality, and scale to the home. The timber floors provide a warm hue to the white walls used throughout the house.

Photography by Remco Photography

65

1 Terrace
2 Living
3 Dining
4 Kitchen
5 Entry
6 Family
7 Bedroom
8 Bathroom
9 Void

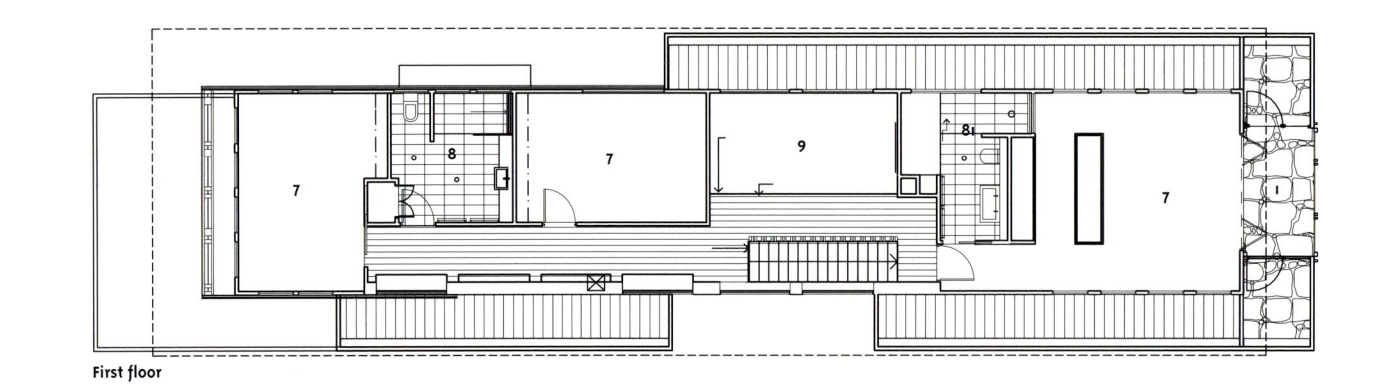

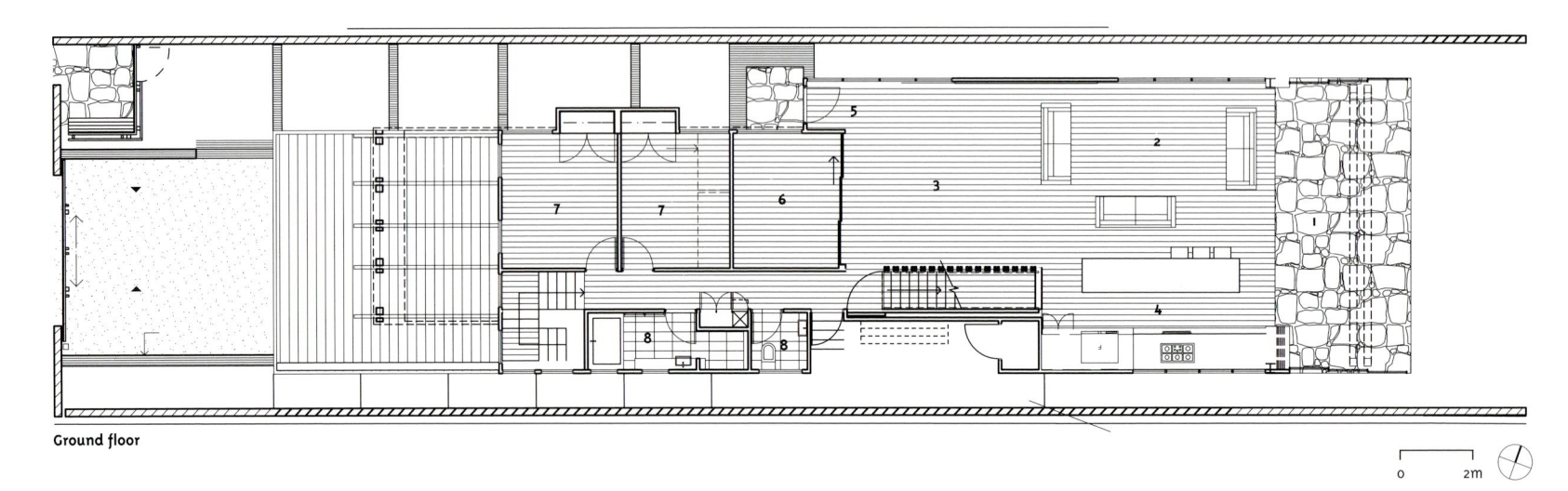

First floor

Ground floor

The Cottage

Elma Bay Residence

Vancouver Island, British Columbia, Canada
Helliwell + Smith: Blue Sky Architecture

Planned as a grand, sweeping crescent-shaped structure opening to spectacular vistas north over a pebble beach, this house and studio was built as a gathering place for an extended family living in England and Canada. While the convex side flows along the shoreline, the opposite, concave side of the plan creates a courtyard that embraces the southern sun.

The sculptural timber roofs float above the walls of glass and cedar. Exposed glulam beams curve through the space, supporting a series of undulating rafters that define and form the roof and highlight the circulation gallery. The curved beams tie into vertical concrete fins, which are exposed on the interior and clad in large bluestone slabs on the exterior. The interior is sparsely detailed and constructed with materials including hardwood floors, architectural concrete, and bluestone.

A transparent link of folding glass walls forms a hallway across the outdoor room and creates an illusion of two homes, one for the parents and one for the children. A series of 5- by 10-foot pivot doors open onto the seaside of the main social spaces. The plan arcs continue outside as unifying landscape elements, tying together the buildings, gardens, forest, and sea. Great attention has been paid to details and craftsmanship resulting in a beautiful home balanced sensitively between the forest and the sea.

Photography by Gillian Proctor and Peter Powles

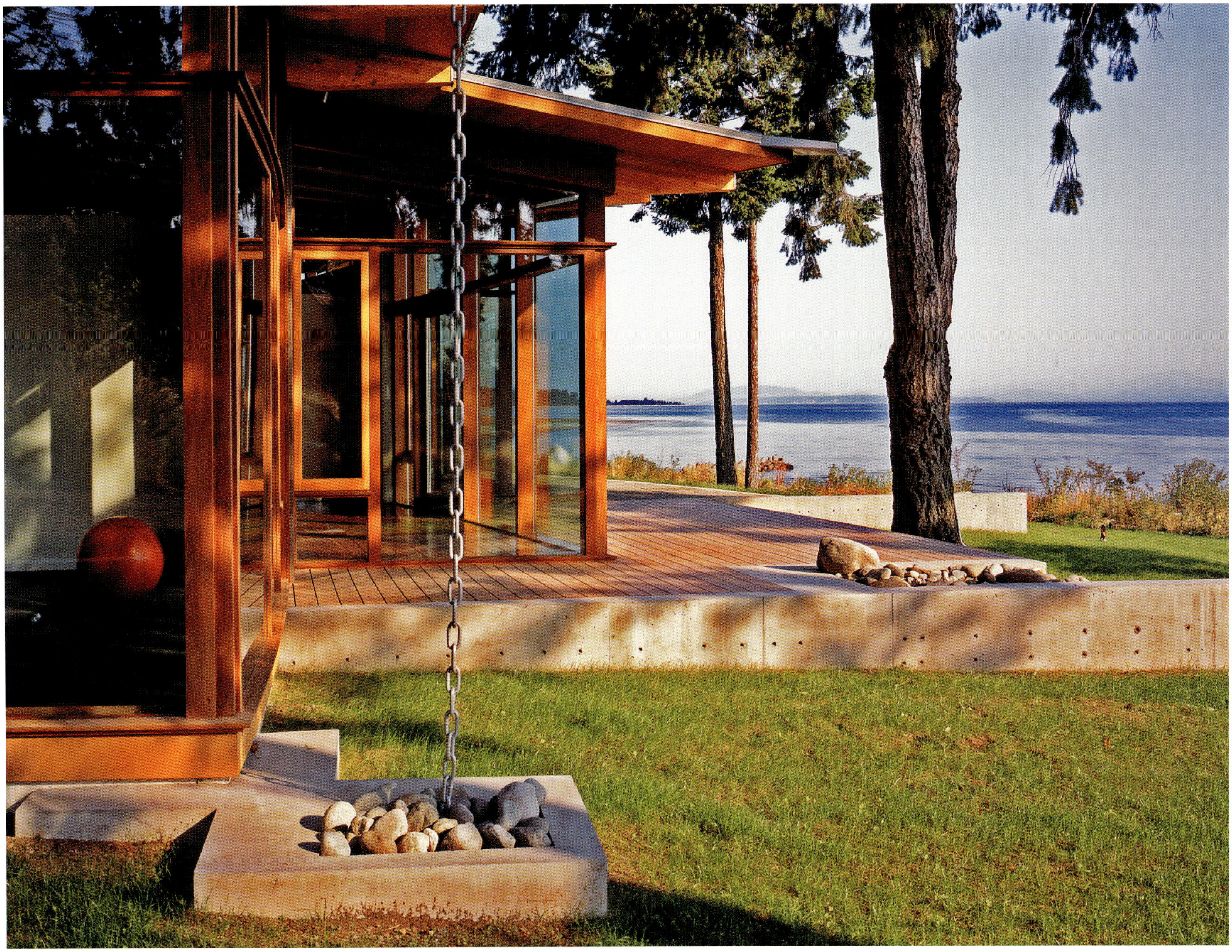

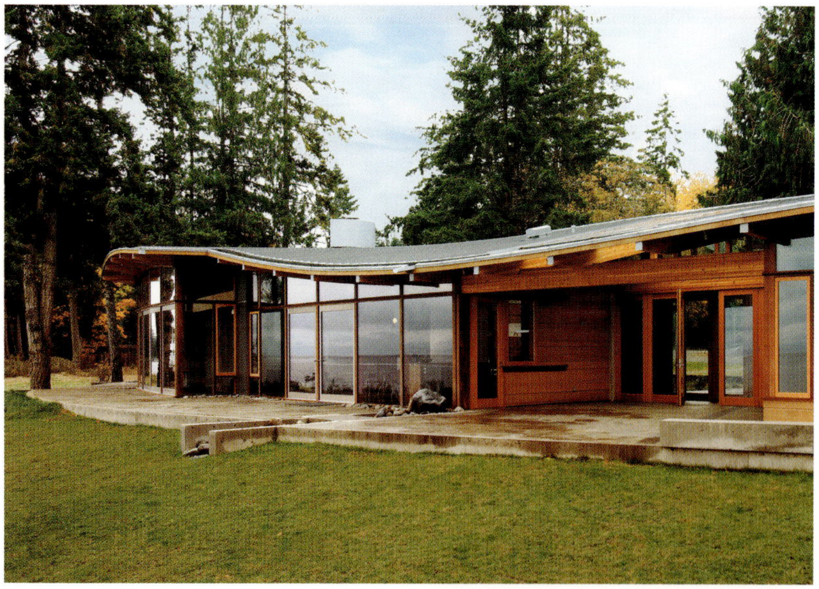

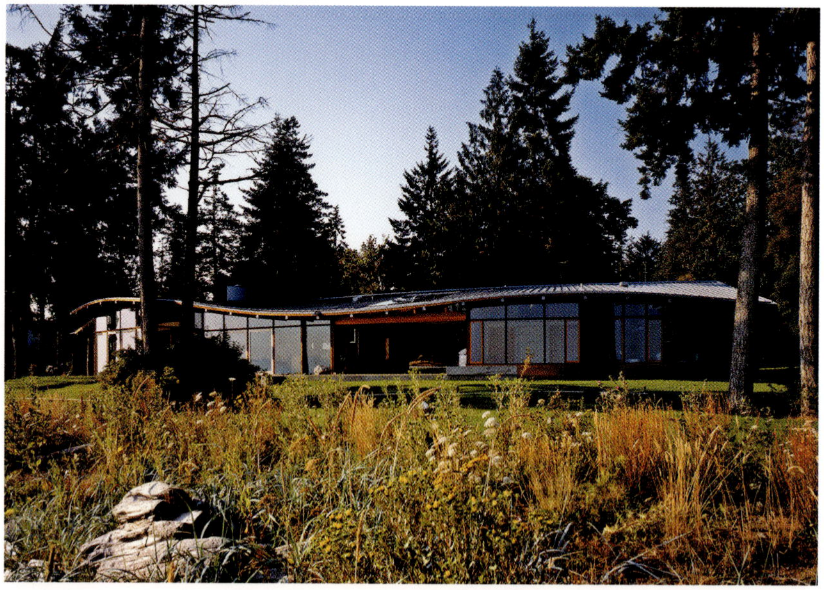

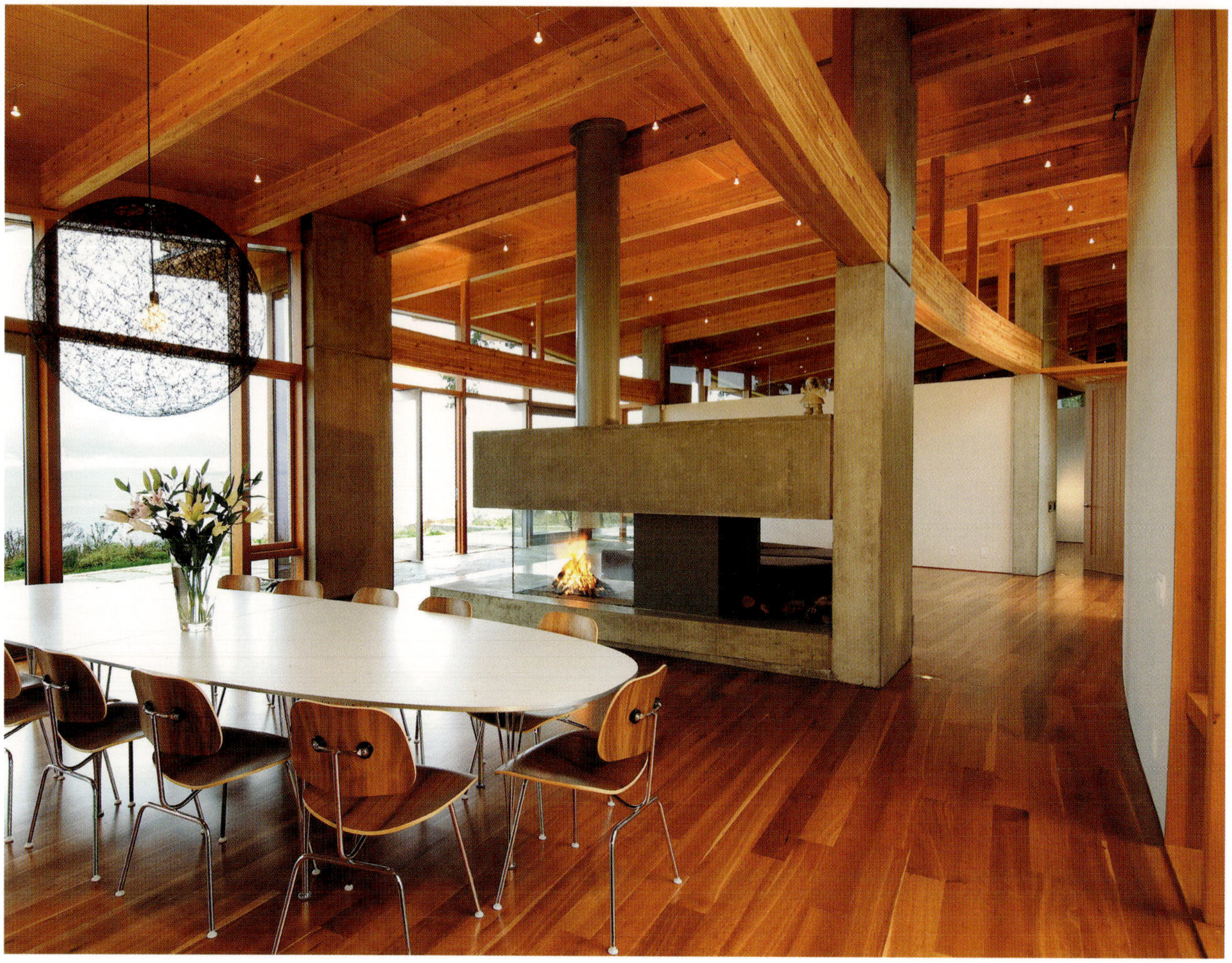

Elma Bay Residence

Emu Bay House

Emu Bay, South Australia, Australia
Max Pritchard Architect

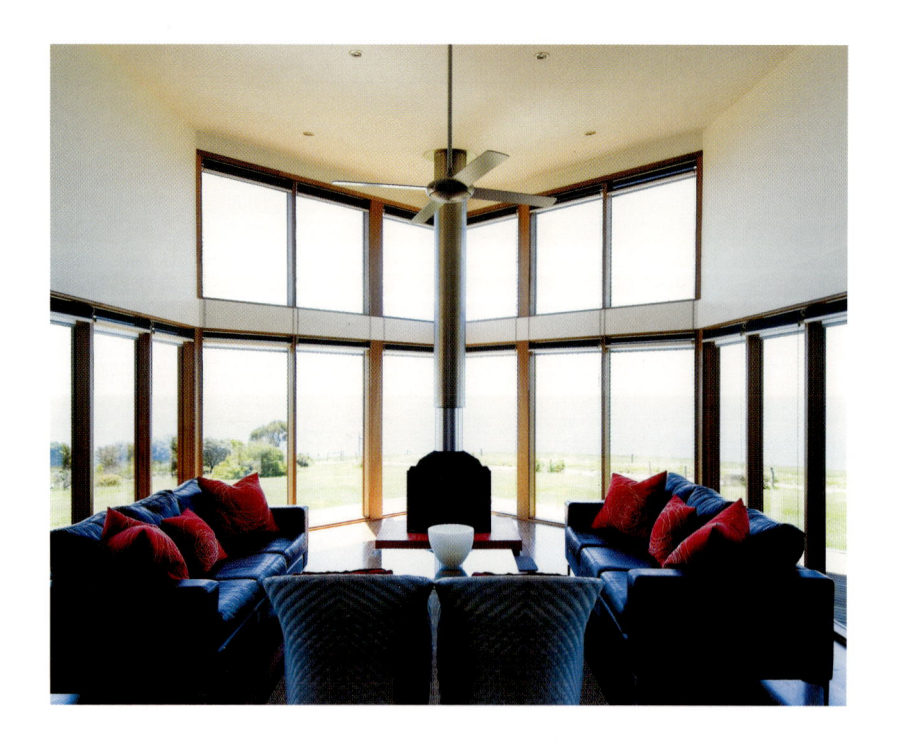

Panoramic sea views and wind protection were strong design determinants of this spectacular holiday home. With an exposed site of sweeping views, the owners of this property required a relaxed holiday home that maximized views but still provided sheltered, outdoor areas.

The house is elevated 3 feet above the ground to maximize the view and reinforce the dramatic form. The living area, with its dominant floating "lid" roof, emphasizes the drama of the exposed site. Two bedroom wings radiate from this core and enclose a rear, sheltered courtyard that features a wood-fired pizza oven. Indented timber decks placed either side of the living area provide further options for outside living and entertaining, with the choice dictated by wind direction.

Double-glazing and high-performance glass, cross ventilation and fans for cooling, and a highly efficient combustion heater have been used to minimize energy use, and hot water is obtained from an efficient electric heat pump. Corrugated colorbond, timber windows, flooring, and decking reinforce the relaxed timeless holiday atmosphere while the floating roof form adds drama to the exposed site.

Photography by Sam Noonan

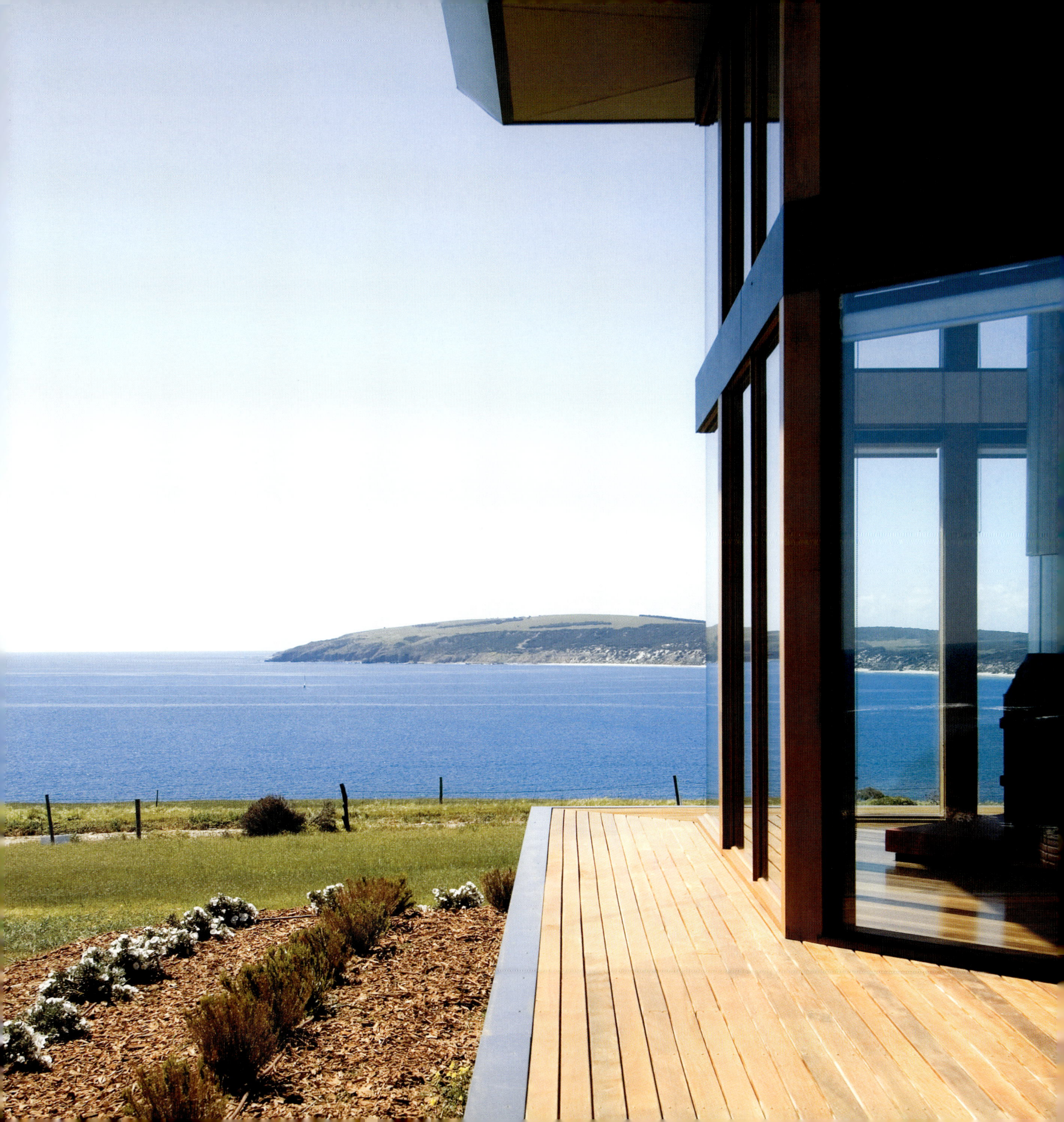

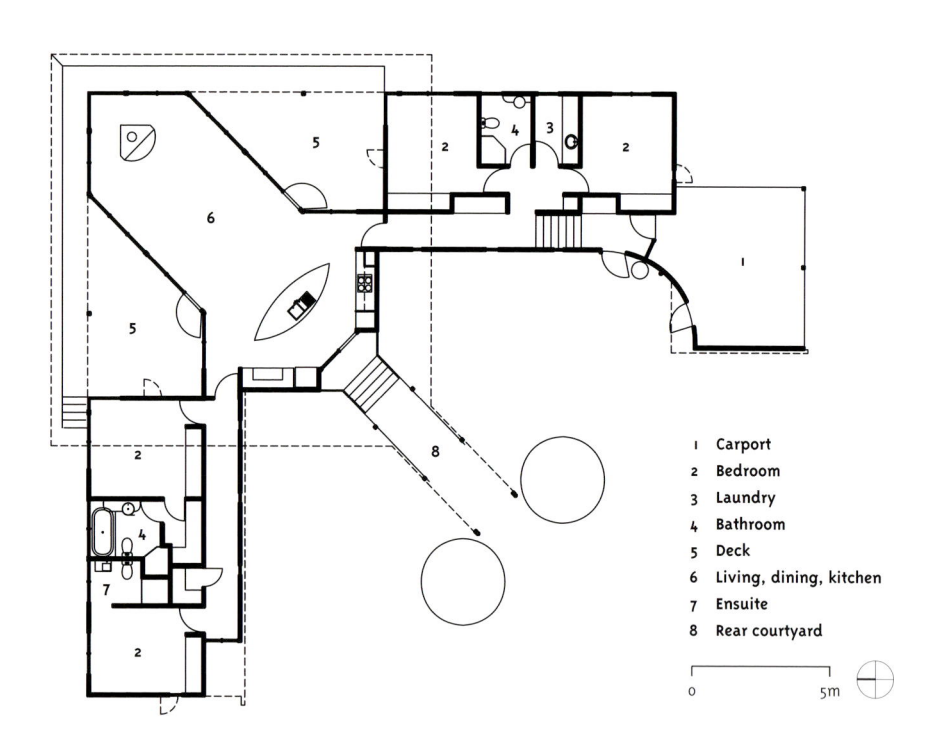

1   Carport
2   Bedroom
3   Laundry
4   Bathroom
5   Deck
6   Living, dining, kitchen
7   Ensuite
8   Rear courtyard

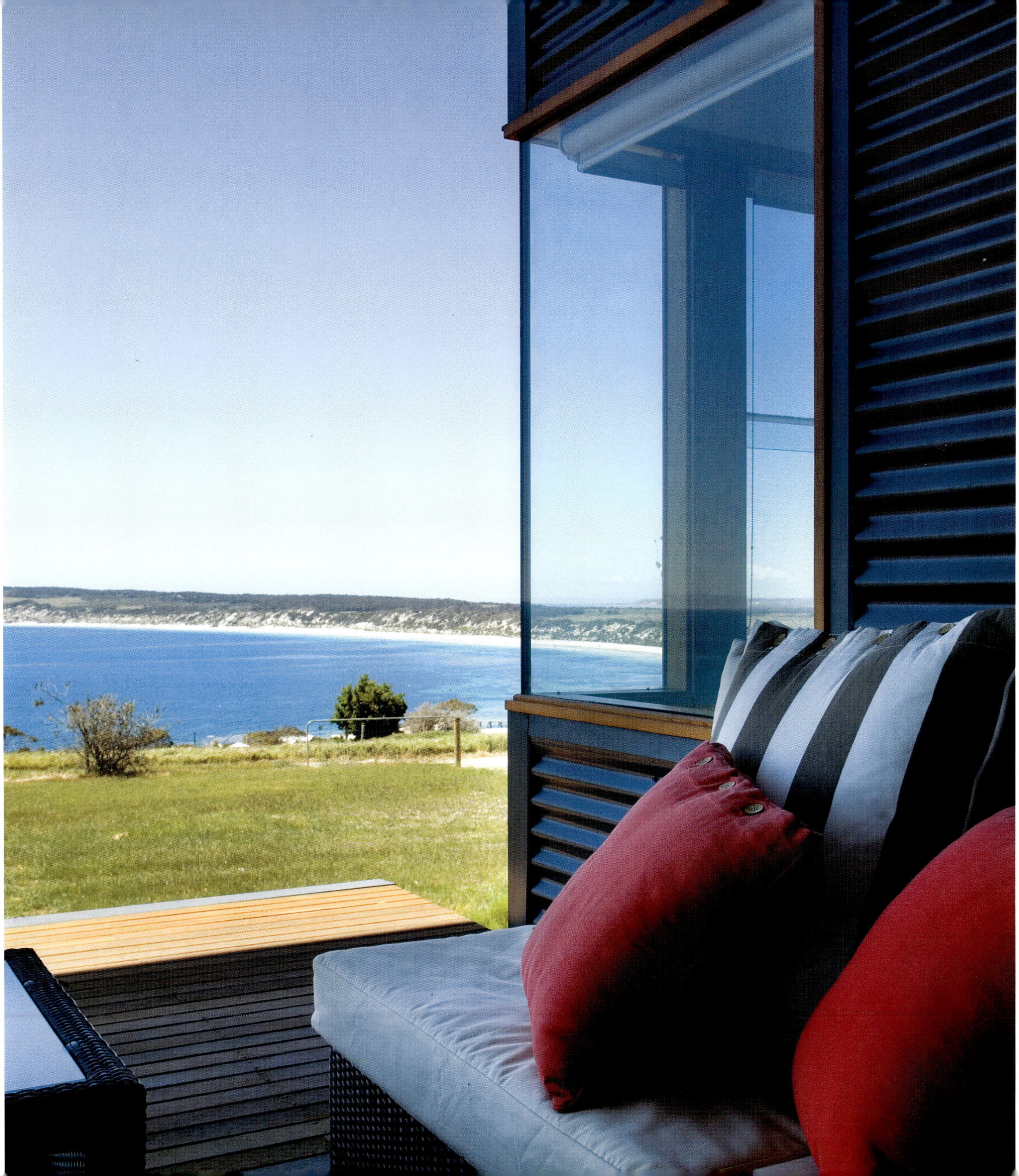

Freshwater House

Sydney, New South Wales, Australia
Chenchow Little Pty Ltd

The 3,500-square-foot beach house is nestled below a sandstone cliff overlooking a beach reserve. The building has three distinct parts—a podium base, a garden/living space, and a screened bedroom volume—each with unique spatial qualities. The basement podium level is introverted and cavernous, concealing a deeply recessed entry vestibule and garage. The living level is sandwiched between the upper and lower volumes and is almost without definition. The weathered timber cladding of the podium continues to this level to form a handrail, the battens of which are angled to maximize the view to the beach. Cabinet pieces within this floor are clad in black mirror, chrome, and a veneer the color of weathered timber.

The space dissolves into a play of views and reflections, with highly reflective surfaces contrasting with the color and texture of the timber. The ceiling above the living space is painted matt black to minimize the glare from the water during the day and to dissolve the ceiling into the sky in the evening, and along with it any sense of enclosure. The top level contains the bedrooms and is veiled by custom-made bi-folding shutters. When the shutters are open the appearance of the building and the experience of the interior are transformed. This house won the Robin Boyd Award for residential architecture at the 2009 National Institute of Architecture Awards.

Photography by John Gollings

77

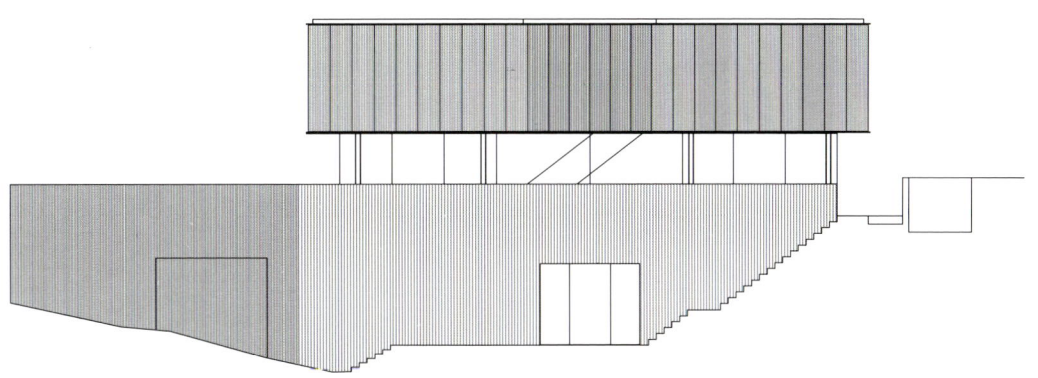

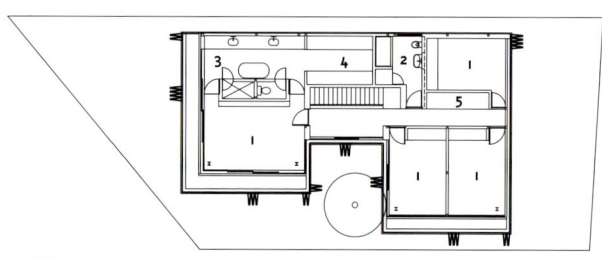

First floor

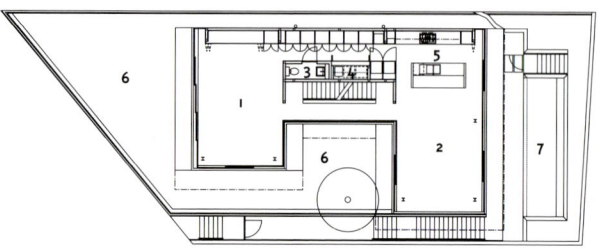

1. Bedroom
2. Bathroom
3. Ensuite
4. Walk-in closet
5. Study nook

Ground floor

1. Living, dining
2. Living, dining
3. Powder room
4. Laundry
5. Kitchen
6. Garden
7. Pool

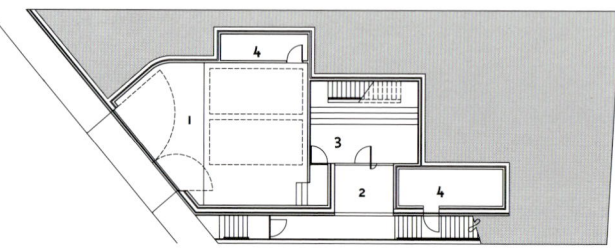

Lower ground floor

1. Garage
2. Entry porch
3. Entry foyer
4. Storeroom, pool room, rainwater tank

Freshwater House

Greenant House

Agnes Water, Queensland, Australia
Middap Ditchfield Architects

This house was designed to be used by one or two family groups as a private retreat that provides a luxury camping or safari-like experience. The intent was to closely connect each part of the building to this remarkable site and take full advantage of dramatic ocean views.

The courtyard plan was developed to create readable private resort character and grew from an initial idea of a campsite of tents positioned around a campfire. The living wing is transparent to allow visual connection from the central courtyard space to the site, beach, and ocean. Each part of the building has been given individual expression, like separate tents, with separate roof structures that provide north-facing, high-level glass to provide maximum controlled day lighting and ventilation.

Sustainability and low environmental impact were important concerns for the design of this house. As such the house generates a minimum 1.5 kW of solar-generated power and all roof water is collected and used for the day-to-day operation of the house, including for the swimming pool. Where possible, building materials for the house were selected for their ecologically sustainable performance.

Photography by Aperture Photography

81

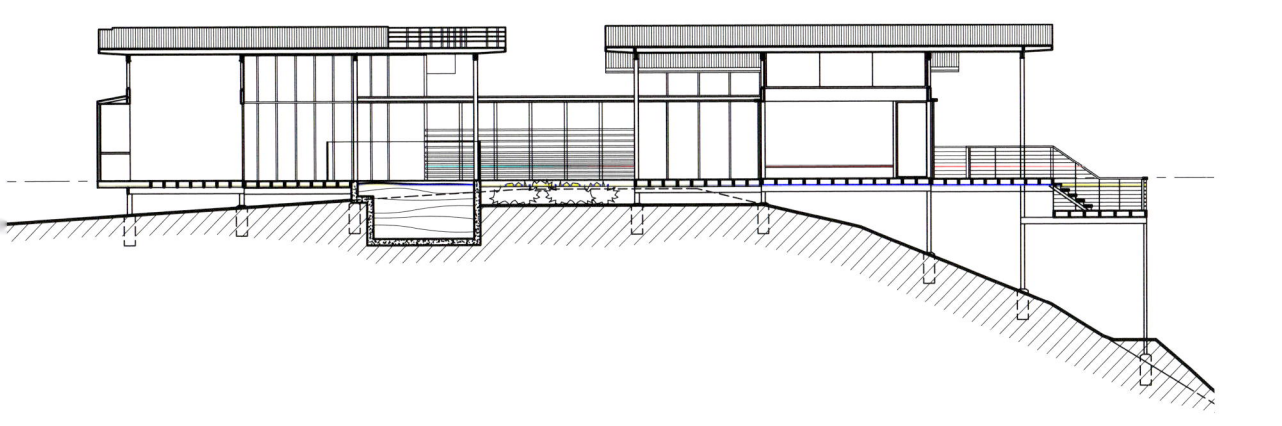

Ground floor

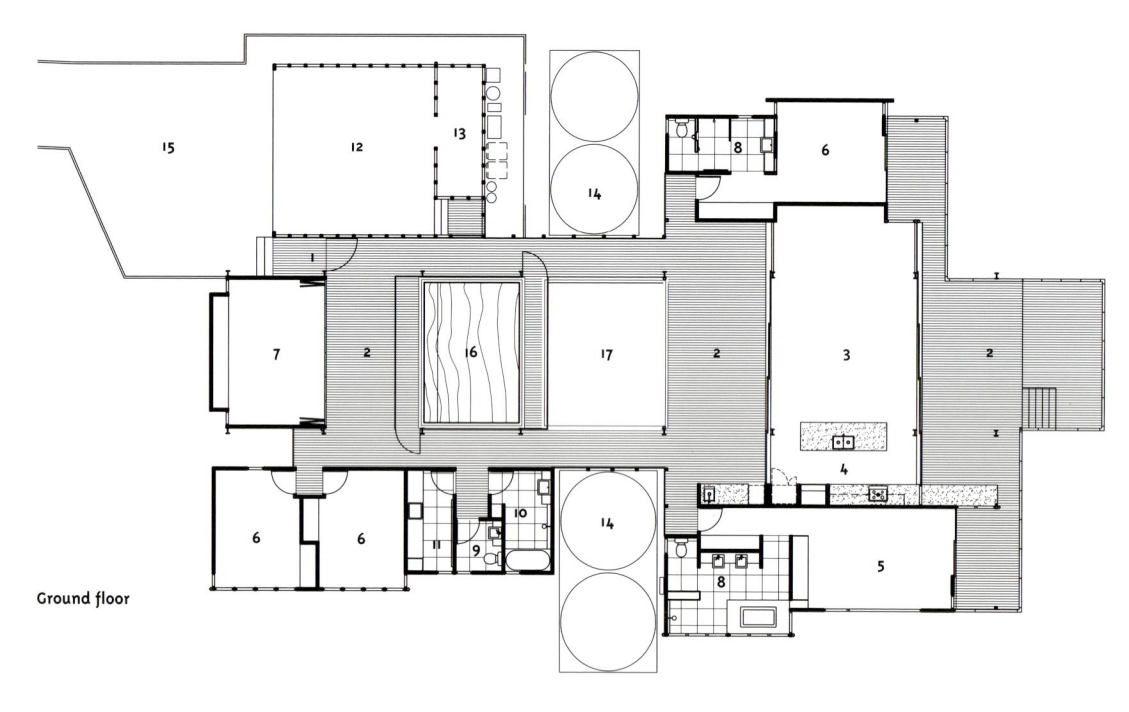

1	Entry	10	Bathroom
2	Deck	11	Laundry
3	Living	12	Garage
4	Kitchen/bar/barbecue	13	Store
5	Master bedroom	14	Water tanks
6	Bedroom	15	Driveway
7	Studio	16	Pool
8	Ensuite	17	Feature garden
9	WC		

Greenant House

Hermosa Beach House

Hermosa Beach, California, USA
KAA Design Group

Located between the Pacific Ocean and a dense residential neighborhood, this home strives to resolve a number of divergent factors. Functionally, the design meets very specific, comprehensive requirements of an active retired couple; architecturally, the design addresses conceptual notions of merging natural light and the erosion of spatial boundaries; and procedurally, the design negotiates stringent and at times contradictory governmental zoning requirements.

The result is a building that incorporates overlapping, interlocking volumes and planes, both horizontally and vertically. The home balances the contemporary notions of maximum views, open flow of internal spaces, and the constant invitation of natural light. Spaces unite to allow for boundless ocean views or more private vistas into introspective areas without compromising privacy.

A contextual and sturdy material palette, which is needed in coastal environments, differentiates the building's massing as it cascades along the structure's primary axis. A centrally located stair forms an important hub with the added benefit of minimizing circulation from room to room.

Photography by Farshid Assassi and Weldon Brewster

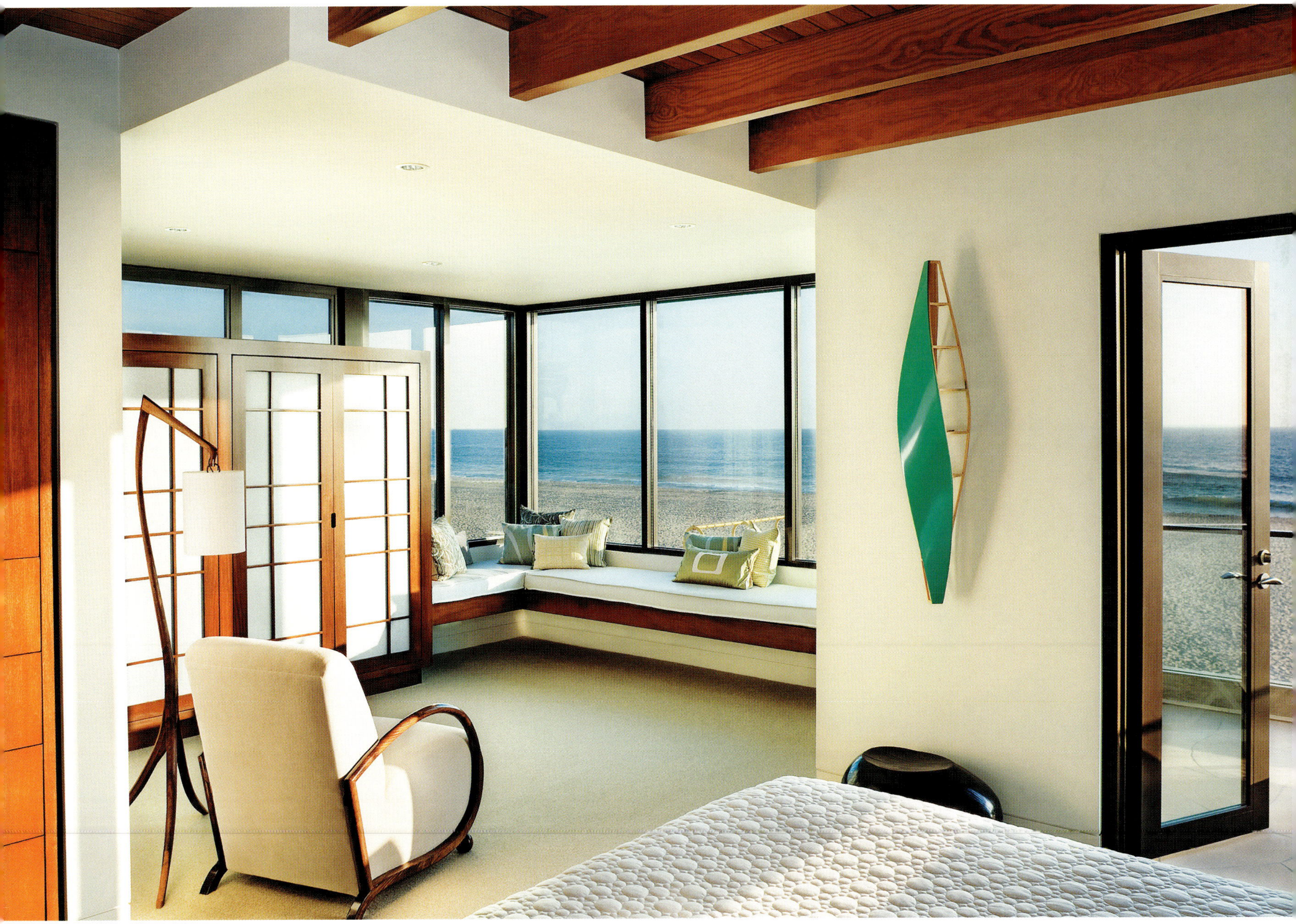

86

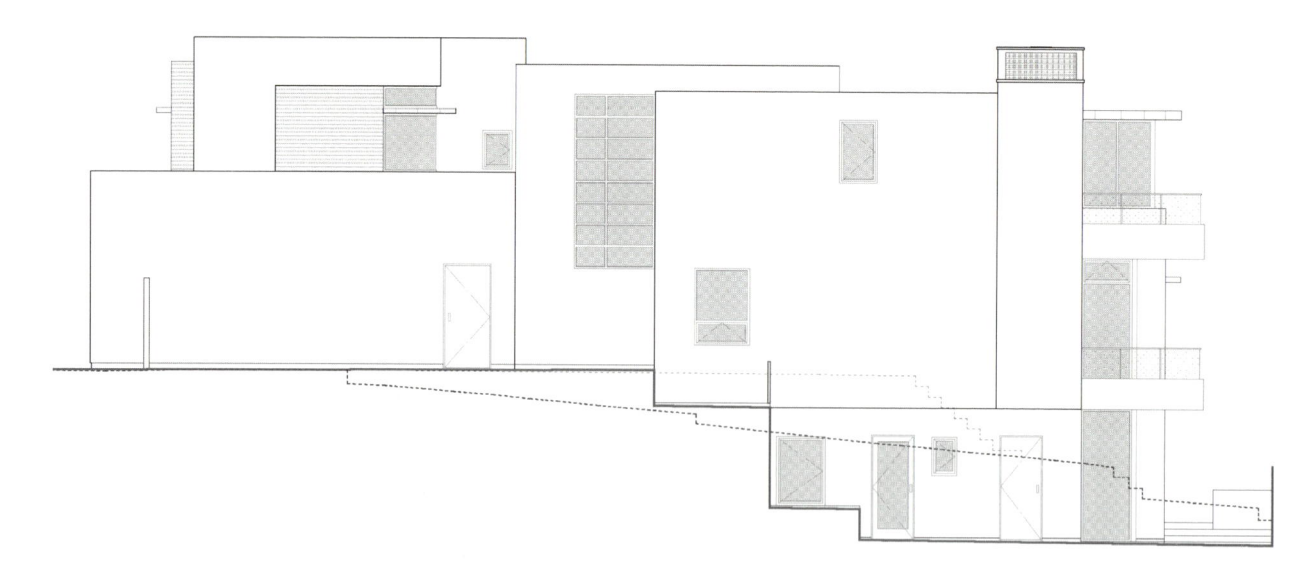

1	Beach room	9	Entry
2	Bar	10	Garage
3	Laundry	11	Kitchen
4	Elevator	12	Sitting area
5	Storage	13	Bathroom
6	Bedroom	14	Office
7	Living	15	Walk-in closet
8	Dining	16	Deck

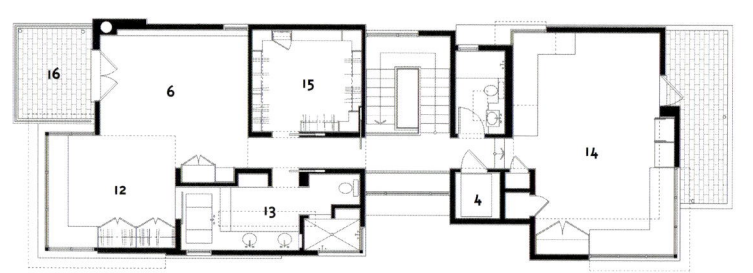

First floor

Ground floor

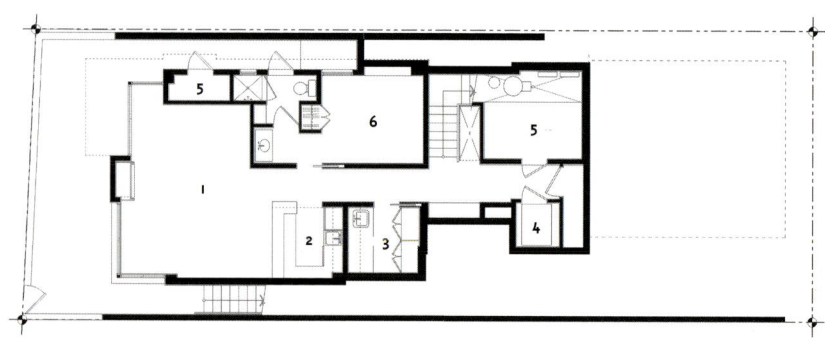

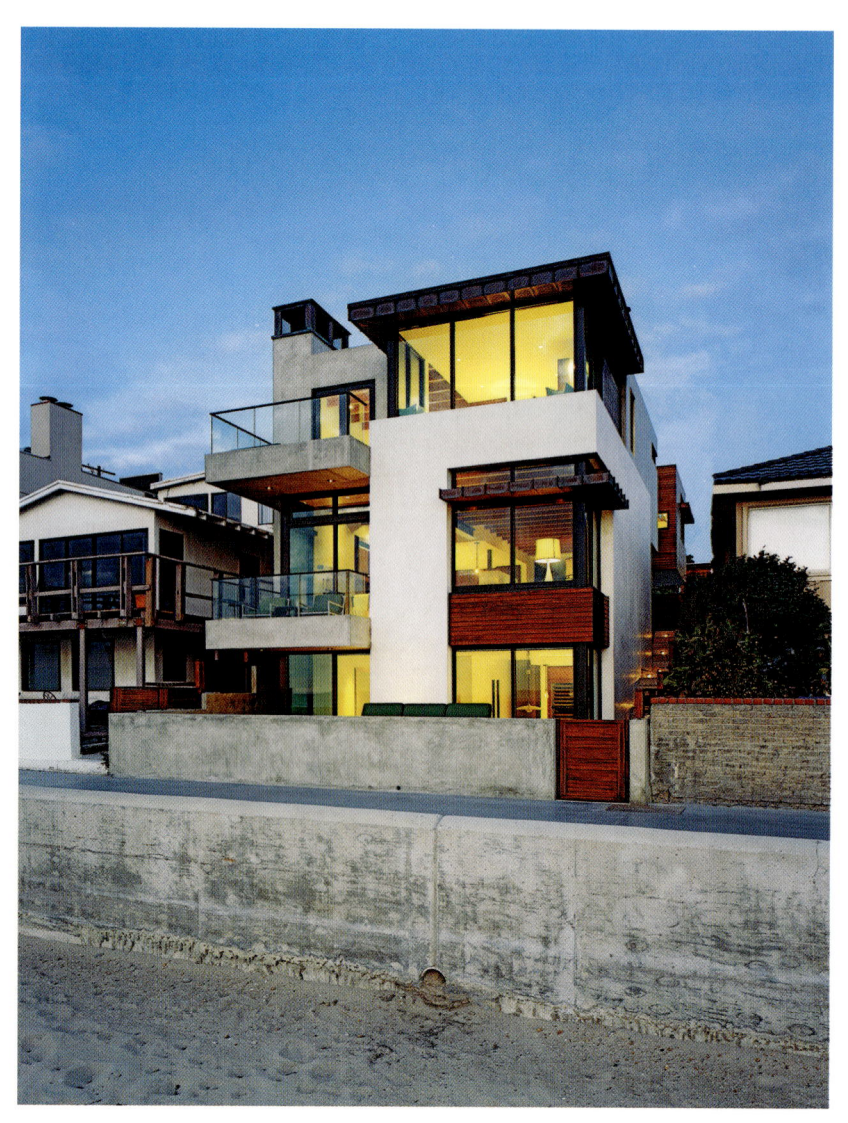

Lower ground floor

Hermosa Beach House

Ingoldsby House

Great Ocean Road, Victoria, Australia
Seeley Architects

The coastal towns that are dotted along the Great Ocean Road in Victoria are where many Melbournians seek their weekend and holiday solace. In one of these towns, sitting alongside a majestic sand-fringed bay, is Ingoldsby House. This robust, generous weekender proudly rises from between the clumps of gnarly gum trees on the site, gently announcing itself as beacon among the sea of fibro and wooden beachside shacks of the locale. After careful consideration of the effects of climate, the architects designed a house that has a sense of being right for its place with a selection of timbers, stone, materials, and colors reflective of its coastal location.

It has been said that "the house is its own person" with an undeniably strong character. However, over time this character will mellow and develop, much like the complexities of a great wine. The cladding of copper and timber will slowly lose its shine, taking on the earthy effects of the environment, a verdigris of tea-tree grey-greens. The rhythm provided by the recycled posts and beams provides both structure and spatial definition to the house, defining rooms, framing views, and providing a sense of forever. These hulks of ironbark, salvaged from a wool store in Adelaide, along with the generous wide blackbutt flooring, demonstrate the architects' commitment to achieving excellence in both design and sustainability.

The program of this house comprises an extroverted form containing the living rooms and several decks, with an intertwined but separate introverted form containing the sleeping and bathing rooms. All sit atop a partial basement for surfboards, a "tinny", a couple of cars, and the obligatory beach gear store. This wonderful retreat captures that often sought after, but rarely achieved notion of a romantic Australian coastal life.

Photography by Shannon McGrath

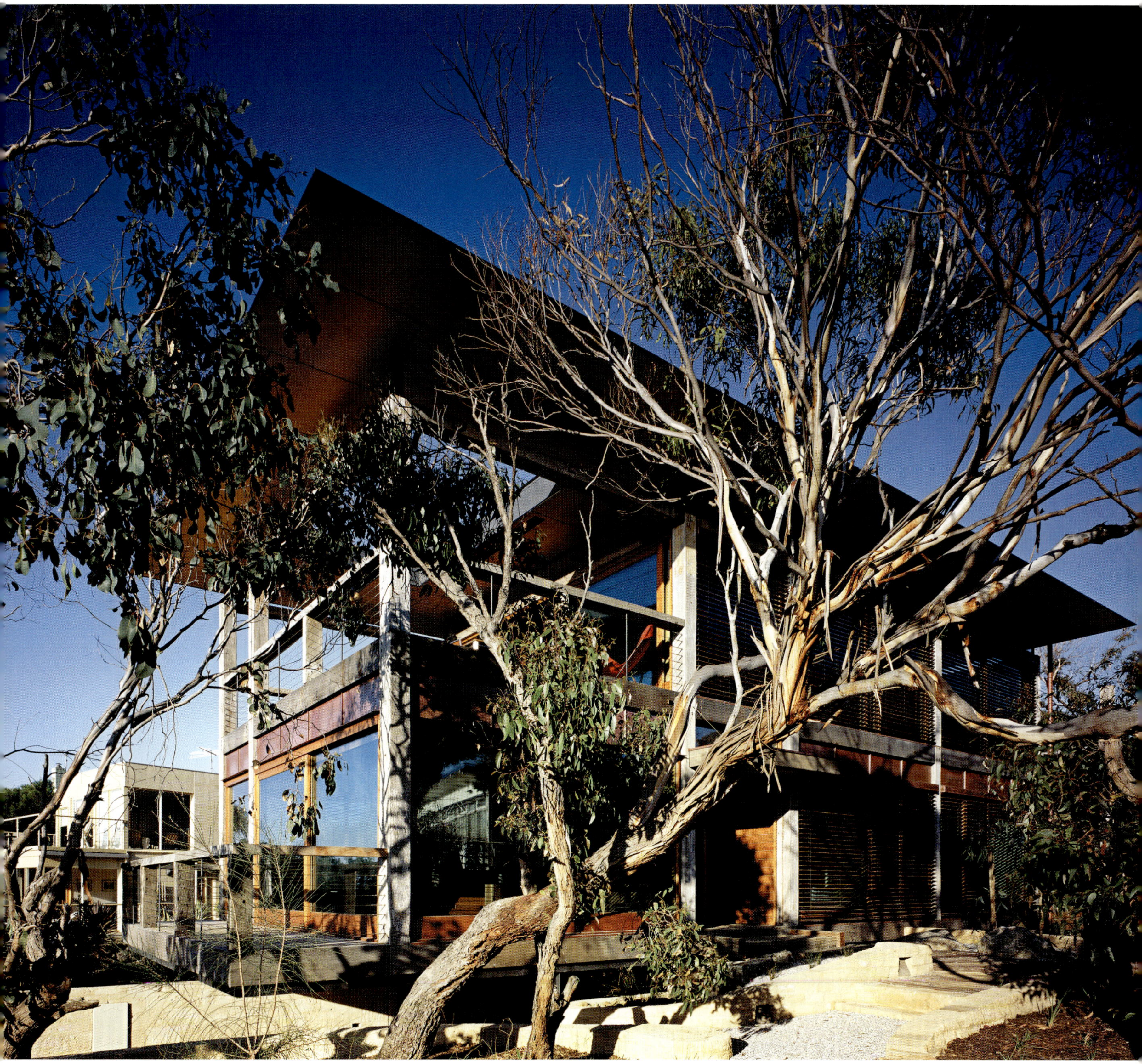

Lower ground floor

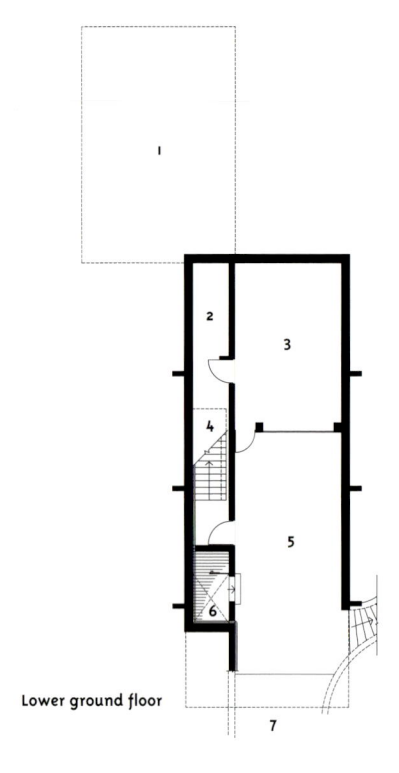

1	Building over	5	Carport
2	Storage	6	Shower
3	Garage	7	Driveway
4	Cellar		

Ground floor

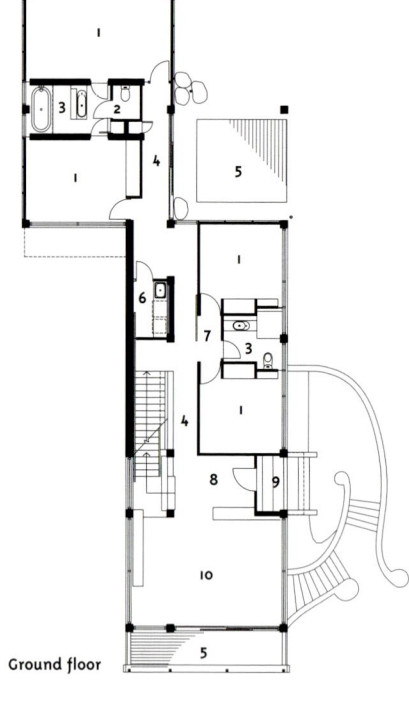

1	Bedroom	6	Laundry
2	WC	7	Vestibule
3	Bathroom	8	Entry
4	Hall	9	Terrace
5	Deck	10	Lounge

First floor

1	Study	6	Bedroom
2	WC	7	Dining
3	Ensuite	8	Kitchen
4	Deck	9	Living
5	Hall		

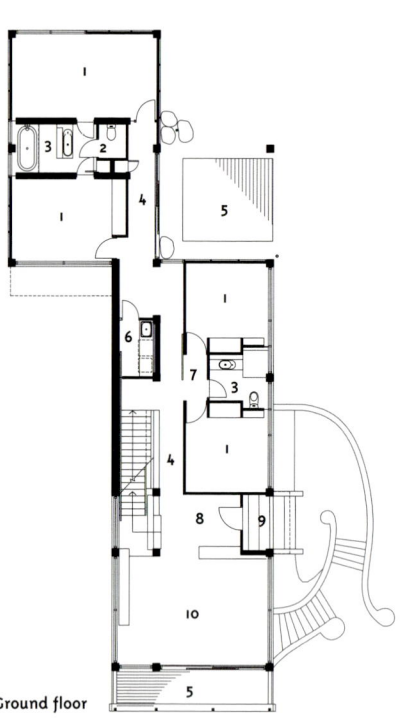

Ingoldsby House

Island Beach House

Kangaroo Island, South Australia, Australia
Architects Ink

Nestled within a sandy dune, this 3,000-square-foot house was built on the site's highest point. The building is oriented to provide solar access to the north and to capture magnificent beach and sea views. From this high position, the site falls away steeply toward the sea, allowing the lower level bedrooms to remain nestled in the scrub, affording privacy and shelter from the beach. The southern side of the lower level is sheltered by earth, which assists the passive design goals by helping maintain stable temperatures and comfort within the house while minimizing the mass of the building from the site's southern approach. The balcony, cantilevered at the northeastern corner, enables immediate access from the kitchen and living areas and provides protection from the prevailing winds.

Designed as a simple linear plan, the house allows for a northerly aspect as well as views from all living areas and bedrooms, thus maximizing exposure to the winter sun and enabling cross ventilation for summer cooling. The polished concrete floors of the living areas act as a heat sink in winter, and these heat gains are retained through the use of high-performance glazing. While this design maximizes solar access in winter, the highly insulated roof provides appropriate overhangs to shade the glass in summer. Adequate ventilation to all interior spaces is provided by large sliding doors and double-hung sashless windows. The house is completely dependent on rainwater, which is collected from the roofs and stored in underground concrete tanks.

Photography by Sam Noonan

93

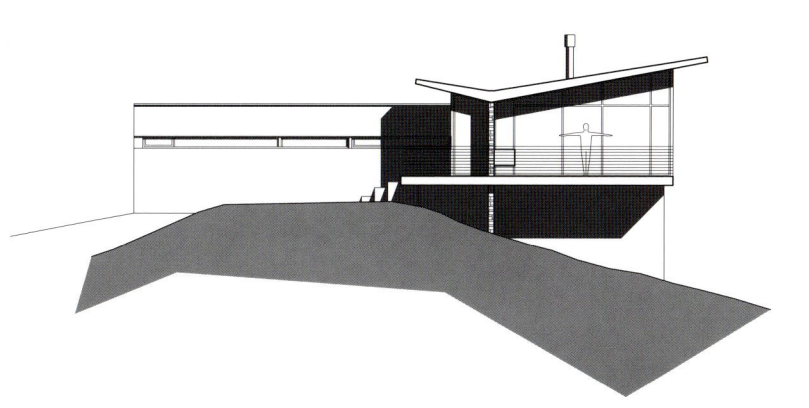

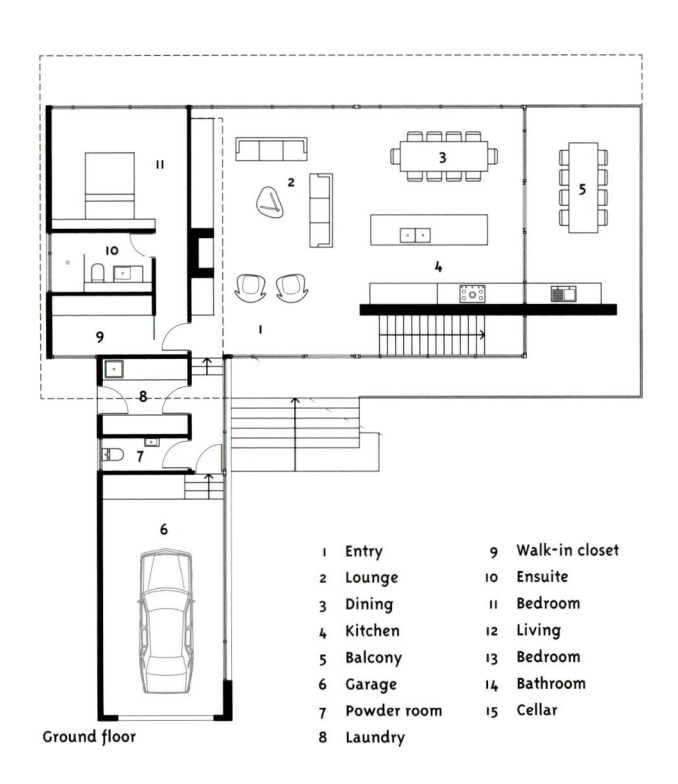

Ground floor

Lower ground floor

1	Entry	9	Walk-in closet
2	Lounge	10	Ensuite
3	Dining	11	Bedroom
4	Kitchen	12	Living
5	Balcony	13	Bedroom
6	Garage	14	Bathroom
7	Powder room	15	Cellar
8	Laundry		

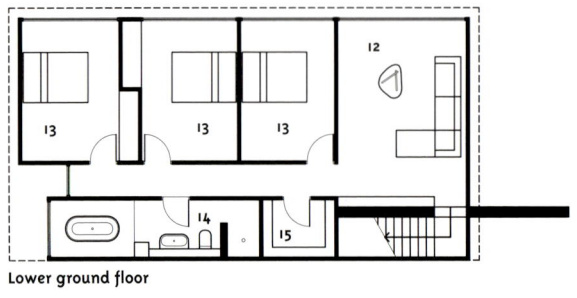

0   5m

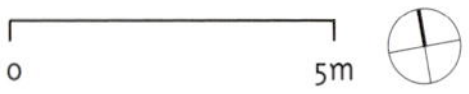

Island Beach House

JZ House

Bahia, Brazil
Bernardes Jacobsen Arquitetura

Built among sand dunes on a beachfront site, this 2,000-square-foot house was positioned to take advantage of natural ventilation and the spectacular sea views. The structure incorporates a variety of indoor and outdoor spaces that allow for a seamless transition to the beach and sufficient room for an extended family to relax in a casual atmosphere.

The main building is connected to the sandy site by a concrete base and the rest of the structure is built from timber. The main area comprises a large living room that has unrestricted views to the beach and garden and has been positioned to ensure that natural sea breezes flow through the space. All other rooms of the house flow from this main living space.

In response to the tropical surroundings, a palette of materials was selected to help the house blend harmoniously with its environment. Locally sourced materials include eucalyptus used for the trellis detailing and beige Bahia marble for the floor coverings. This marble, which is a similar shade to the surrounding sand, is also used for the solarium and beachfront swimming pool.

Photography by Leonardo Finotti

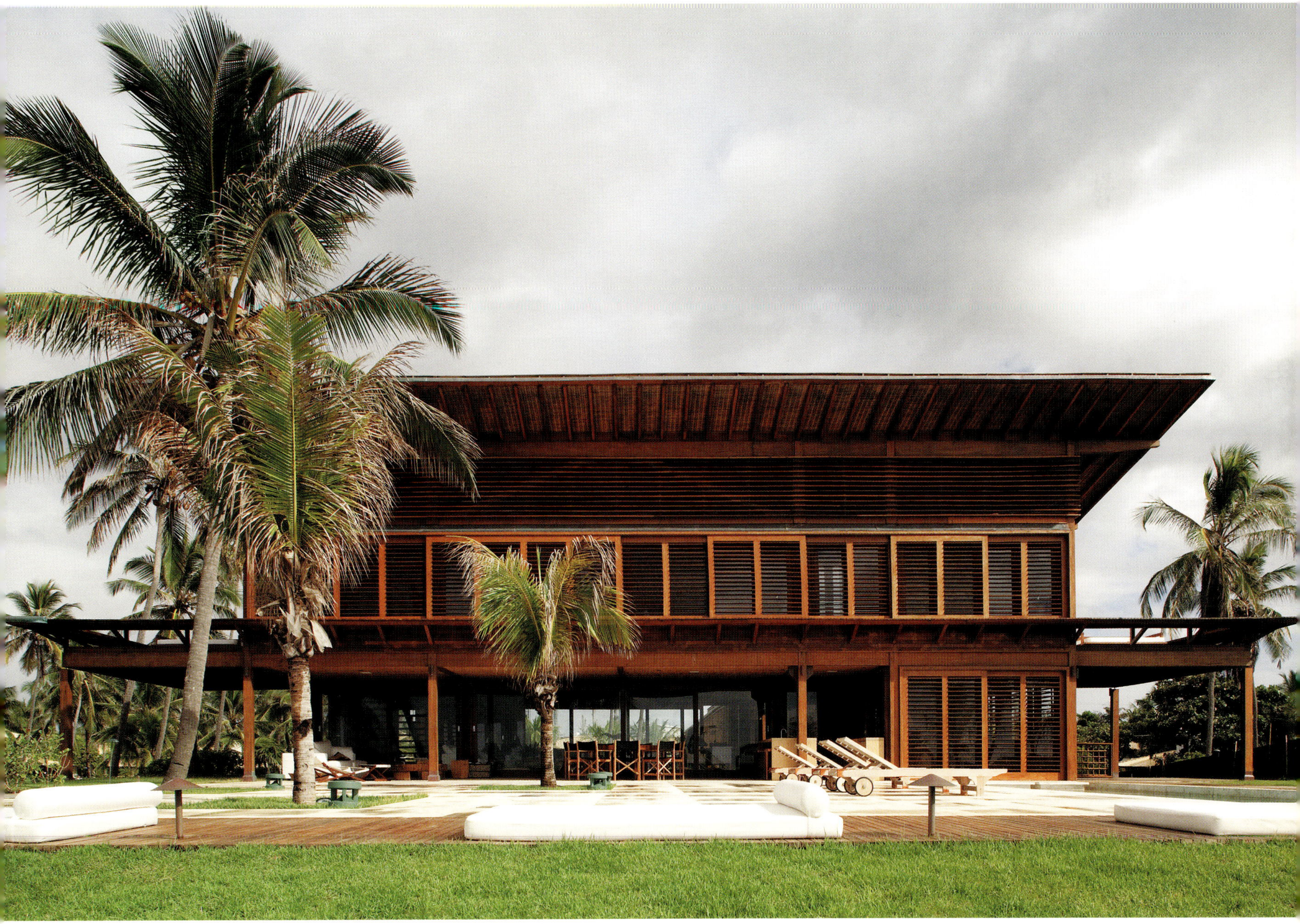

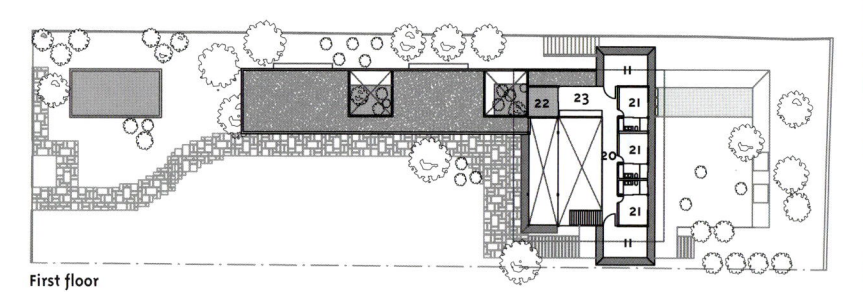

First floor

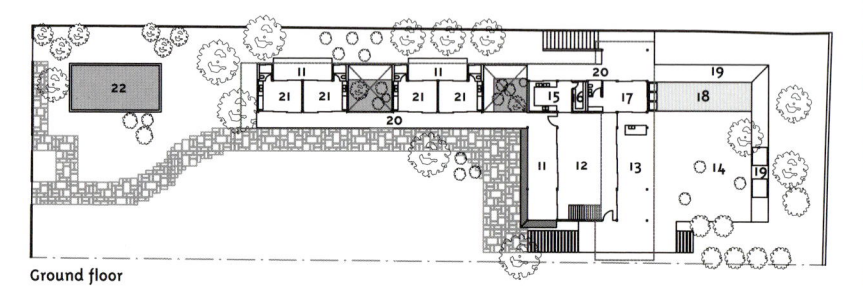

Ground floor

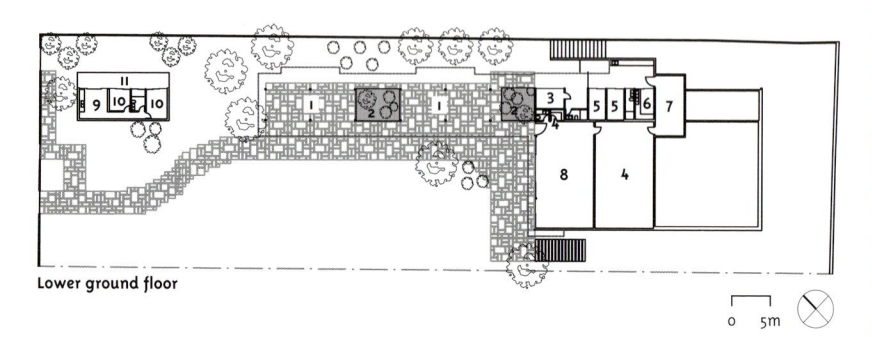

Lower ground floor

0   5m

1 Garage	9 Kitchen/living	17 Living
2 Garden	10 Bedroom	18 Swimming pool
3 Sauna	11 Veranda	19 Deck
4 Storage	12 Living/dining	20 Circulation
5 Staff bedroom	13 Covered veranda	21 Ensuite bedroom
6 Laundry	14 Sunroom	22 Rooftop garden
7 Services	15 Kitchen	23 Study
8 Children's room	16 Pantry	

99

JZ House

Kenny House

Omaha Beach, Auckland, New Zealand
Godward Guthrie Architecture

The exposed location of this beachfront property required the architect to ensure privacy from the adjoining coastal public walkway and provide adequate shelter from the wind and sun. To achieve this, the main indoor and outdoor living spaces were conceived as a detached raised pavilion, placed high enough to achieve views to the bay but low enough to ensure an easy connection to the lawn and beach path beyond. The living area is almost entirely wrapped in sliding, full-height glazing panels that open onto a beach-facing terrace to the northeast and a sheltered courtyard behind. An exterior stair leads from the courtyard up to a large roof-deck living space, which offers wide views to the bay.

Sleeping areas are located in three separate zones—the children's rooms adjoining the lawn, the parents' area on the second level, and the guest rooms located above the garage. All rooms utilize a system of sliding glazed openings behind a layer of sliding, adjustable louver screens. In fact, cavity sliding doors are used throughout the interior of the house, some of which are automated, as is the pivoting front entry door that is fabricated from a huge single sheet of aluminum. In the living pavilion, the screens slide vertically up to the roof deck level, enabling the room to be opened entirely to the exterior, closed down fully to a shining metal case, or any variation between. Similarly, a pair of sliding, frameless glass panels allows the living area to be fully or partially connected to the rest of the house, or completely detached by the courtyard space. This adjustability, along with flush floor tiling throughout, serves to minimize distinctions between internal and external space.

Photography by Patrick Reynolds

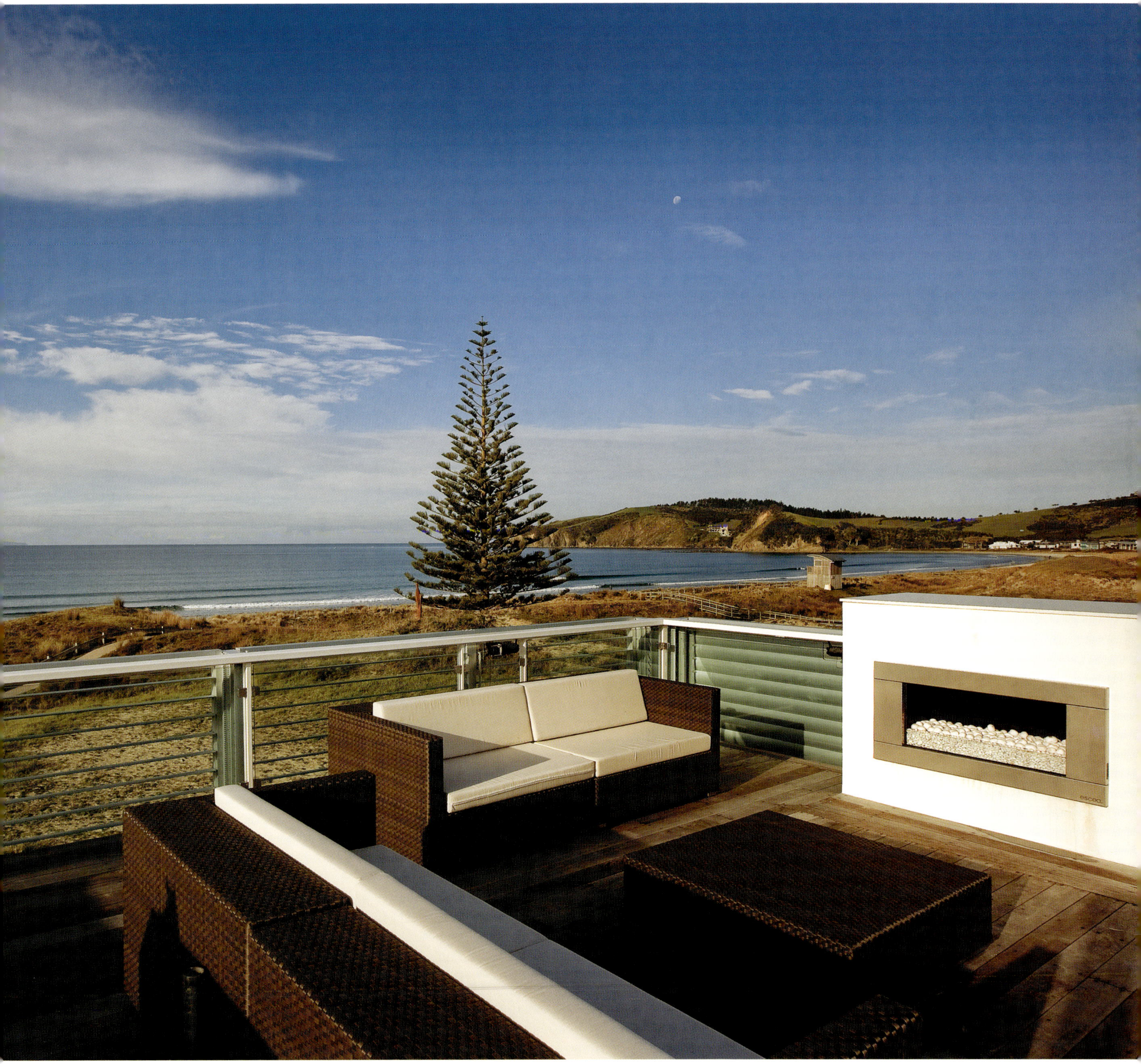

102

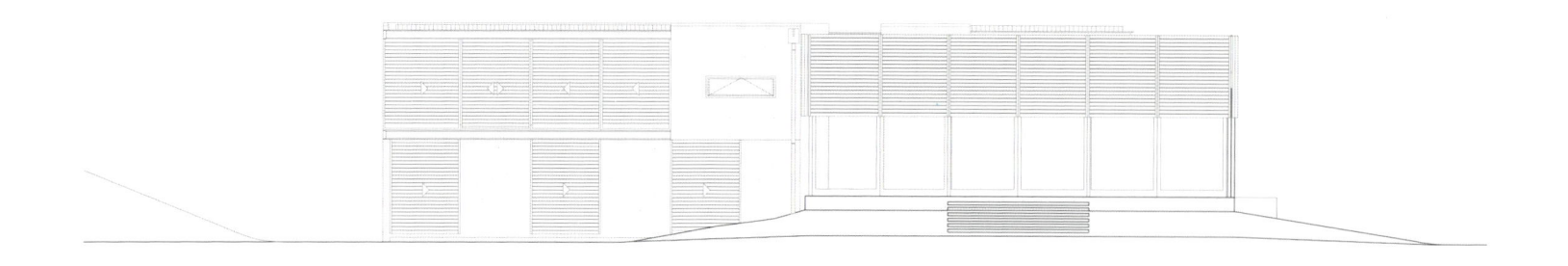

Kenny House

Le Fevre House

Punta Misterio, Peru
Longhi Architects

This 5,500-square-foot beach house, located 70 miles south of Lima, was conceived as a meeting point between the Peruvian desert and the Pacific Ocean. Sand garden roofs located on the eastern part of the house act as an extension of the desert, while lap and recreation pools on the western section provide a connection to the ocean. An in situ concrete structure joins the architecture to the rocky cliff top as an extension of the natural environment.

The materiality of the house's components gives order to the design, transforming the natural to the artificial. For example, the natural rock at the lap pool area is sculpted to create a terrace bordered by natural rock while the floor and steps are formed by crafted pieces of stone. A counterpoint to the connection between the natural rocks of the site and man-made architecture is found in the sophisticated use of a green stone sourced from the Peruvian Andes. The stone is used throughout the house and transitions from rough to fine when moving from exterior to interior.

Vertical circulation is provided by an open staircase, comprising stainless steel and timber steps, that cantilevers out from a wall finished with green stone. The house also includes a wine cellar and a living room located under the external swimming pool, where the exposed natural rock is accompanied by sophisticated architectural design. The glass box housing the living room, which offers a 180-degree view to the ocean and nearby cliffs, hangs from the structure to symbolize the relationship between sand and water.

Photography by CHOlon Photography

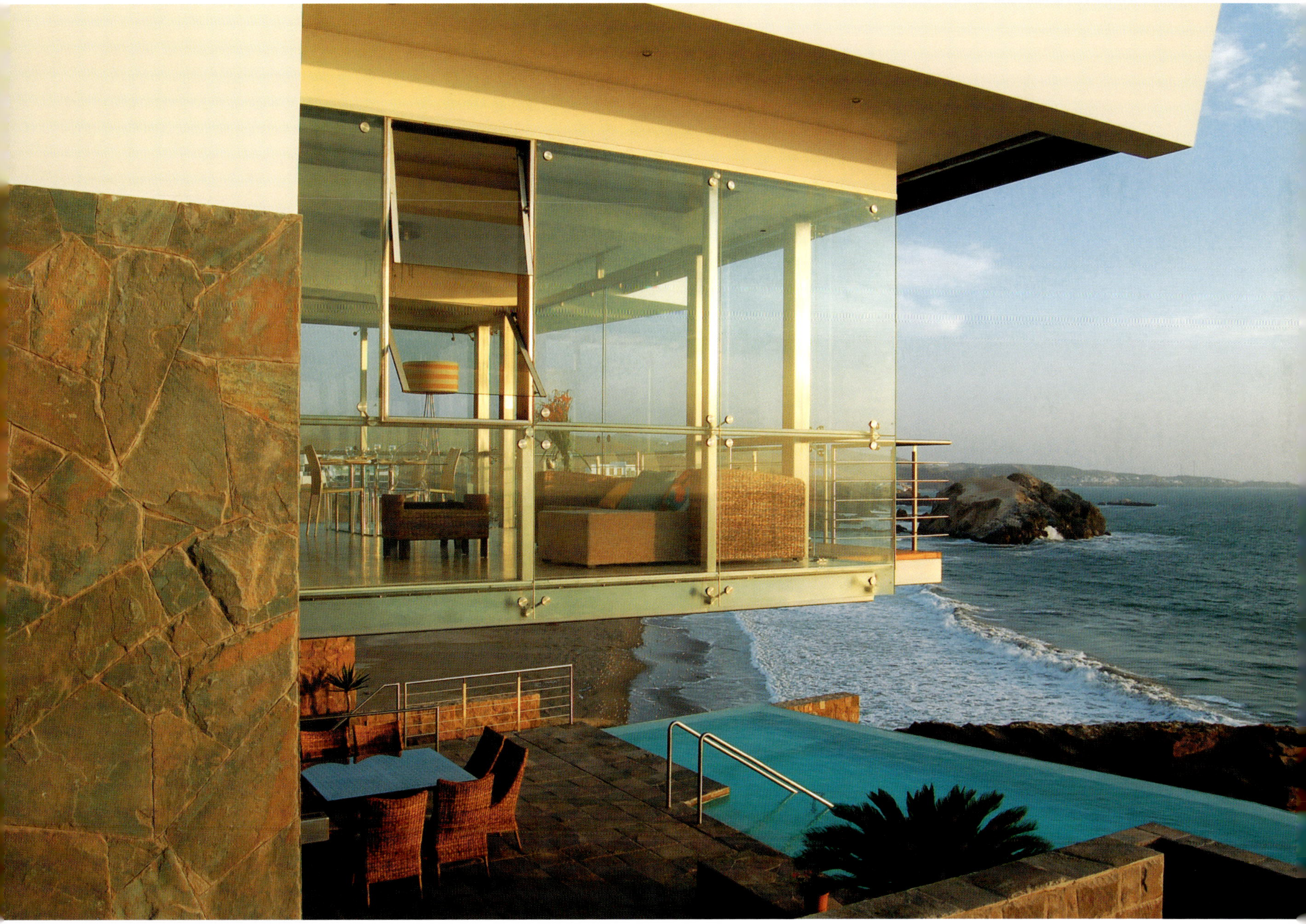

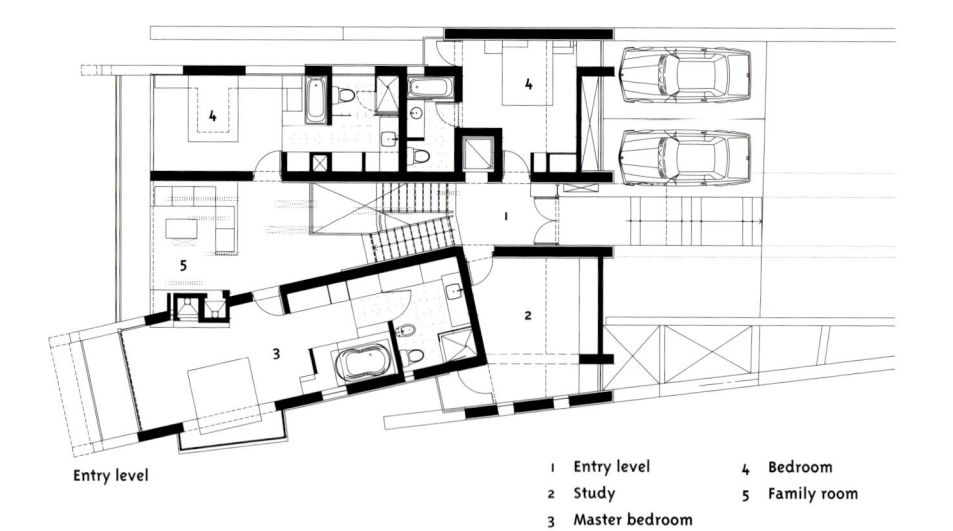

Entry level

1. Entry level
2. Study
3. Master bedroom
4. Bedroom
5. Family room

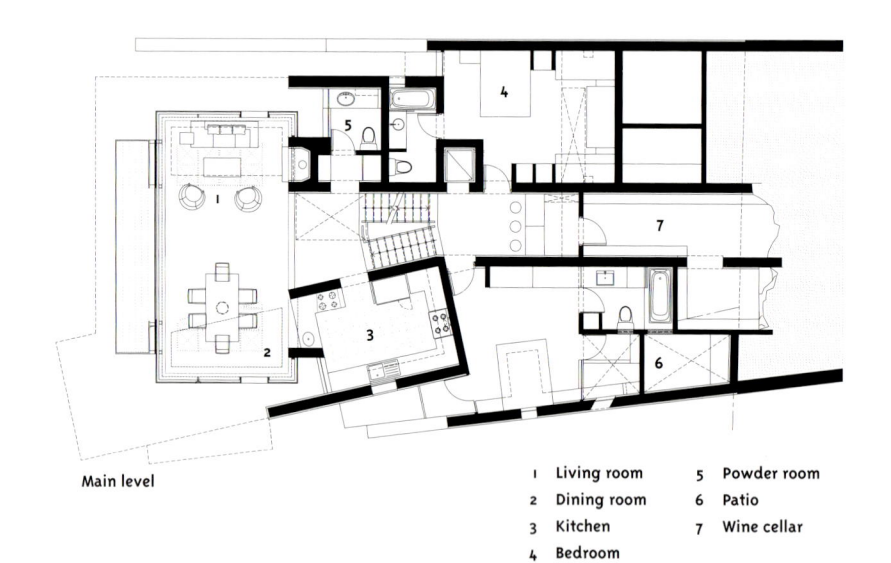

Main level

1. Living room
2. Dining room
3. Kitchen
4. Bedroom
5. Powder room
6. Patio
7. Wine cellar

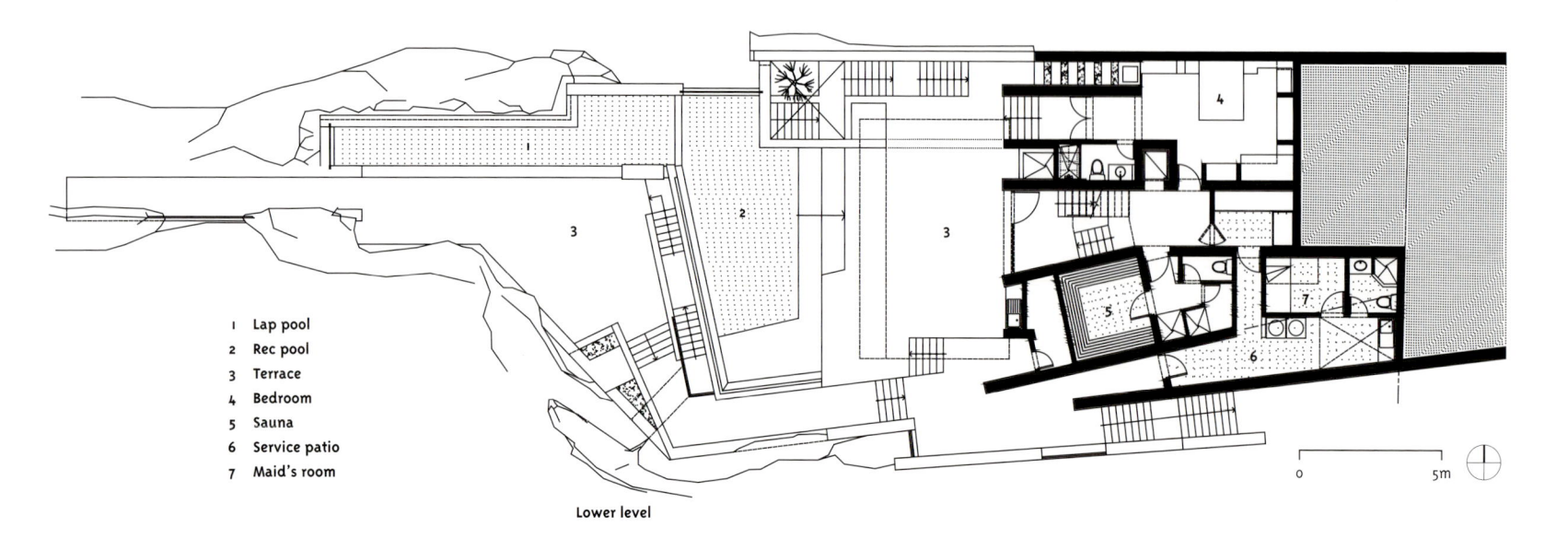

Lower level

1. Lap pool
2. Rec pool
3. Terrace
4. Bedroom
5. Sauna
6. Service patio
7. Maid's room

107

Le Fevre House

Martin House

Inverloch, Victoria, Australia
Techne Architects

Overlooking Anderson Inlet and Bass Strait beyond, this 4,500-square-foot house was designed for a semi-retired couple who needed a substantial residence to accommodate their own activities as well as those of their extended family. The dramatic entrance acts as a "knuckle" between the two wings of the house, and this glazed, double-height area also includes a bridge at the upper level linking the private and public spaces. In addition, an elevator links both levels and ensures ongoing ease of access. The bedroom wing comprises guest rooms on the ground level, with the main bedroom suite located above. The living wing, which sits at 90 degrees to the bedroom wing, contains a split-level, open-plan kitchen, living, and dining area on the upper level; the lower level houses the entertainment room and bar, laundry, and garage.

The house was designed to take full advantage of seaside living on a stretch of coastline with strong, cold winds. Contemporary in design, the house was constructed from materials including Alucobond cladding, honed concrete blocks, and spotted gum timberwork. The interior and exterior living and activity areas were conceived for use at different times of the day, according to the season, and to facilitate socializing, accommodating, and entertaining guests in this stunning coastal location.

Photography by Vince Destefano

109

1 Entry
2 Billard room
3 Bar
4 Laundry
5 Bathroom
6 Children's bunk room
7 Bedroom
8 Garage
9 Swimming pool
10 Living
11 Dining
12 Kitchen
13 Terrace
14 Parents' retreat
15 Ensuite
16 Main bedroom
17 Study
18 Powder room
19 Lift

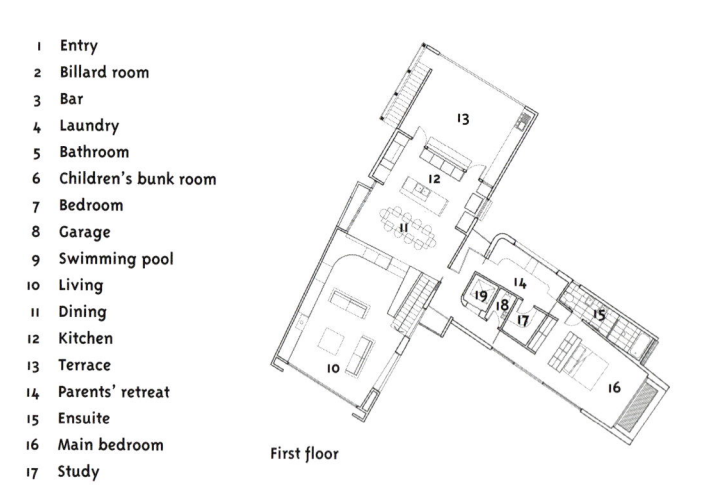

First floor

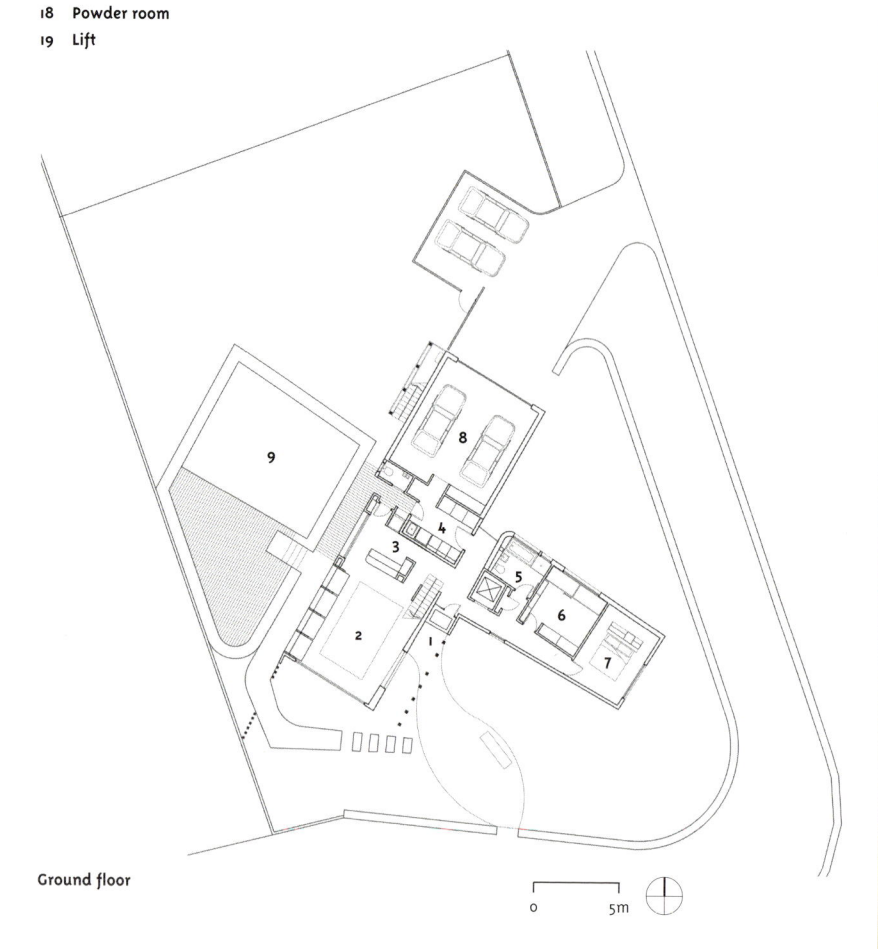

Ground floor

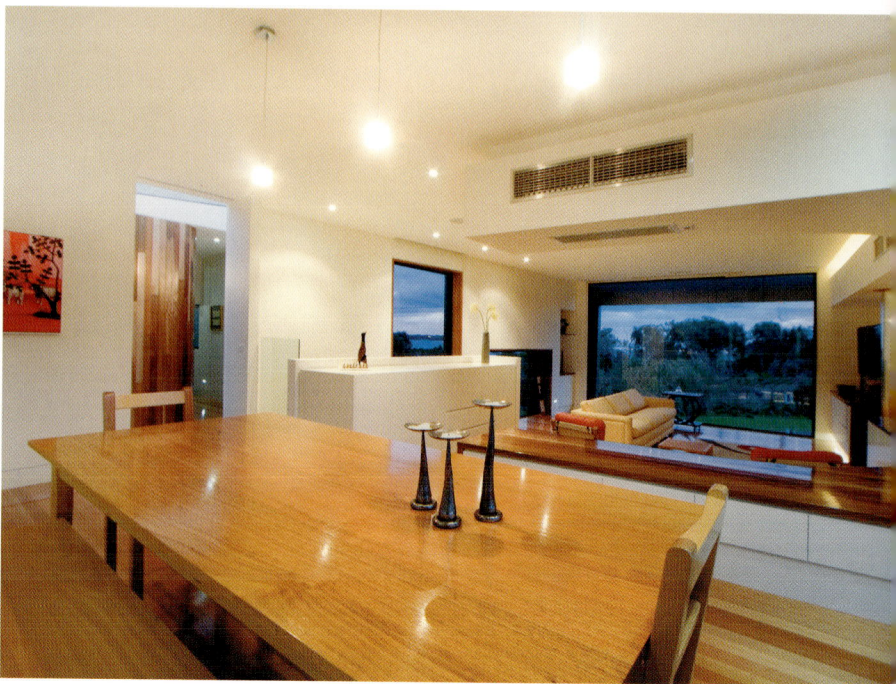

Martin House

Metamorphosis

Tunquén, Casablanca, Chile
Ulloa Davet + Ding

This striking, 1,900-square-foot, cliff-top house is the result of an extension and renovation of an existing structure. The existing roof has been transformed into a panoramic deck offering views along the coastline. This viewing deck is open to the public and is accessed via an independent stair.

The layout of the existing house was maintained and reinforced, and the south façade, located in the central area of the structure, was enlarged to provide a new living area with ocean views. A new bedroom is cantilevered over the entrance, with the absence of columns reinforcing the dynamics of the volume and protecting the space below from sun and rain. The addition is made from Oregon pine, while radiata pine is used for the rest of the house.

The master bedroom, located in the lower east area of the house, was renovated to relocate a bathroom that obstructed the central circulation axis. To assist circulation, an additional entrance on the east façade allows a direct connection to the adjacent valley. The façade is designed as a ventilated skin that affords greater durability and thermal stability, protecting it from the harsh coastal conditions. The timber façade is constructed in a three-four rhythm, where every three planks change a module and every four modules change a set. This design generates a natural texture and is interrupted only by the square-shaped openings.

Photography by DD-JUD

113

1. Master bedroom
2. Ensuite
3. East door
4. Breakfast terrace
5. Lounge
6. South sea-view terrace
7. Dining room
8. Kitchen
9. Living room
10. Bathroom
11. Bedroom
12. Main entrance
13. Porch

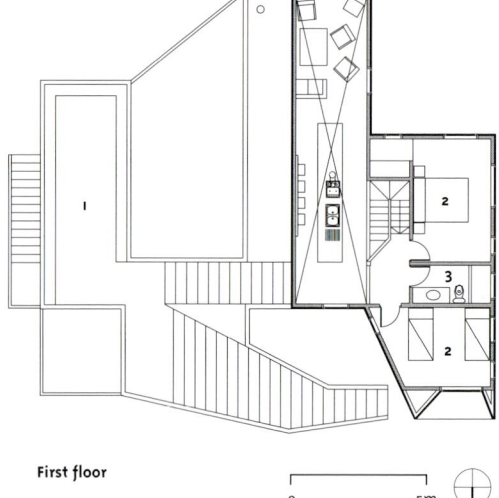

Ground floor

1. Deck
2. Bedroom
3. Bathroom

First floor

0 5m

Metamorphosis

Mount Eliza House

Mount Eliza, Victoria, Australia
Graham Jones Design

Located on Mount Eliza's Golden Mile, an exclusive residential area on the shores of Port Phillip Bay, this stylish contemporary home makes the most of its stunning coastal views. Creating enormous challenges for the designers, the sub-divided, narrow, steep site also had many restrictive covenants placed upon it to protect neighboring houses' stunning water views and amenity.

Huge terraces and retaining walls located on side boundaries, plus a six-car underground garage, were necessary in order to maximize the land usage of the small envelope available for construction. The building shape was designed using two simple pavilions, manipulated and layered to create functional spaces and architectural interest. These pavilions are located on separate levels and are linked by a glass bridge, providing magnificent views to the northwest from all major rooms of the home. Clean lines, flowing spaces, and detailed attention to all internal and external fittings and finishes are notable features of this contemporary beach house.

The house was designed around entertaining at the beach, therefore a "resort-style" design approach was adopted for the external areas. Large stone terraces surround the magnificent clean lines of the black mosaic-tiled, infinity pool and spa area, which flow into a rectangular reflection pond stretching out toward Port Phillip Bay. Upper terraces overlook the entertaining area, which features an undercover outdoor kitchen complete with temperature controlled wine fridges, wet-bar, and barbecue.

Photography by Chris Groenhout

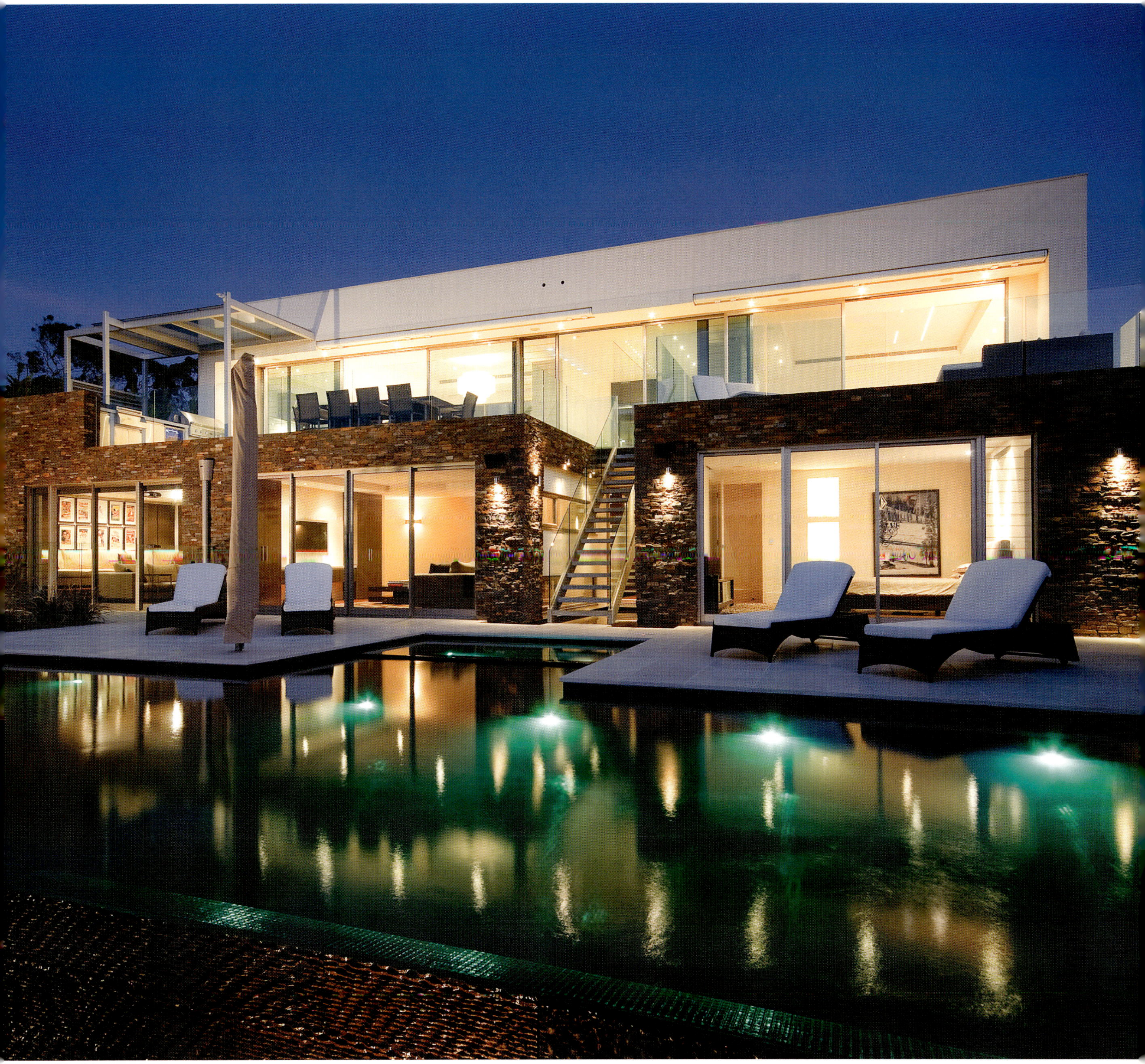

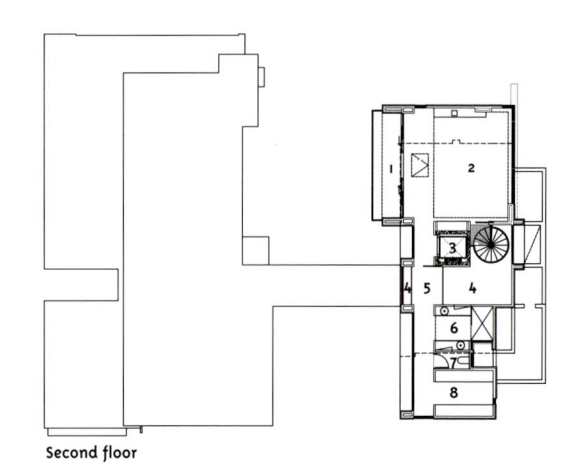

1 Balcony
2 Master bedroom
3 Lift
4 Void
5 Bridge
6 Ensuite
7 WC
8 Walk-in closet

Second floor

1 BBQ/bar
2 Terrace
3 Kitchen
4 Pantry
5 Dining
6 Void
7 Living
8 Link
9 Office
10 Lift
11 Entry 1
12 Bridge
13 Pond
14 Powder room

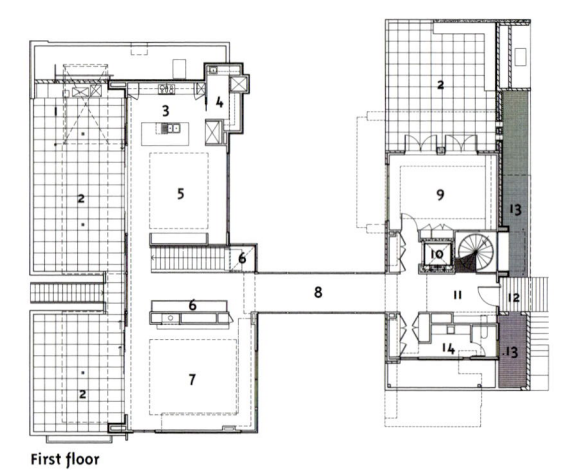

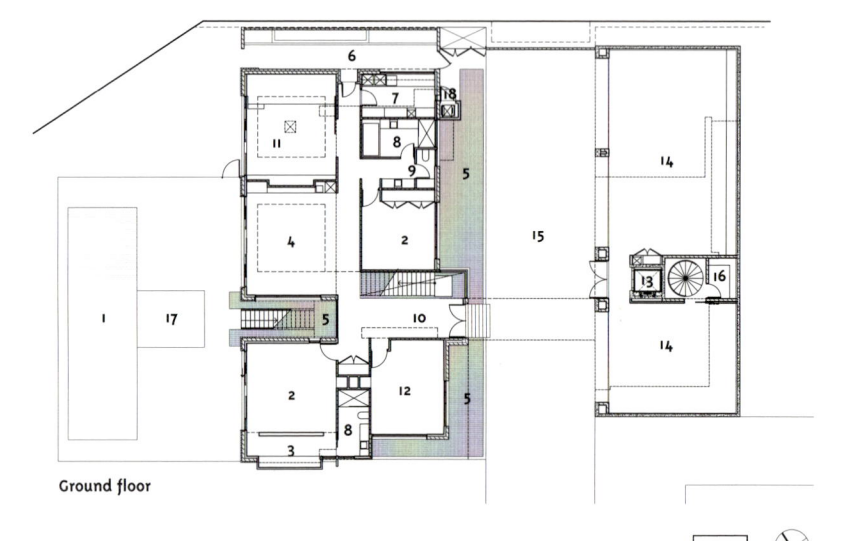

First floor

Ground floor

1 Pool	7 Laundry	13 Lift
2 Bedroom	8 Bathroom	14 Garage
3 Walk-in closet	9 Powder room	15 Driveway
4 Rumpus room	10 Entry 2	16 Cellar
5 Pond	11 Theater	17 Spa
6 Service courtyard	12 Gymnasium	18 Garbage shute

0 3m

Mount Eliza House

Northwood House

Sydney, New South Wales, Australia
Cullinan Ivanov Partnership

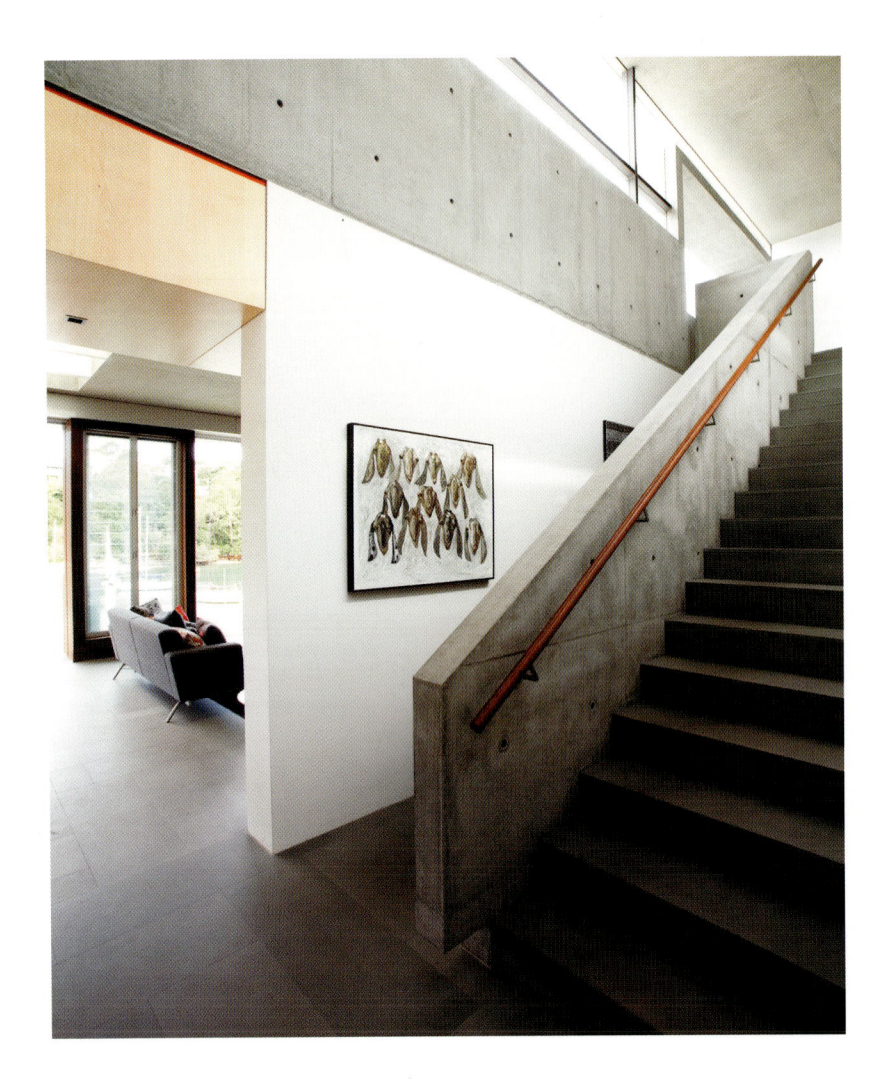

Built on a 7,500-square-foot foreshore site, this four-bedroom house comprises an open-plan living, dining, and kitchen area and enjoys extensive water views to the east. The house is split over three levels: the entry, main, and lower levels. The entry opens up to the east, allowing for framed and controlled views to the water. To the north, a low, clear-glazed corner brings in reflected northern light from a pond and provides privacy from the neighboring house. The main level comprises two pavilions with a courtyard in between.

The eastern pavilion contains the living, kitchen, and dining spaces and affords the best views over the water. To the south, separated by four steps is the master bedroom, which shares similar, uninterrupted views. The western pavilion houses the children's areas, including the playroom, bedrooms, and bathrooms. This pavilion arrangement allows for a number of openings that provide a high level of controlled natural cross-ventilation. The thermal mass of the concrete helps keep the house at comfortable temperatures all year round. The lower level contains the rumpus room and a self-contained flat to the north and a study to the south.

Photography by Giles Westley

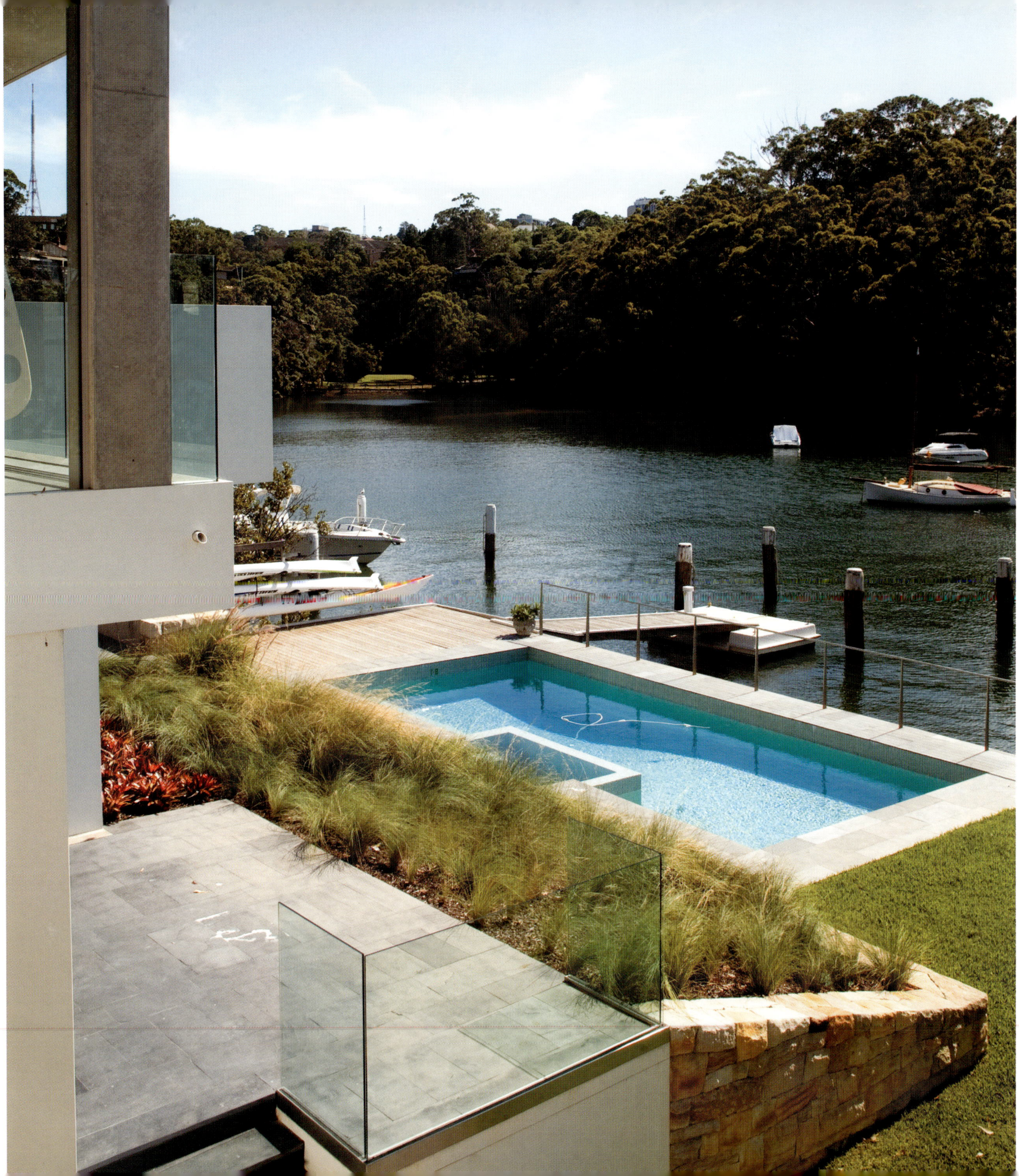

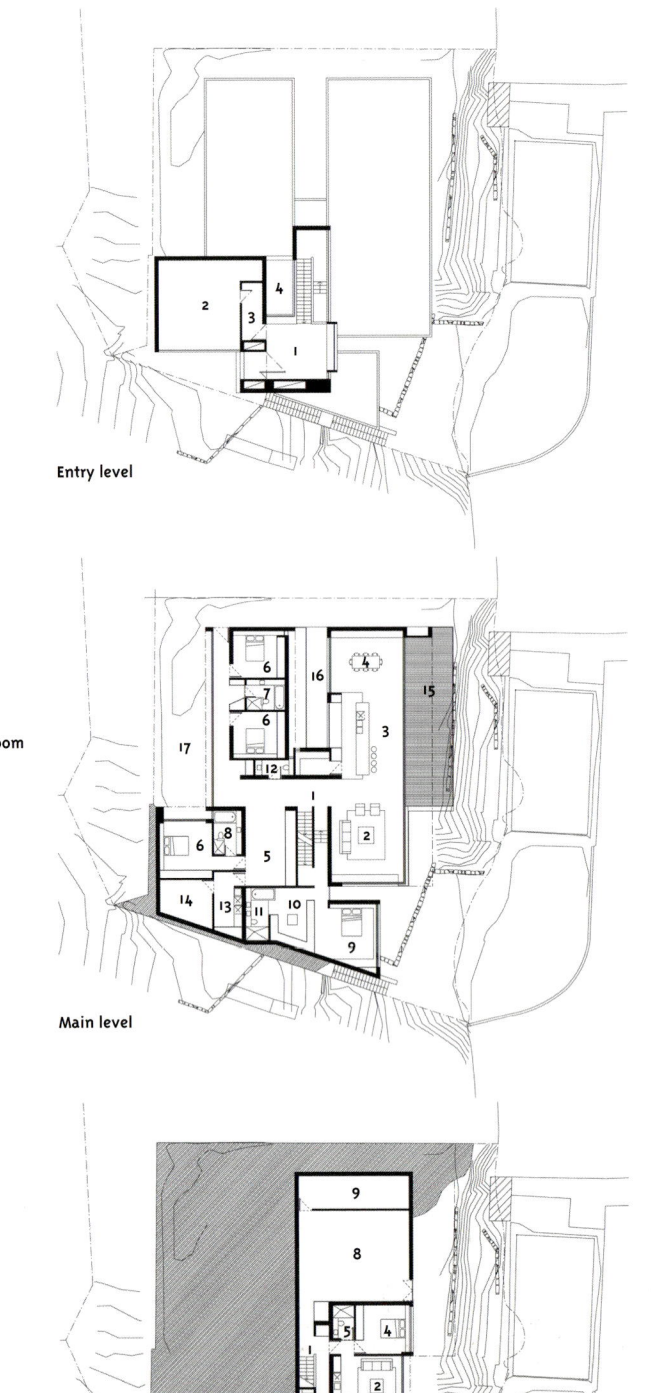

1 Entry
2 Garage
3 Cloak room
4 Reflective pond

Entry level

1 Stair landing
2 Living
3 Kitchen
4 Dining
5 Children's playroom
6 Bedroom
7 Bathroom
8 Ensuite
9 Master bedroom
10 Walk-in closet
11 Ensuite
12 Guest WC
13 Laundry
14 Cellar
15 Deck
16 Light courtyard
17 Children's lawn

Main level

1 Landing
2 Living
3 Kitchen
4 Bedroom
5 Ensuite
6 Study
7 Study WC
8 Store room
9 Plant room

Lower level

0 5m

Northwood House

Ocean House

Hawaii Island, Hawaii, USA
Olson Kundig Architects

Inspired by traditional Balinese palaces and temples, this contemporary residence is sited on a beautiful promontory of exposed lava. A river of hardened lava runs through the site, symbolically connecting the house to the great Hawaiian sources of energy—the mountains and the sea.

Though modern, the house uses tropical design concepts to fit naturally into its setting and to take advantage of time-honored building practices. Broad overhangs protect the large expanses of sliding window walls from the sun, yet allow the house to be cooled by sea breezes. Windows are arranged to maximize cross ventilation, and a combination of shutters, screens, and doors allow the owners to adjust the temperature inside.

A lava rock base anchors the house to the site, while the roof planes appear to float in the sky. The house is built with long-lasting materials—stone, teak, bronze, steel, and copper—to stand up to the harsh coastal weather. The restrained elegance of the material palette serves as a quiet backdrop for the owners' collection of Asian art and artifacts as well as modern art.

Photography by Paul Warchol

125

Ground floor

0 20ft

1	Auto court	8	Guest room
2	Courtyard	9	Kitchen
3	Entry	10	Terrace
4	Gallery	11	Garage
5	Great room (living, dinning, sitting)	12	Game room
6	Master bedroom	13	Lanai
7	Den	14	Pool

Ocean House

Ocean View House

Fire Island Pines, New York, USA
Bromley Caldari Architects

This spacious, open vacation residence was designed to minimize distinctions between interior and exterior areas. The overall structure comprises the main house, a guesthouse and dining pavilion linked by timber boardwalks, and a pool and adjoining cabana. The main house is the primary living area and is oriented to command optimal views of the Fire Island oceanfront. The interior of the house was designed by Jenkins Baer Associates.

A timber boardwalk leads to the understated main entrance of the house, which then opens up to a large, double-height living area with high ceilings, large windows and skylights. This centrally located, ground-floor room is the main room of the house. On the first floor, the master bedroom features a "window in the wall" pivoting panel that opens to a view into the double-height living room. The poolside cabana features an outdoor daybed, bathroom, shower, and changing room, while the guesthouse comprises three bedrooms, a gym, and a full kitchen. The dining pavilion is accessed via a timber path that runs between the guesthouse and the main residence. The light colors and natural palette used throughout the interior and exterior make for crisp summery spaces that provide striking contrast to the surrounding coastal vegetation and beach landscape.

Photography by Mikiko Kikuyama, Nathan Kirkman, and Bromley Caldari

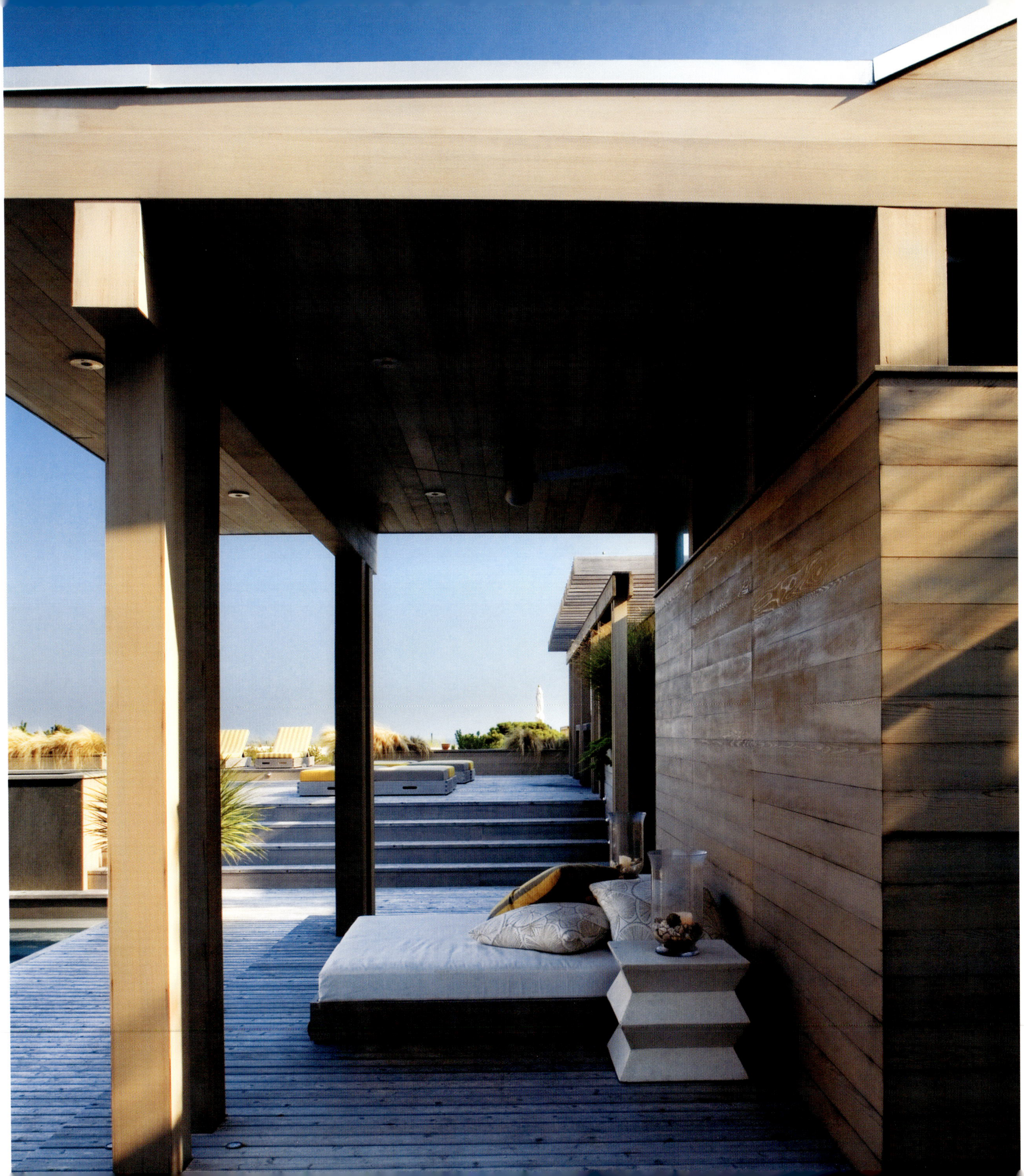

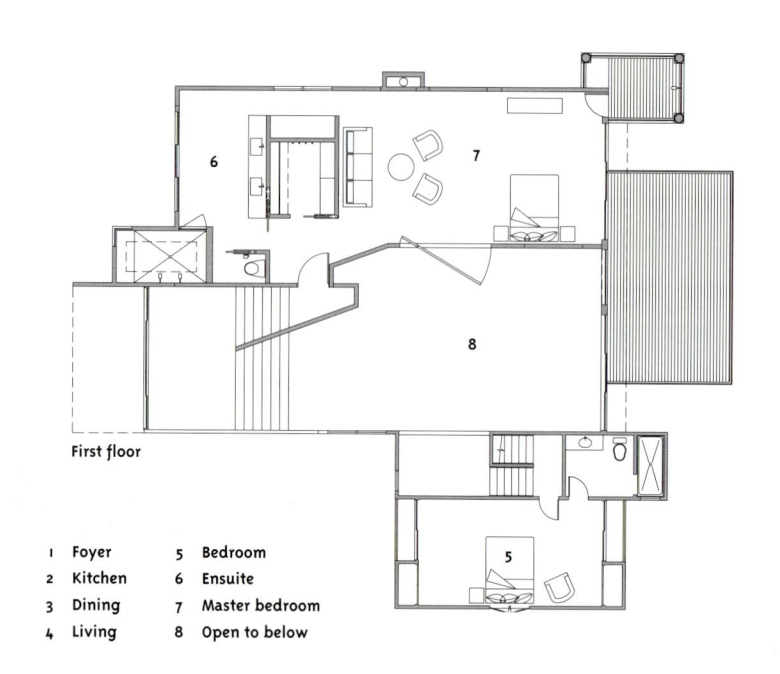

130

First floor

1. Foyer
2. Kitchen
3. Dining
4. Living
5. Bedroom
6. Ensuite
7. Master bedroom
8. Open to below

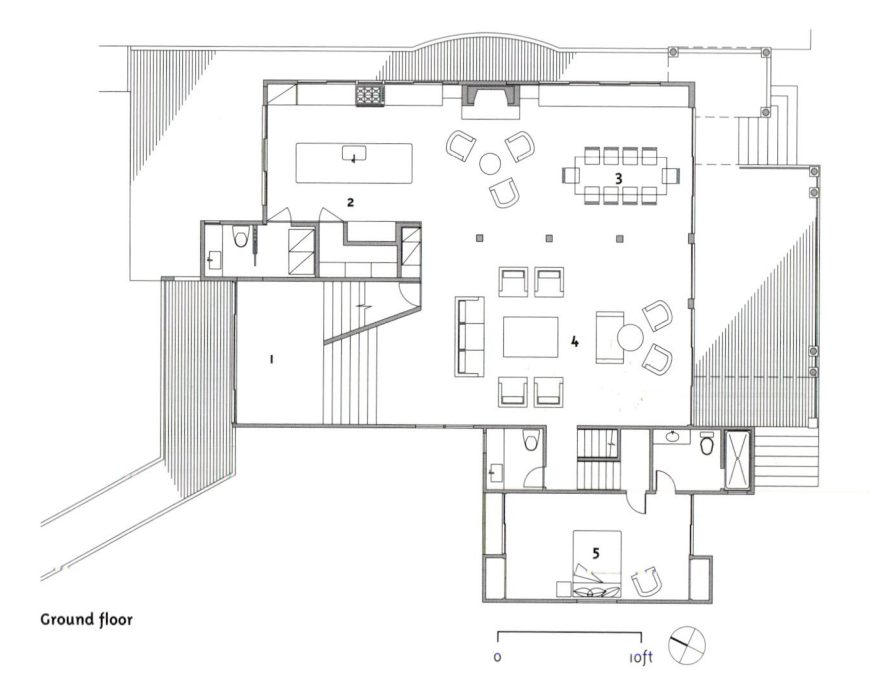

Ground floor

0   10ft

131

Ocean View House

Ocean Weekender

Flinders, Victoria, Australia
Graham Jones Design

To achieve a connection between this structure and the local rural and coastal environments, the designers conceived the house as a "lightbox" with continuous glazing that allows for a total viewing experience. The glass curtain wall and galvanized steel portal skeleton provide a seamless backdrop to the vast southern ocean and ever-changing seasonal landscape.

Perched on the highest point of the site is a simple, tubular-designed plywood-clad weekender. The upper tube cantilevers over the lower for the full length of the building on the southern side and comprises the kitchen, dining, and principal living area, which then opens onto a large deck angled directly toward the ocean to the east. A solid wall to the north provides privacy from the neighboring properties, and solar access is achieved by angling the roof and inserting highlight windows.

An open-tread staircase splits the tubular design internally at the rear of the kitchen, creating a separate zone for the master suite that contains a small study area opening onto a private north-facing rear deck. An internally glazed ensuite takes in a 180-degree rural view beyond the master bedroom. A guest room, multipurpose room, and bathroom on the lower level also enjoy the site's spectacular scenery.

Photography by Chris Groenhout

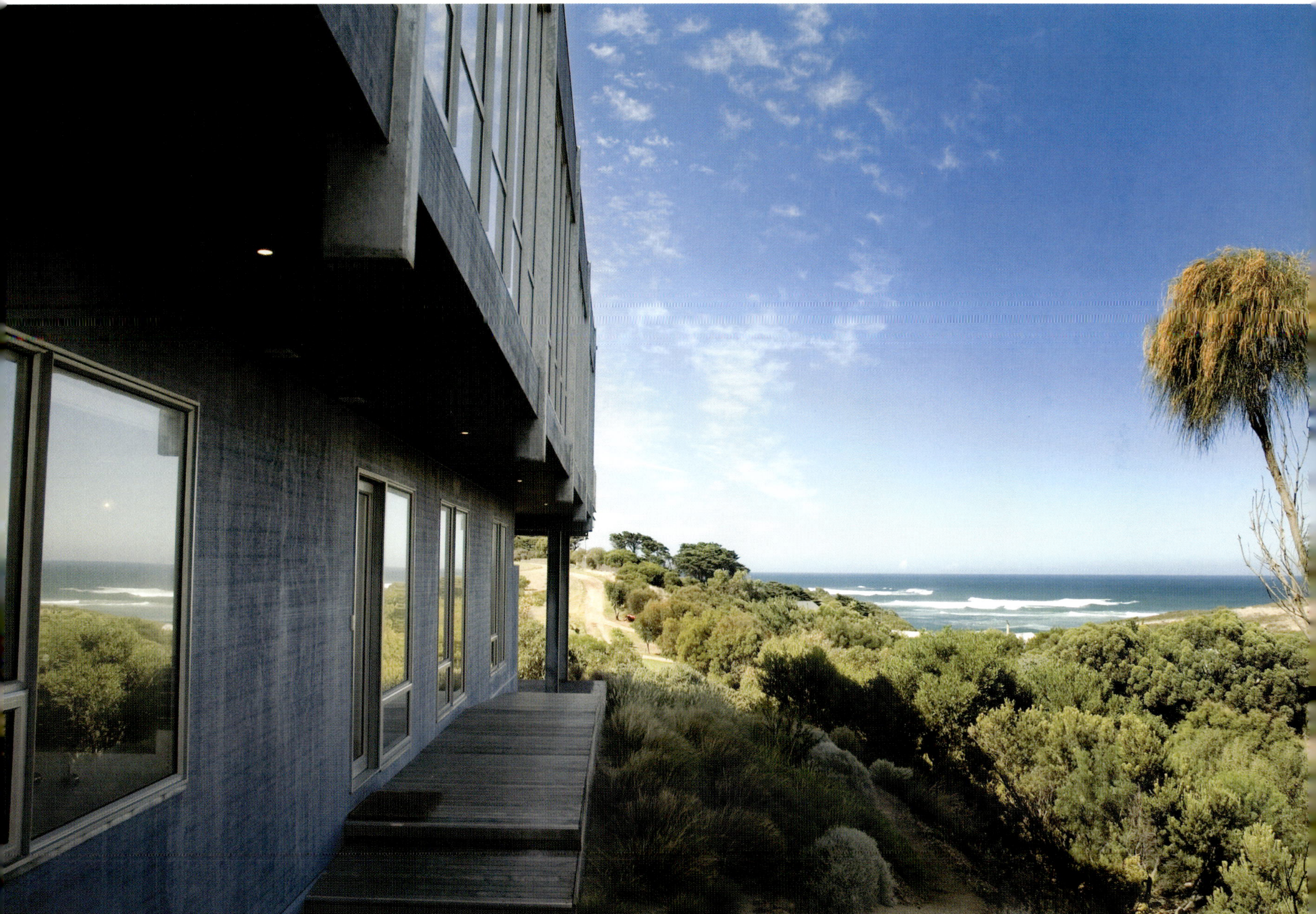

First floor

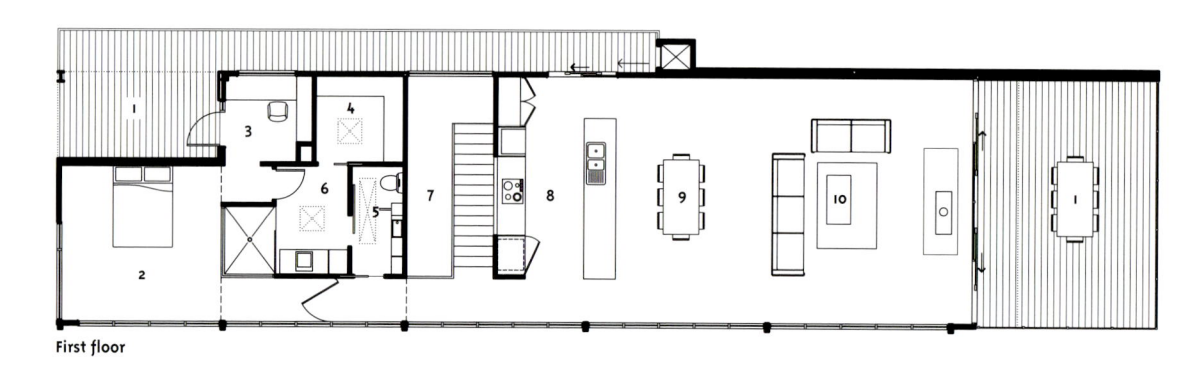

1. Deck
2. Master bedroom
3. Study
4. Walk-in-robe
5. Powder room
6. Ensuite
7. Void
8. Kitchen
9. Dining
10. Living

Ground floor

1. Water tank
2. Laundry
3. Bathroom
4. WC
5. Entry
6. Bedroom
7. Multipurpose
8. Workshop
9. Carport

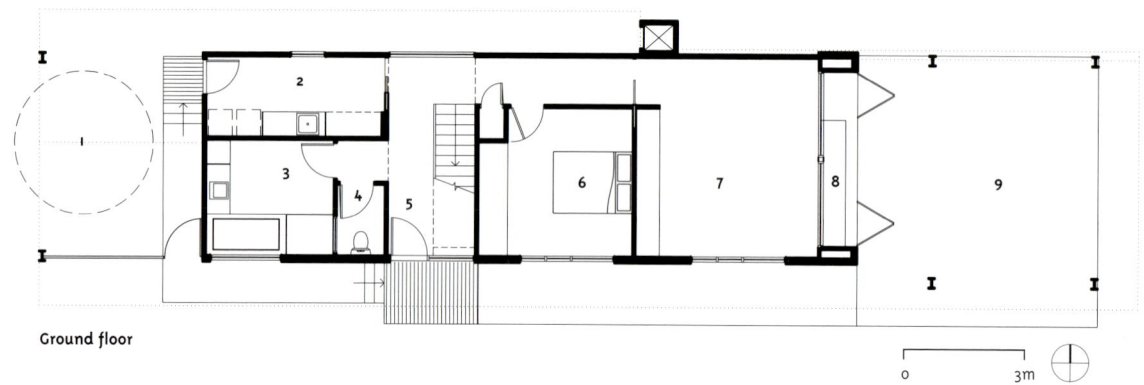

Ocean Weekender

Onetangi House

Onetangi Beach, Waiheke Island, New Zealand
Stevens Lawson Architects Ltd

This black timber house is situated beside a rocky outcrop at the eastern end of the beach. Dug into the base of a steep slope, the house is partially concealed behind a mature pohutukawa tree. The main living areas and bedroom are elevated to the first floor and open out onto decks on two sides, affording striking views down the beach and providing separation from the boating and beach activity below.

The house has an irregular, angular form that is responsive to its location and suggests an air of informality appropriate for a vacation home. The living spaces form a crescent shape that wraps around the pohutukawa tree and encloses an outdoor room with a fireplace. The irregular, carved timber fins have an organic, textured quality that animates the building edge while providing screening from the road and a sense of enclosure to the upper deck and living areas. The simple roof is created from a single tilted plane trimmed to fit the angular plan form, resulting in interior spaces with unusual geometries. This house has been imbued with a strong local flavor through the use of local materials and references to the local vernacular and natural environment.

Photography by Patrick Reynolds

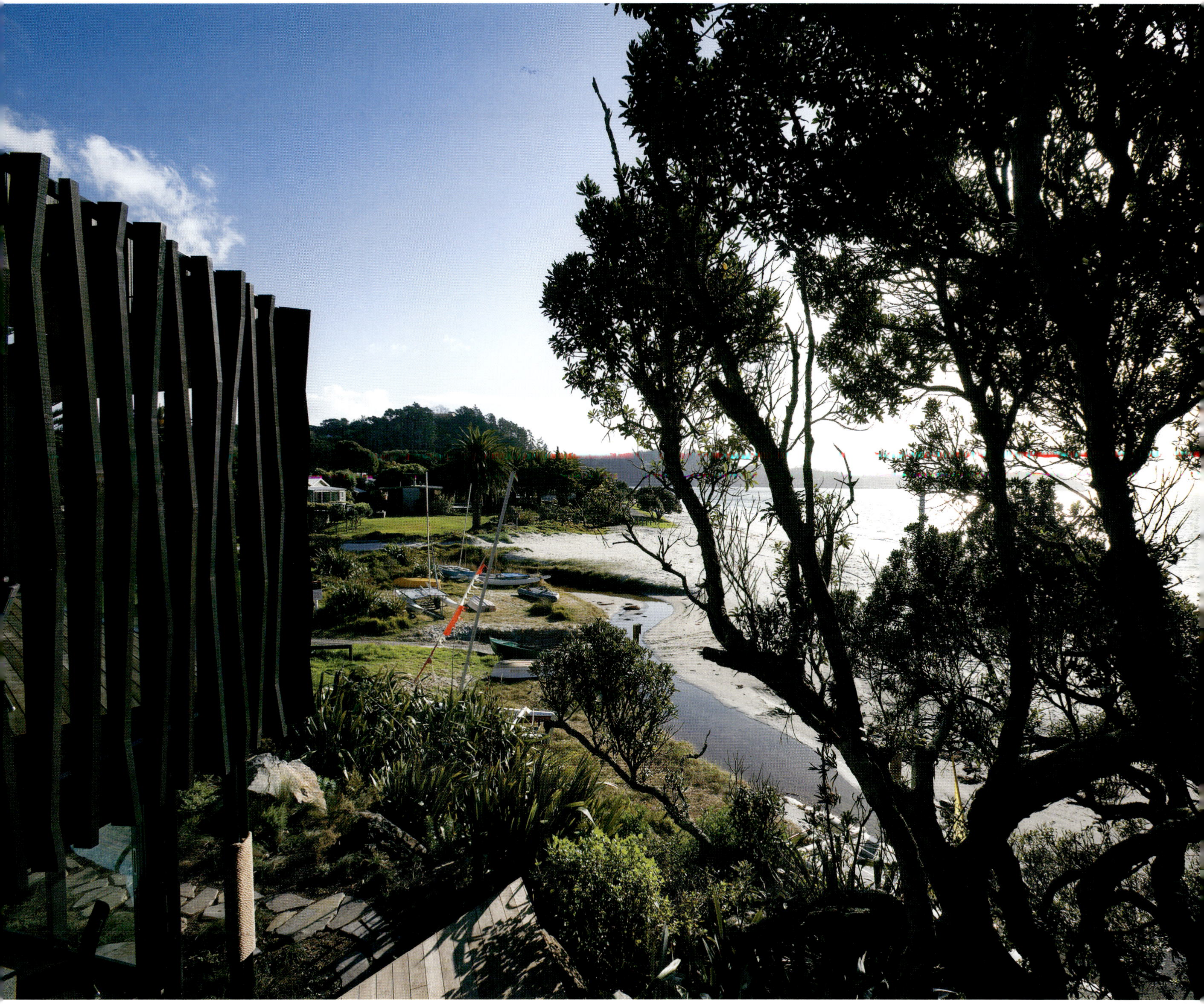

1 Entry
2 Living
3 Dining
4 Kitchen
5 Master bedroom
6 Dressing room
7 Ensuite
8 Bedroom
9 Garage
10 Deck

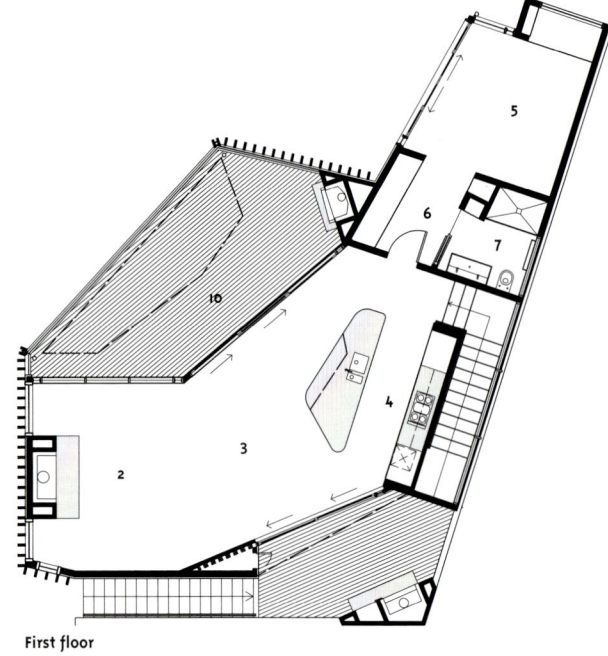

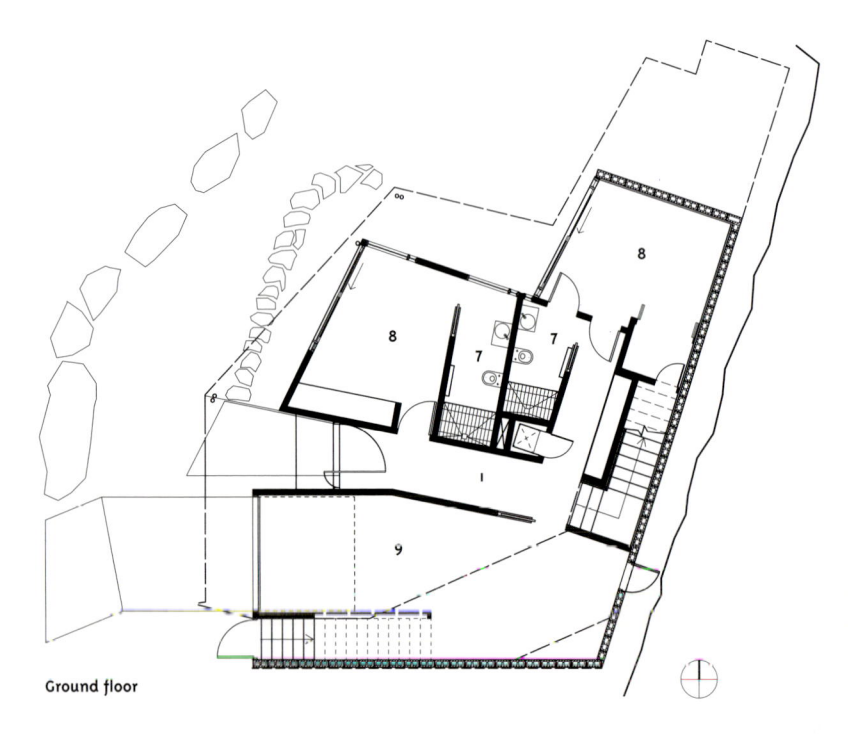

First floor

Ground floor

Onetangi House

Palmasola

Puerto Vallarta, Mexico

Girvin Associates and Manolo Mestre

Located just north of Puerto Vallarta, Mexico, Palmasola was built as a private residence on 2.25 acres within the Punta Mita Resort. Comprising 11 separate structures in a tropical, village-like setting, the residence offers 25,000 square feet of spacious living on a pristine beach.

Flanked by a Jack Nicklaus Signature golf course and a Four Seasons Hotel, Palmasola's authentic Mexican architecture and classic tropical landscape provide an unforgettable setting. A 200-foot-long undulating infinity edge pool provides security and visually connects outdoor spaces to the Pacific Ocean. Stepping stones float across the pool surface and provide access to the beach and a romantic dining palapa.

Lush, tropical landscaping offers privacy and shade from the hot Mexican sun while creating and separating outdoor spaces. Meandering walkways, stands of mature planting, and stone walls direct views and provide intimacy throughout the site, taking advantage of the "borrowed" landscape to give the compound scale and context. Service paths are strategically located to provide separation from primary circulation corridors.

Photography by Michael Calderwood and Mark Callanan

141

142

143

Palmasola

Parmela Residence

Gold Coast, Queensland, Australia
Paul Uhlmann Architects

This project, originally a 1970s beachfront residence, was reduced to its necessary structure, remodeled, and replanned to suit a modern beachside lifestyle. The internal living area, kitchen, dining room, and master bedroom were located on the first floor and were designed to achieve an open living space while encapsulating the beach views. Sliding doors between the living areas and the master bedroom were incorporated to provide privacy for the occupants when required.

The existing, expansive first-floor beach terrace was maintained and enhanced by extending an outside living area into this space, thus allowing the occupants to take full advantage of the beachfront location. Large sliding doors are retracted to combine the internal and external spaces, and the large, folded roof structure encapsulates the deck using solid, transparent, and adjustable louvers to allow the occupants to control both views and privacy. A floating timber roof plane provides intimacy and warmth to the deck. While the renovation is modern and minimal in its design, the use of natural timbers in the built form and furnishings, combined with the utilization of the existing travertine floors, softens the spaces and contributes rich colors and textures.

Photography by Kylie Hood

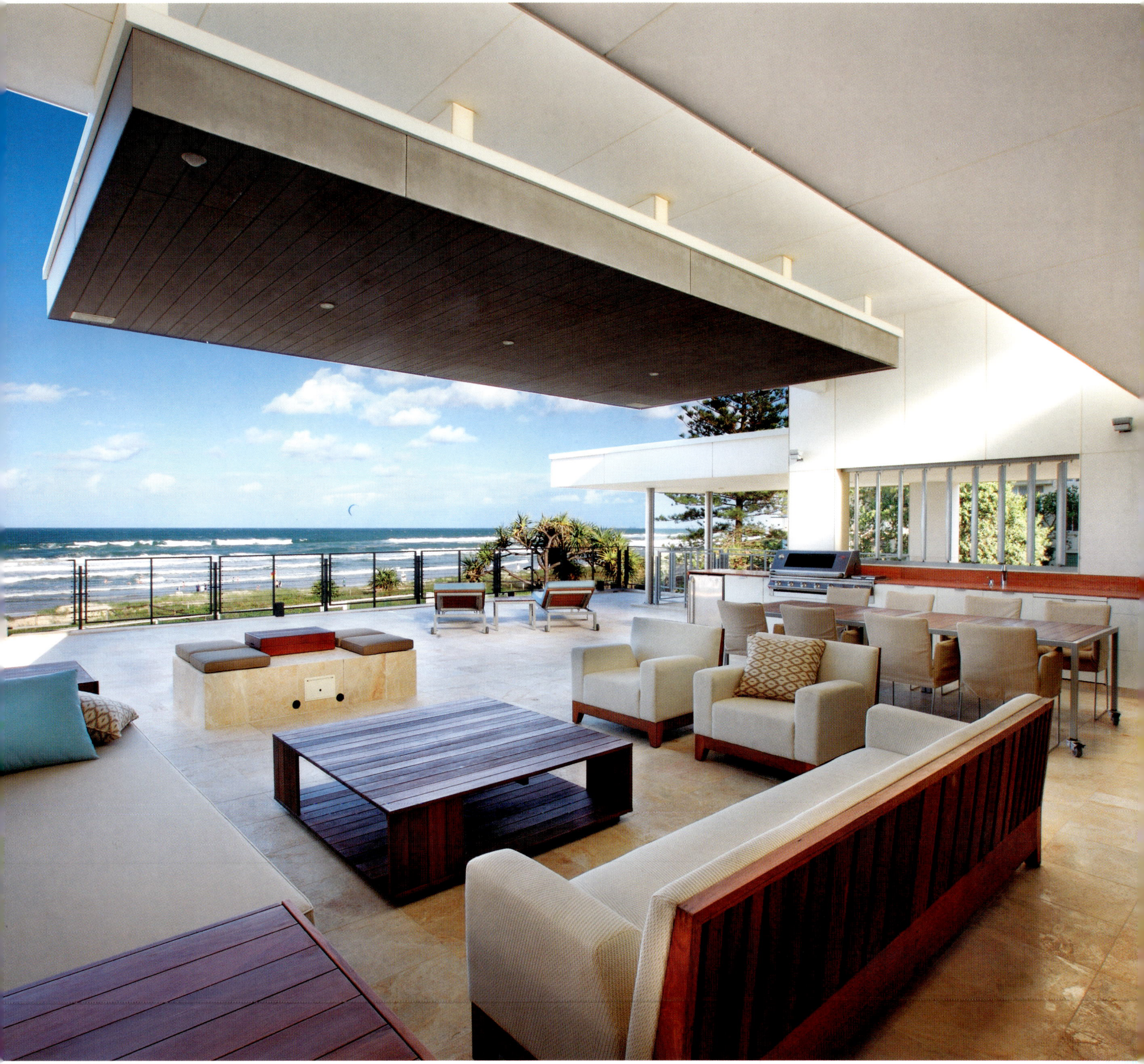

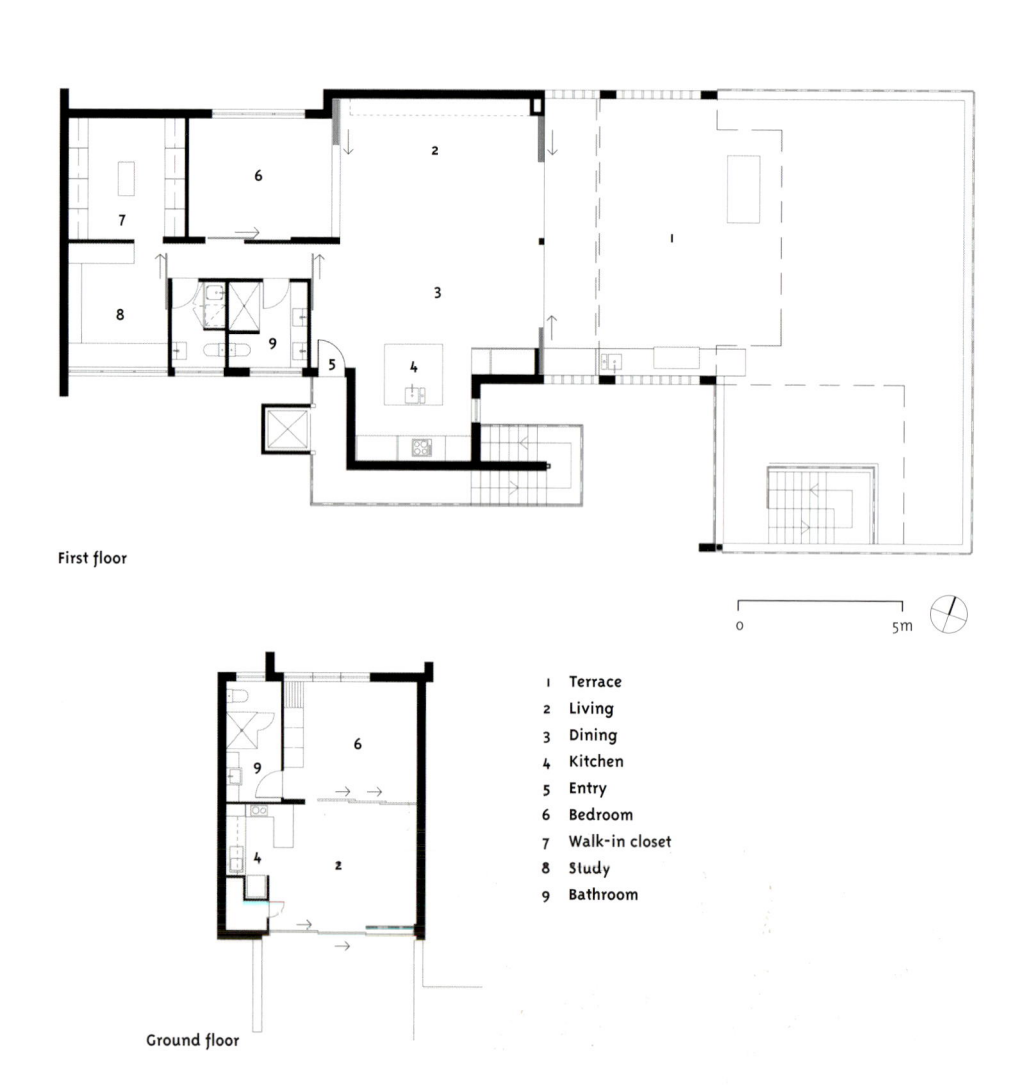

First floor

Ground floor

0 5m

1. Terrace
2. Living
3. Dining
4. Kitchen
5. Entry
6. Bedroom
7. Walk-in closet
8. Study
9. Bathroom

Parmela Residence

Peloponnese House

Peloponnese, Greece

Alexandros N. Tombazis and Associates Architects Ltd

This 2,000-square-foot house is built on a hillside overlooking the Gulf of Corinth. Due to the natural slope of the ground it was built over three levels—a basement with ancillary spaces, a ground floor comprising the main living spaces, and a mezzanine level above the kitchen—and resembles a cube perched on a sloping site.

The residence was developed according to bioclimatic design principles and has a solar chimney incorporated in its south façade. The main living areas create a unified open space and feature a two-sided, energy-efficient fireplace placed in the middle of the mezzanine railing, partly hanging over the living room. Special care was taken to ensure the gradual transition from interior to exterior areas. To achieve this the architect oriented the verandas toward both the sea and mountain views and positioned windows to allow natural lighting of all spaces throughout the day.

Fair-faced concrete was chosen for the exterior to better blend the building into the colors of the natural environment, and the roofs are planted. All interior walls are painted white and are complemented by various shades of gray throughout the house, punctuated by vividly colored doors and furniture.

Photography by Alexandros N. Tombazis

149

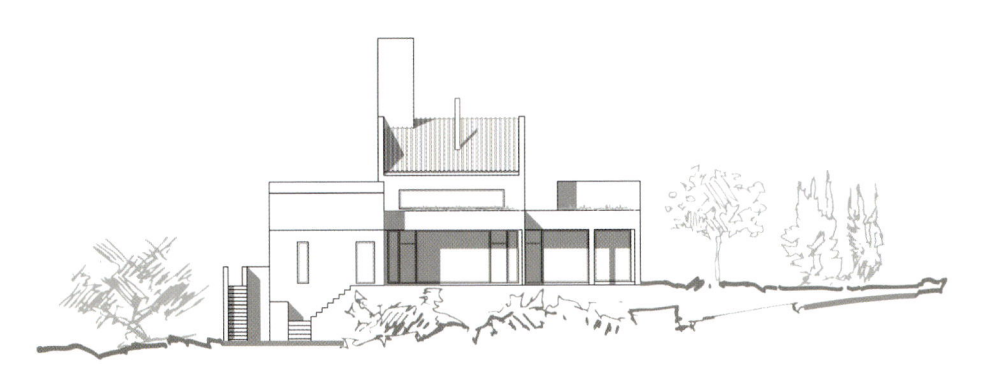

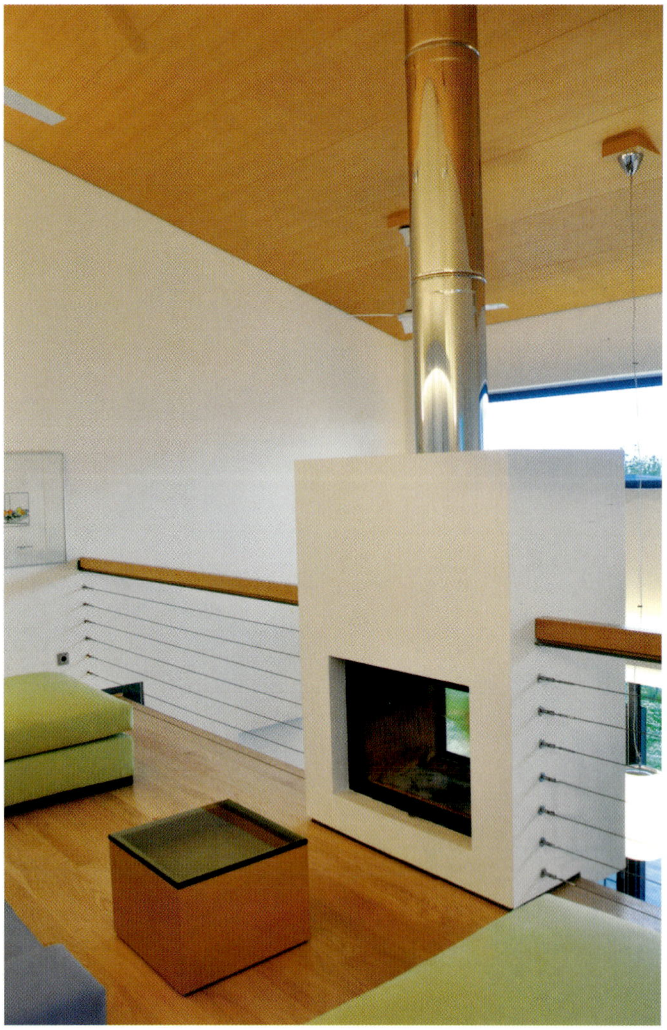

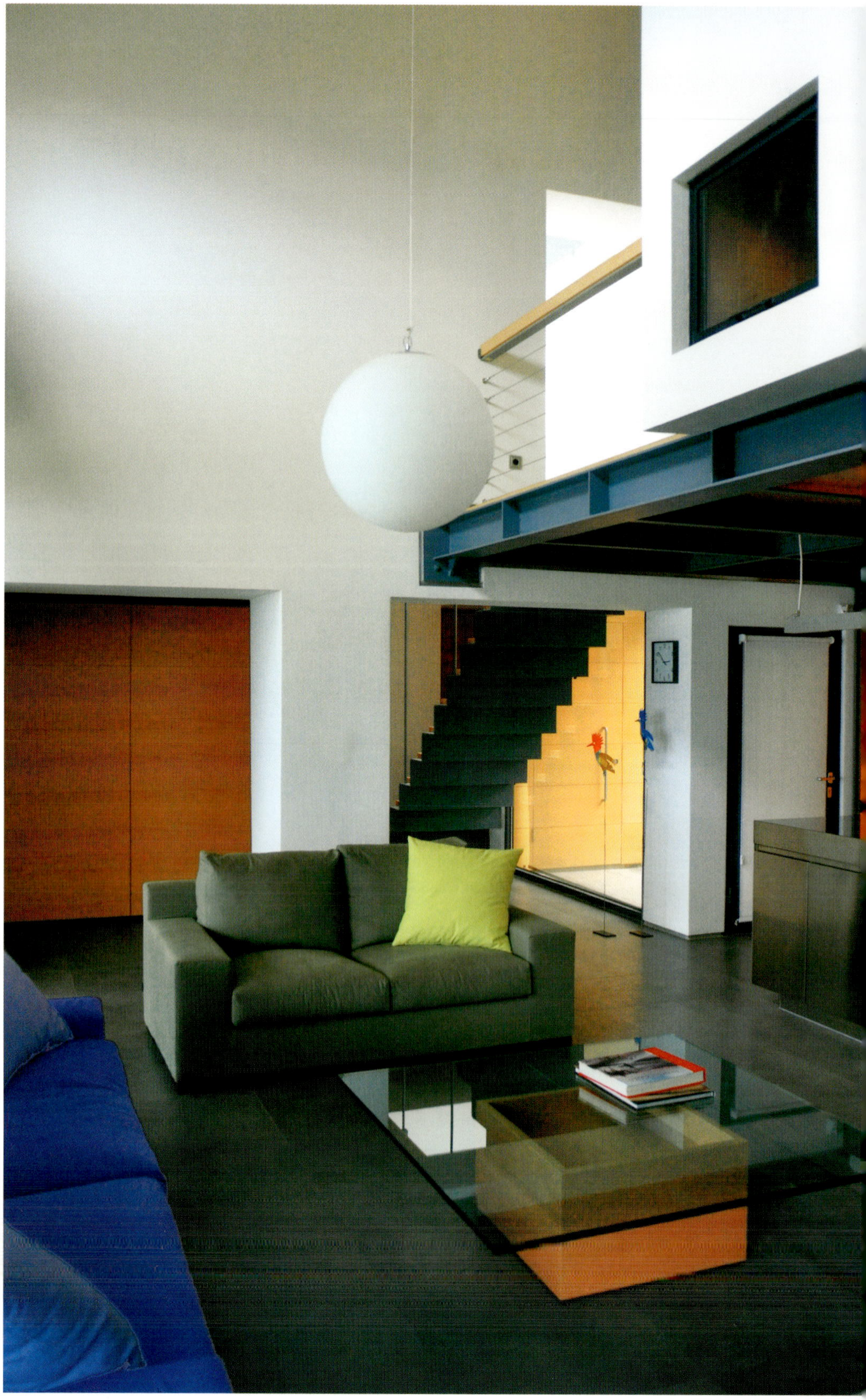

Peloponnese House

Peregian Beach House

Peregian Beach, Queensland, Australia
Middap Ditchfield Architects

This vacation house is located on an elevated site overlooking Peregian Beach and foreshore. The house steps down the site to take full advantage of dramatic ocean views, which also helps to connect internal and external spaces to the ground plane. Courtyard spaces have been introduced to reduce building bulk, capture north light, and promote through-building viewing opportunities to the pool, ocean, and other areas of the house.

Where possible, the building has been designed to be a single room in width to maximize natural light and cross ventilation. A central circulation spine is flanked by an off-form concrete wall, which continues for the length of the house. This is the structure's key feature and provides thermal mass for natural climate control and defines the circulation spine, while the off-form board finish presents a weathered driftwood character.

Large wall openings in the living areas are achieved by a series of sliding, stack-away doors that give a transparent quality while allowing easy access to the exterior spaces, which feature a raised pool and spa at the same level as the main outdoor living area. External materials were chosen for their low maintenance and robust characteristics. Solar hot water systems have been installed and roof water is collected in above-ground tanks for reuse.

Photography by Aperture Photography

153

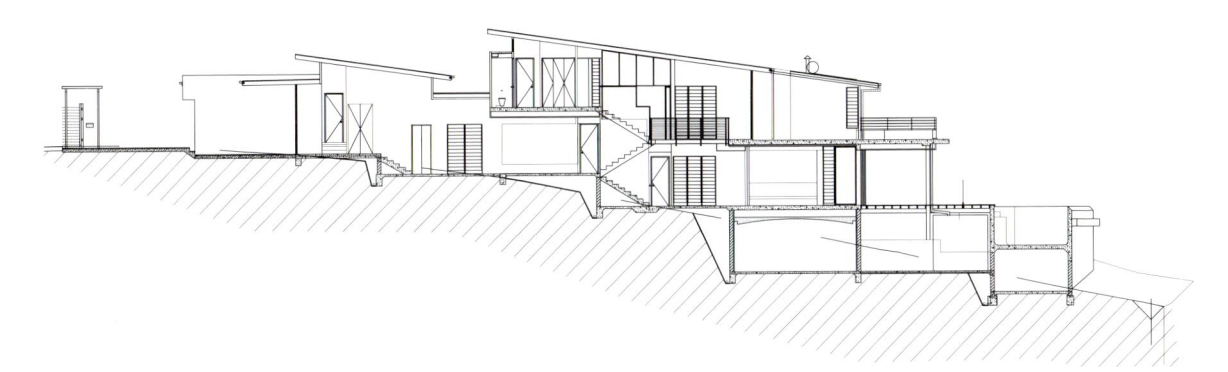

154

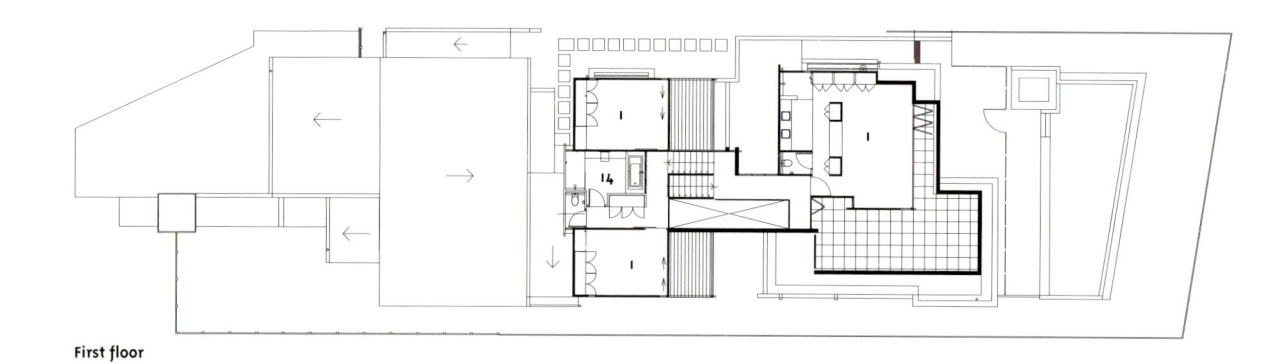

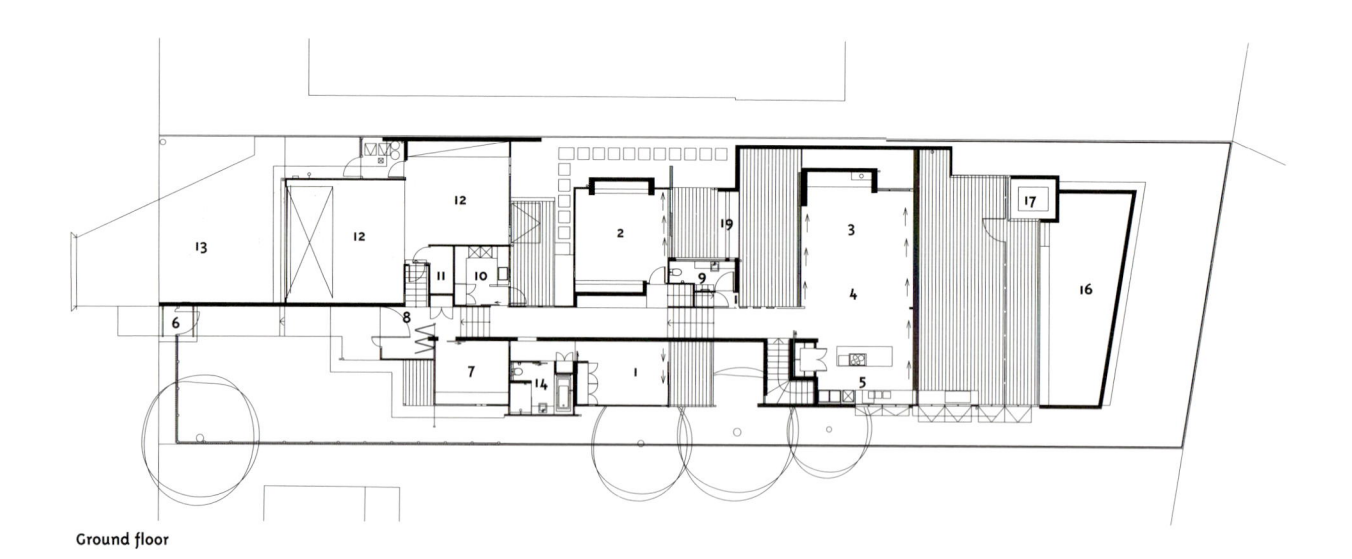

First floor

Ground floor

1	Bedroom	11	Storeroom
2	Media room	12	Garage
3	Living	13	Driveway
4	Dining	14	Bathroom
5	Kitchen	15	Cellar
6	Gatehouse	16	Pool
7	Office	17	Spa
8	Entry	18	Water storage
9	Powder room	19	Water feature
10	Laundry		

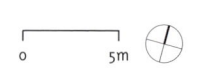

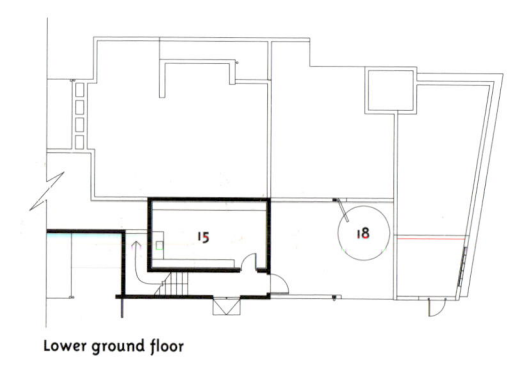

0 5m

Lower ground floor

Peregian Beach House

Phillip Island Beach House

Phillip Island, Victoria, Australia
Pleysier Perkins

The 6,000-square-foot residence is sited between a national park and cliff edge on the northwest coast of the island—a dramatic and rugged coastline subject to major climatic shifts and constant winds. The architect's design response to this environment is a solid and robust, double-story, L-shaped building that wraps around a protected pool garden.

The building is composed of two tectonically opposing wings. The wing clad in solid timber contains a double-height entry hall and sleeping quarters, including an upper-floor terrace off the master bedroom protected by a semi-transparent timber screen. The timber façades are articulated by long, vertical slot windows that capture slices of the landscape and create dynamic interior lighting effects.

The other wing contains extensively glazed living areas protected by deep eaves and terraces. The living areas in this wing are contained by a concrete block wall with open fires on both levels and an external fire on the upper-floor terrace. The kitchen and main living spaces are located upstairs to maximize the stunning ocean views.

Natural materials were selected that would age gracefully in the harsh coastal environment and include spotted gum timber, black zinc, concrete, black anodized aluminum, and glass. The natural and robust approach is carried through to the interior with concrete fireplaces, timber ceilings, and timber wall panels.

Photography by Berit Barton

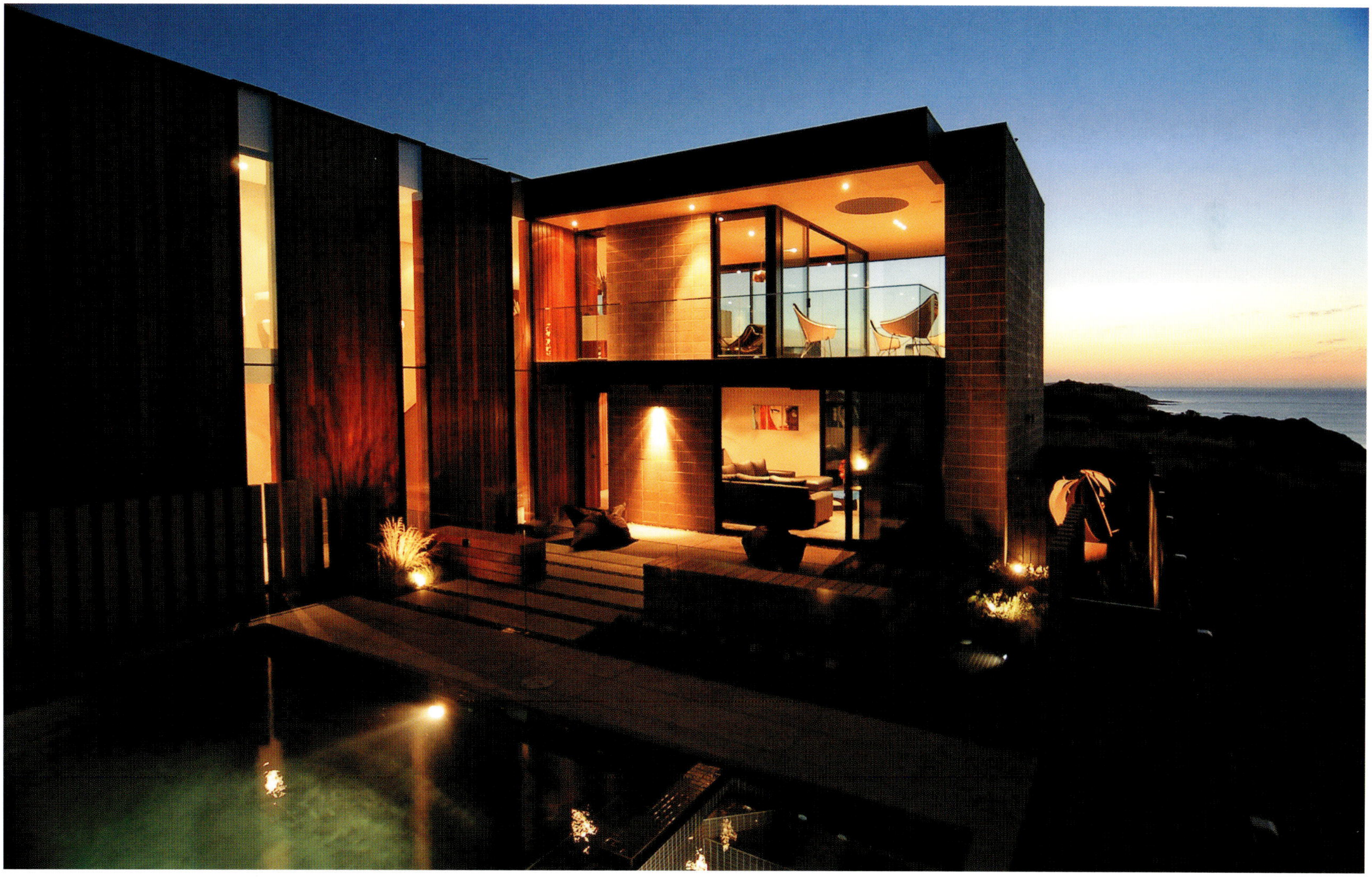

1	Entry	9	Loggia
2	Living	10	Living
3	Billiards	11	Meals
4	Bar	12	Kitchen
5	Bedroom	13	Pantry
6	Laundry	14	Study
7	Garage	15	Balcony
8	Pool		

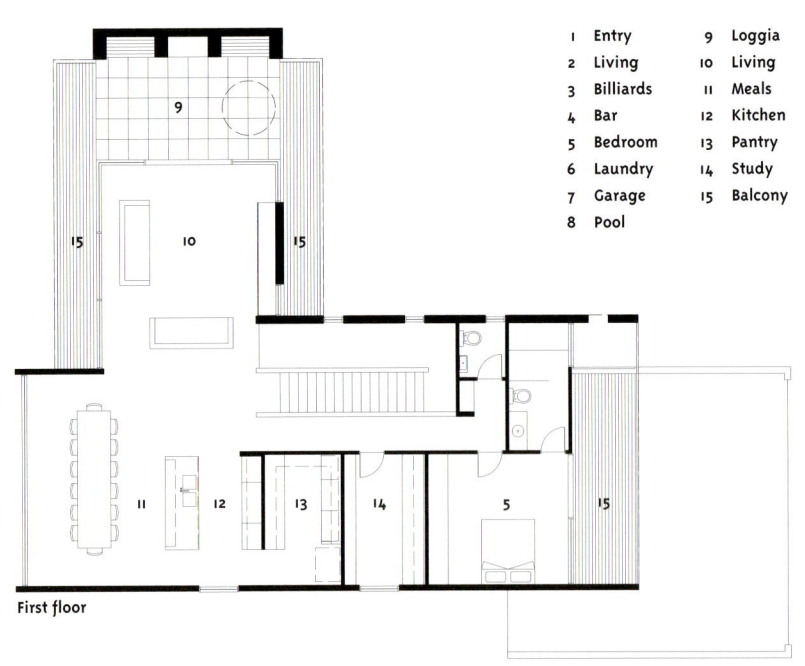

First floor

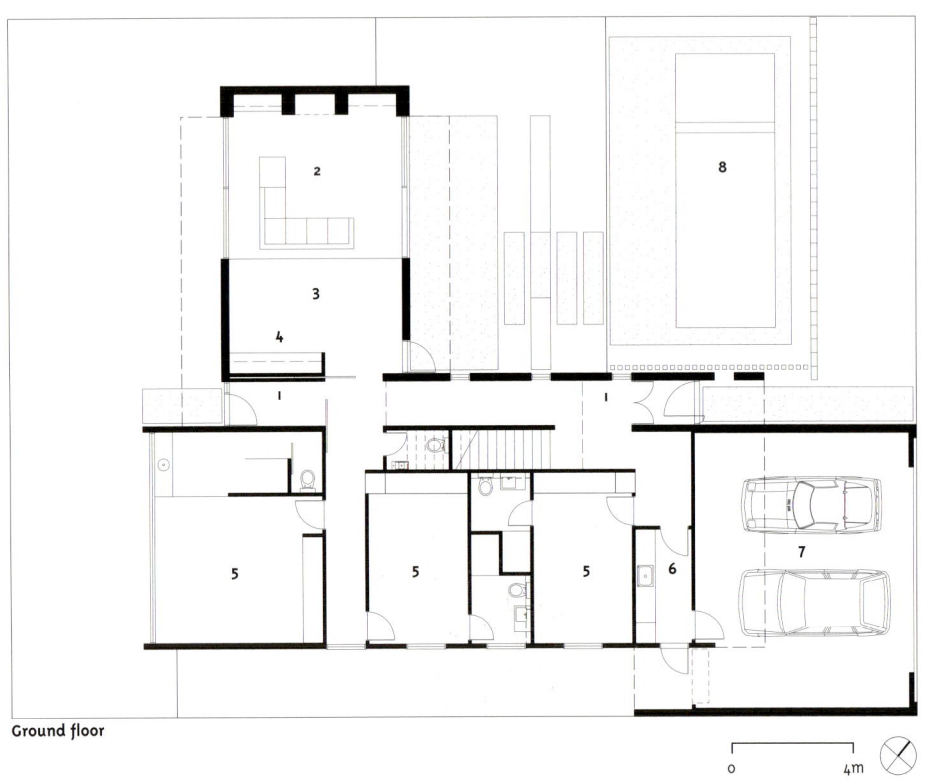

Ground floor

0   4m

Phillip Island Beach House

Portrane Residence

Portrane, County Dublin, Ireland
Damien Murtagh Architects

This 9,500-square-foot energy-efficient house consists of a double-story elongated spine, off which two additional arms extend at either end to form a private sunny courtyard. An open-plan layout was adopted by the architect, in which voids, frameless glass railings, and sliding walls allow playful interaction and communication throughout. Externally, dry stonewalls, brilliant white stone rendering, patinated copper, and cedar cladding blend effortlessly together and into their surroundings.

A recessed alcove, set at the juncture of the protective dry stonewall and the spinal core, forms the main entrance to the house. From here, access is gained to the first floor and basement levels, ground floor bedrooms, and swimming pool. The open-plan kitchen, dining, and living rooms are accessed through a large sliding door, with the dining area featuring double-height frameless corner glazing. Off the dining area is a raised living space; the dining and living areas are separated by a cantilevered, white corian-encased second stair with frameless glass rail.

Located on the second floor are a study that overlooks the dining area and the sitting room, which is the most dramatic room in the house. With its exposed single-pitch ceiling cantilevered on the coastal side, the room is afforded breathtaking views through a wall of frameless, floor-to-ceiling glass. The roof terraces are accessed from this room through large sliding doors, and external steps connect the terraces to the courtyard below.

Photography by Michael Taylor and Anthony Hopkins

161

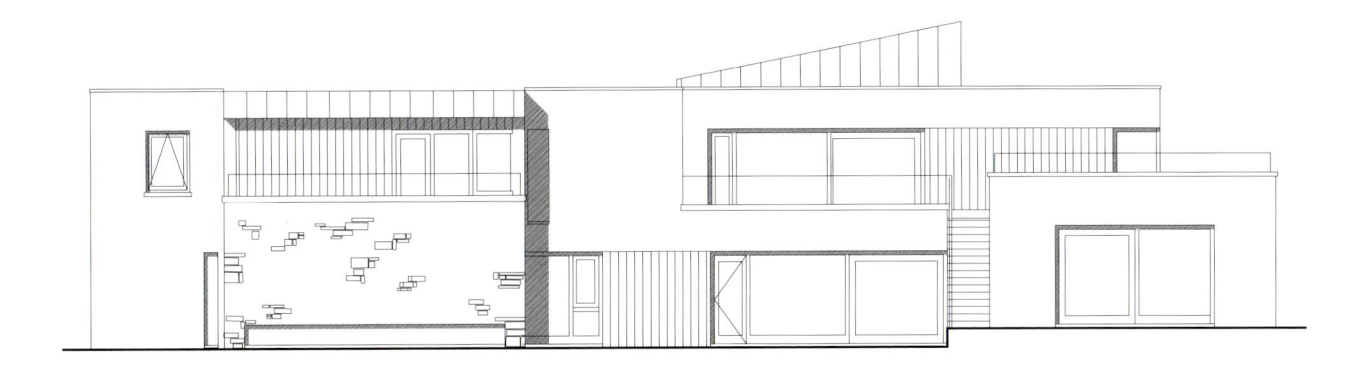

1 Entry
2 Pool
3 Kitchen
4 Dining
5 Living
6 Bedroom
7 Ensuite
8 Bathroom
9 Pantry
10 Master bedroom
11 Wardrobe
12 Sitting room
13 Study
14 Roof terrace
15 Service room
16 Utility room
17 Naturally lit gym and cinema
18 Garage
19 Steam room
20 Sauna
21 Entrance courtyard
22 Courtyard

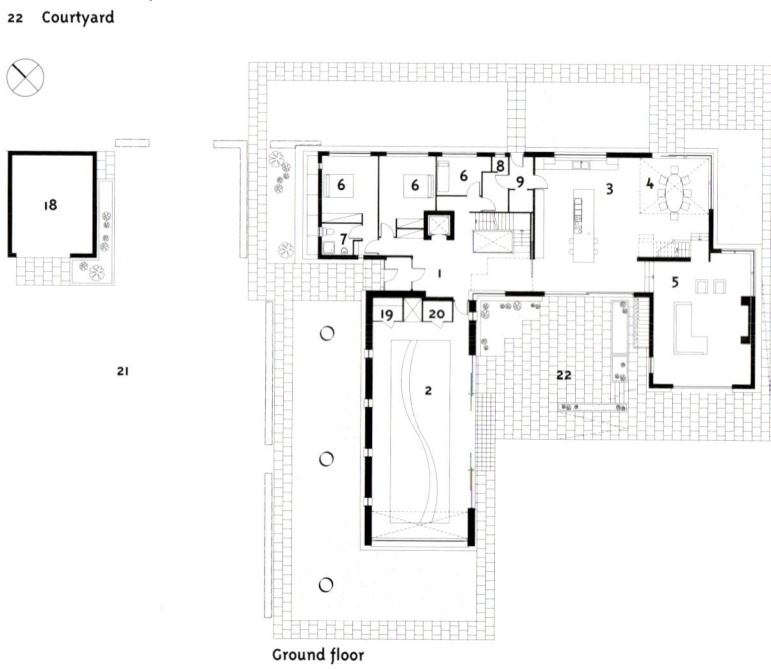

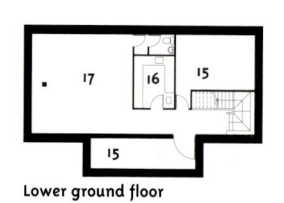

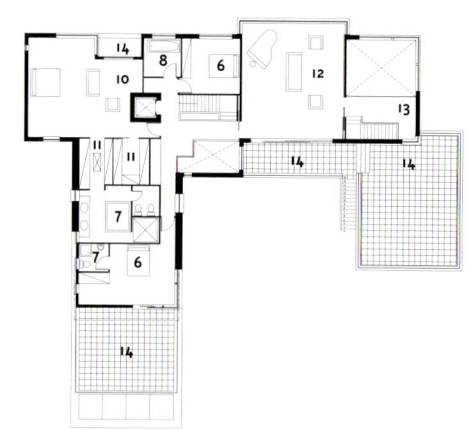

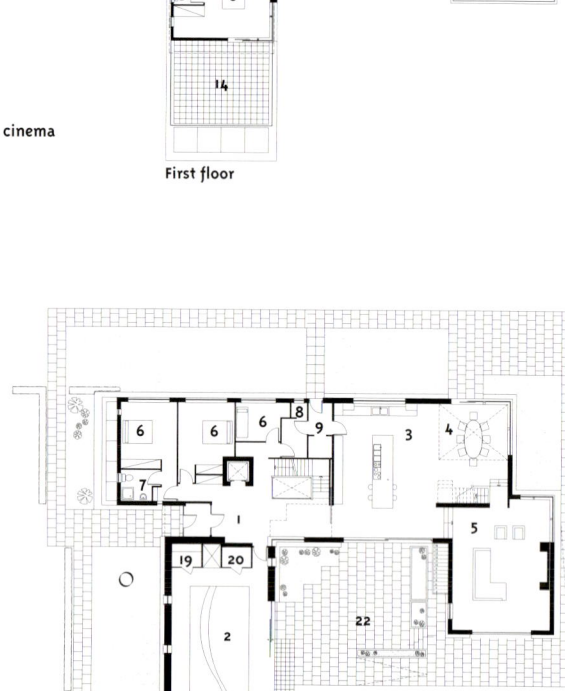

First floor

Ground floor

Lower ground floor

Portrane Residence

Point Dume Residence

Malibu, California, USA
Griffin Enright Architects

This house manipulates the typical paths of domestic movement, weaving the exterior landscape and site into the house while enhancing natural airflows and views. The 60,000-square-foot property and 6,550-square-foot house are accessed from below by a driveway.

The entry is placed in a gap between the garage and guest bedroom volumes and descends into a narrow vertical hall below two curved clerestory windows that twists sinuously toward a panoramic view of the ocean. This main interior path runs through the living area under an eco resin, custom-fabricated light box and extends to an outdoor terrace that curves around to the lap pool.

The open living area has 11-foot-high ceilings and the kitchen, dining, and living areas have a loft-like feel. The living area extends to the exterior with two large sliding doors that reveal an 11-foot-high by 22-foot-wide opening to the exterior. An over-scaled system of horizontal louvers extending along this edge of the residence controls light, incorporates library shelving, and also forms the railing system for the master bedroom terrace above. The second floor is peeled away from the louvered plane to reorient to distant ocean views and create a private master bedroom terrace. At the far end of the master bedroom terrace, a large catwalk twists around an oculus-like aperture allowing views to the outdoor terrace and pool below.

Photography by Benny Chan – Fotoworks

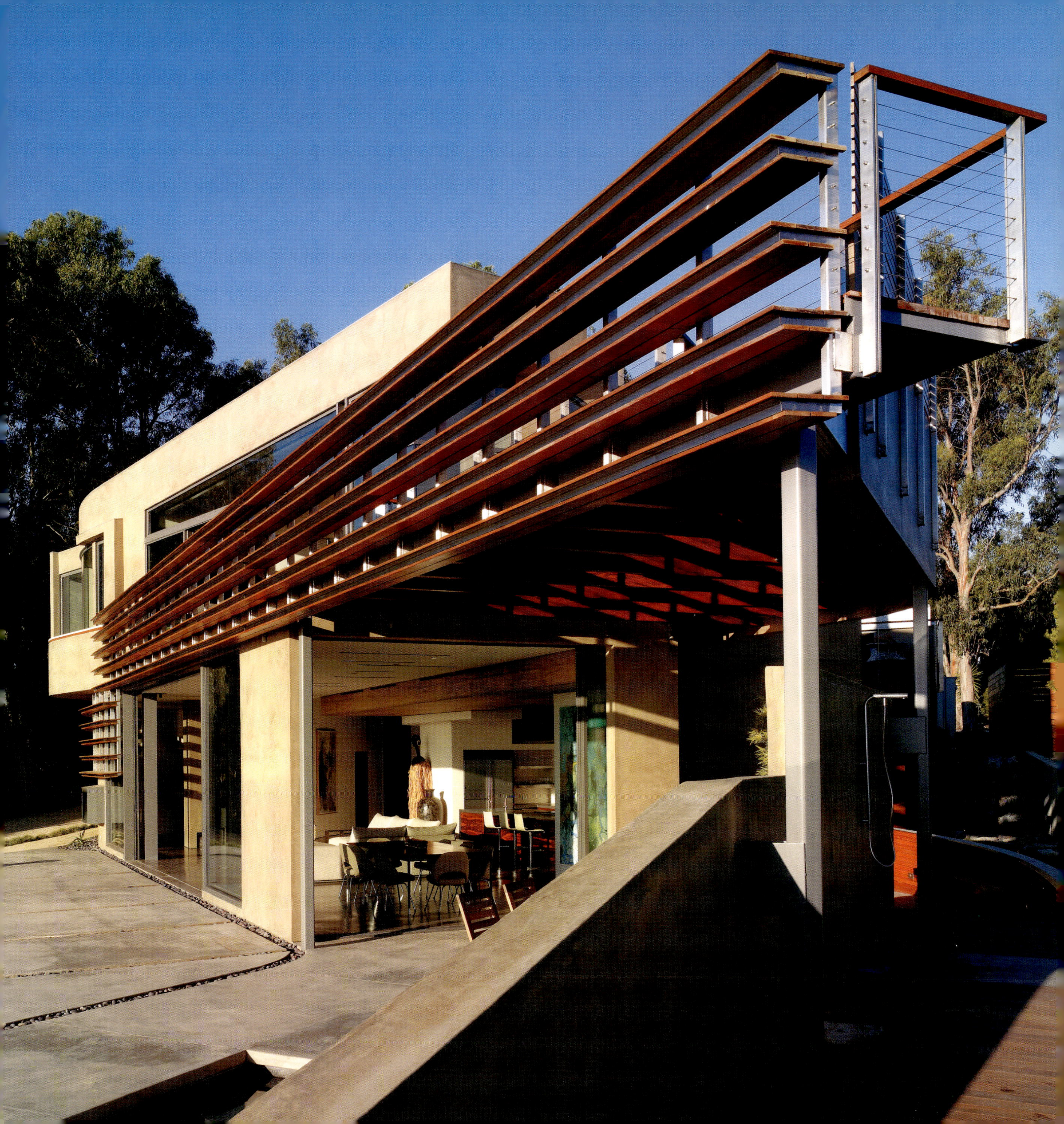

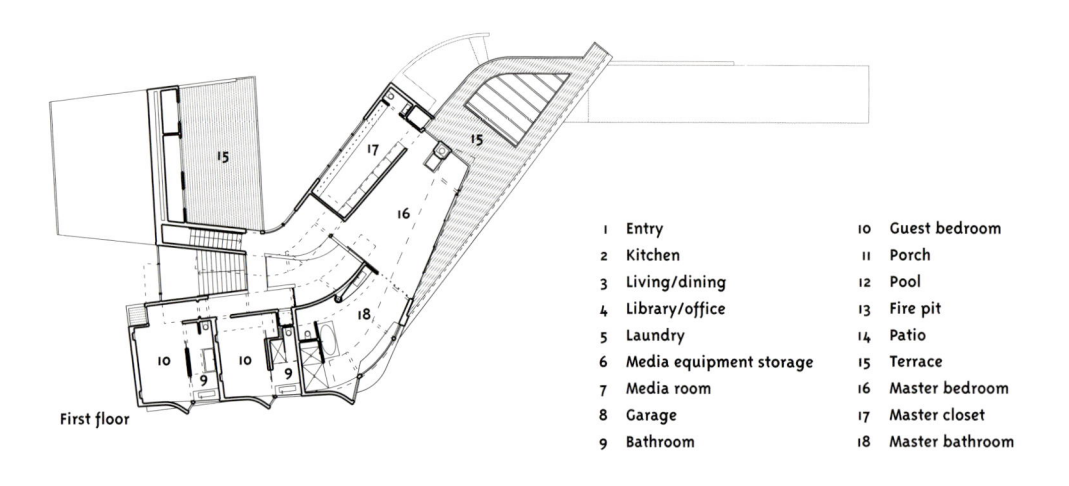

1	Entry	10	Guest bedroom
2	Kitchen	11	Porch
3	Living/dining	12	Pool
4	Library/office	13	Fire pit
5	Laundry	14	Patio
6	Media equipment storage	15	Terrace
7	Media room	16	Master bedroom
8	Garage	17	Master closet
9	Bathroom	18	Master bathroom

First floor

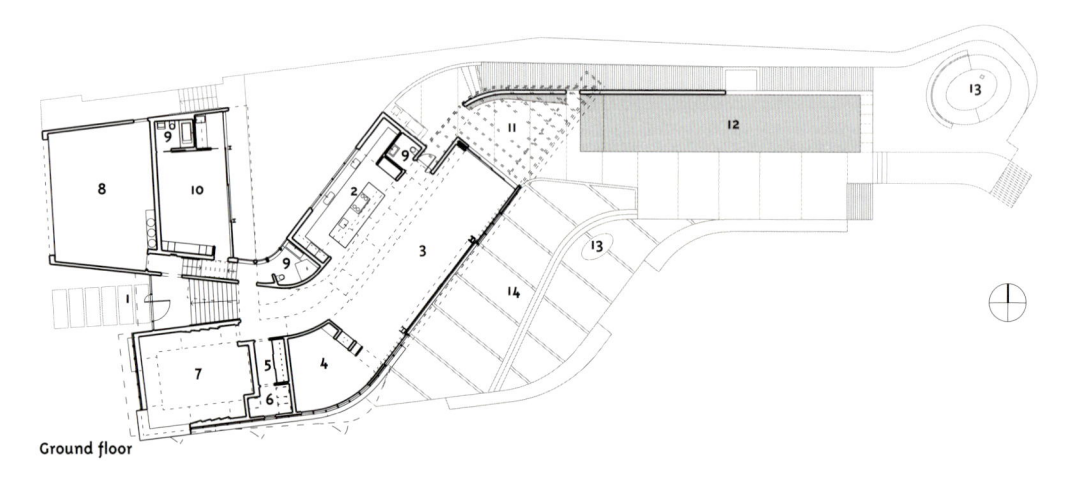

Ground floor

Point Dume Residence

Raumati Beach House

Raumati South, Kapiti Coast, New Zealand
Herriot + Melhuish: Architecture Ltd

Accessed by a steep driveway, this beachfront house is removed from the localized suburban environment, confronts the westerly sea view, and is bounded by trees to the north and south. The home was conceived as a simple arrangement around a central entrance spine and transverse timber skylight that anchors the center of the house. The sculpted timber form of the central skylight, as well as admitting sun and light in the morning hours, acts as a storage and display zone between the entry, bedroom, and living areas. The kitchen/dining/living space spans the breadth of the west elevation, opening up to the view. In contrast, the bedrooms are more closed, with aspects to north and south via controlled openings and high-level clerestories.

A simple palette of exterior materials includes painted board and batten, local river stone, hardwood timber slats and screens, combined with aluminum windows and doors. Some external finishes extend into the interior to accentuate the connection with the outside. Exposed timber framing elements, revealed within some interior walls and ceilings, refer back to a more traditional beach house typology.

Photography by Paul McCredie

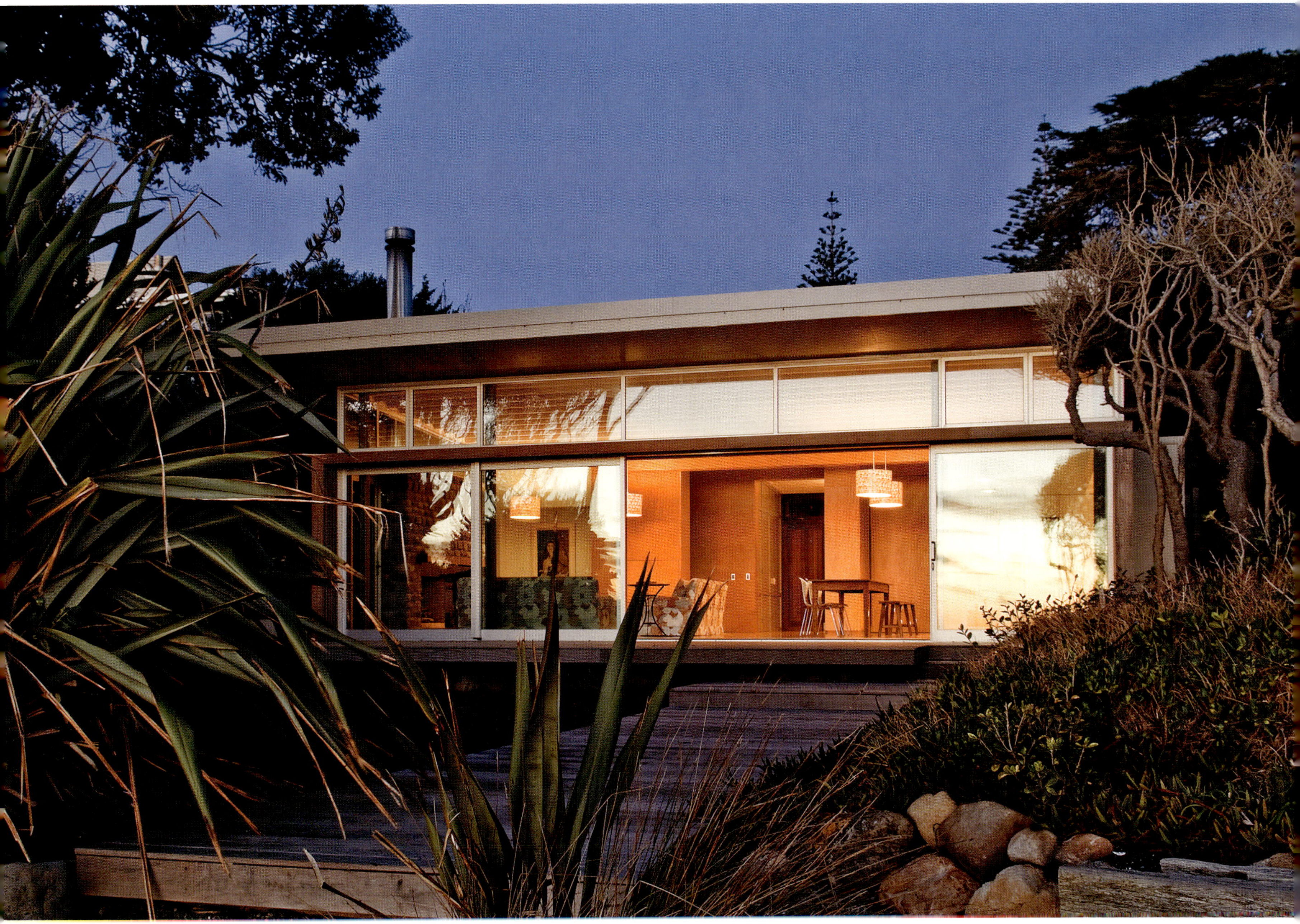

Ground floor

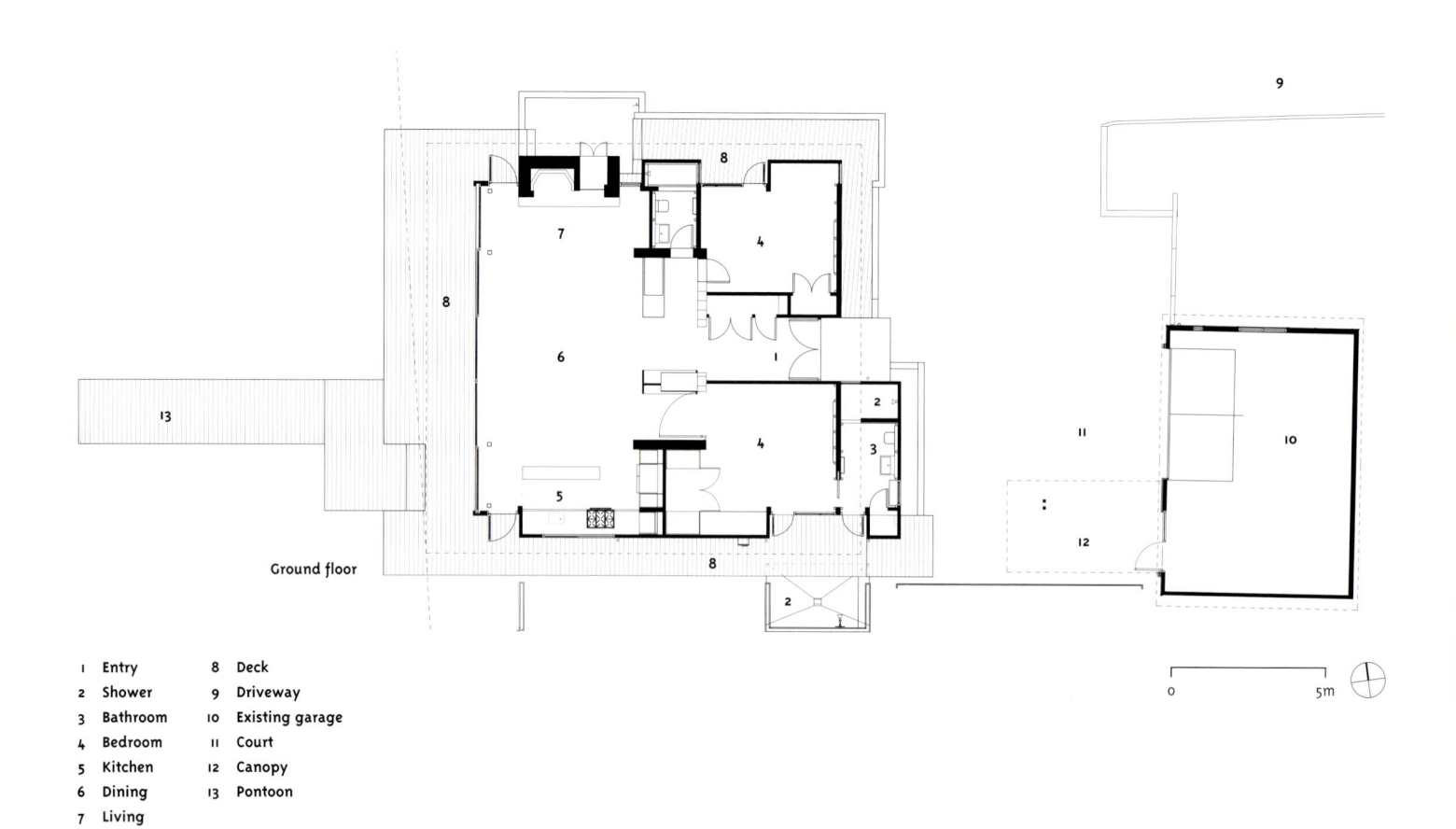

1	Entry	8	Deck
2	Shower	9	Driveway
3	Bathroom	10	Existing garage
4	Bedroom	11	Court
5	Kitchen	12	Canopy
6	Dining	13	Pontoon
7	Living		

Raumati Beach House

Rubinsztein House

Sydney, New South Wales, Australia
Rolf Ockert Design

This house is located on a small but stunningly located site with panoramic views of the Pacific Ocean. To the east, the house opens up almost completely to large decks that overlook the water, with the sliding doors designed to allow many different configurations for the internal–external connection of spaces. A generous, open-plan living/dining/kitchen area at entry level is the central focus of the house, with the children's areas located below and the master bedroom above. A series of stairs, including the open, main stair running across the short length of the site, connects all levels effortlessly.

The centerpiece on the upper level is the freestanding bathtub in the middle of a room that offers uninterrupted views across the ocean. A large, curved sliding door closes off the otherwise open bedroom area for acoustic and visual privacy. The lower floor is the children's realm, comprising three large bedrooms and a play area with direct access to the lower garden and pool.

The main, middle level has a large kitchen, a dining area in its own protruding pocket, and the main seating area located under a curved void. Some design decisions, made on site after experiencing the play of light through holes in the roof formwork as it was laid, resulted in design features that help define the house, such as the three skylights over the void and the hole-filled wall to the garage.

Photography by Sharrin Rees

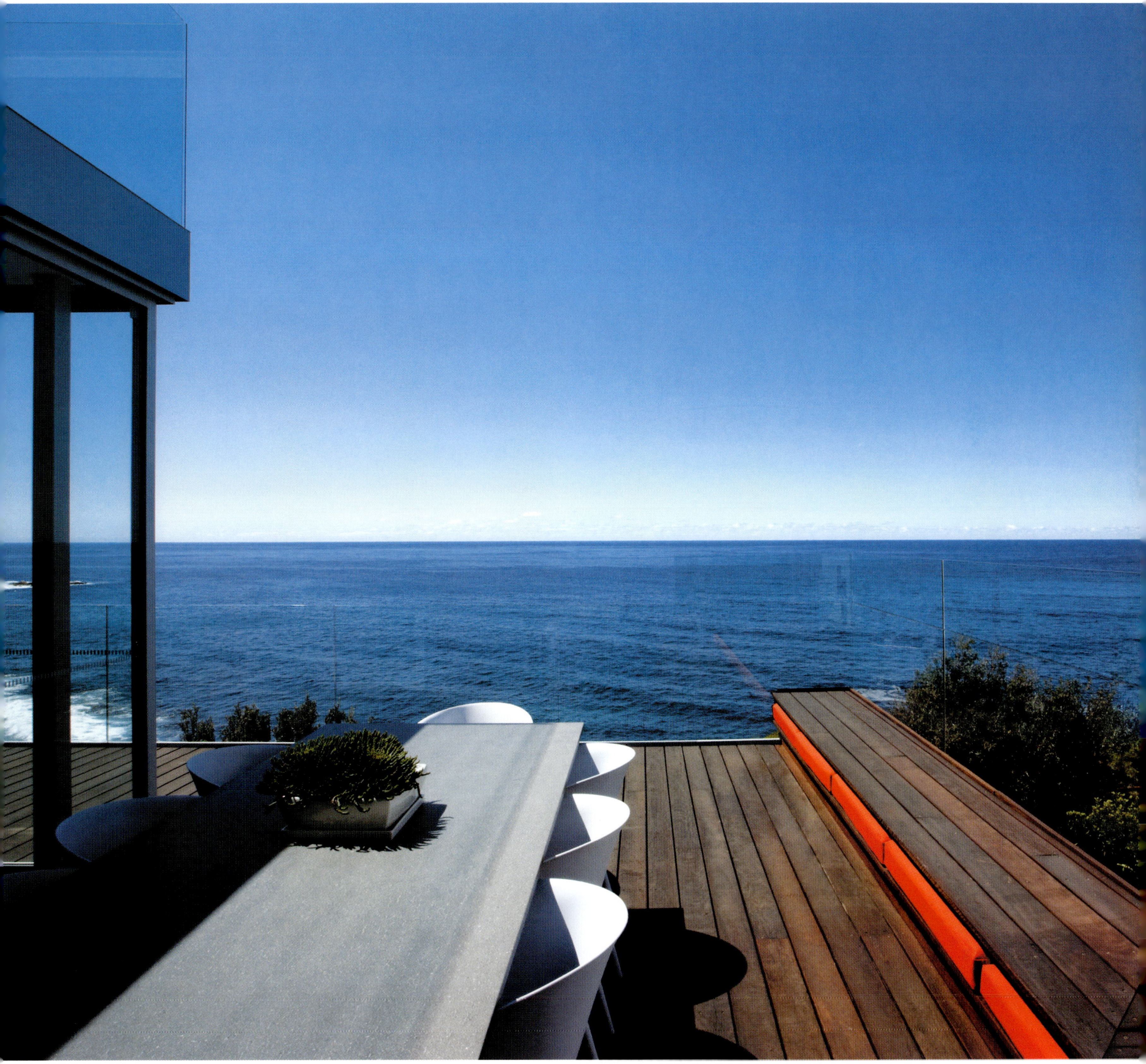

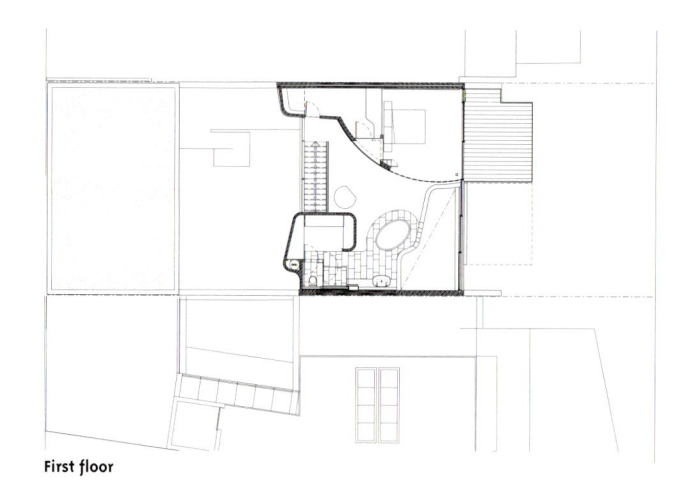

174

First floor

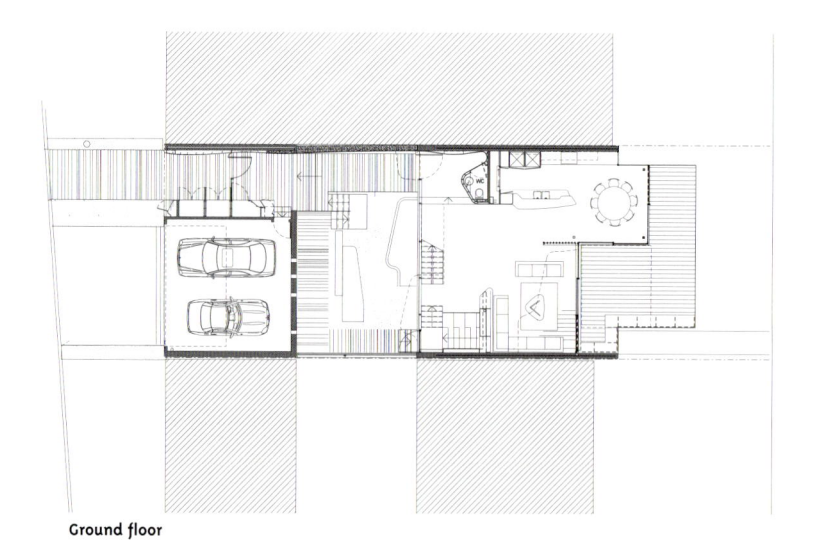

Ground floor

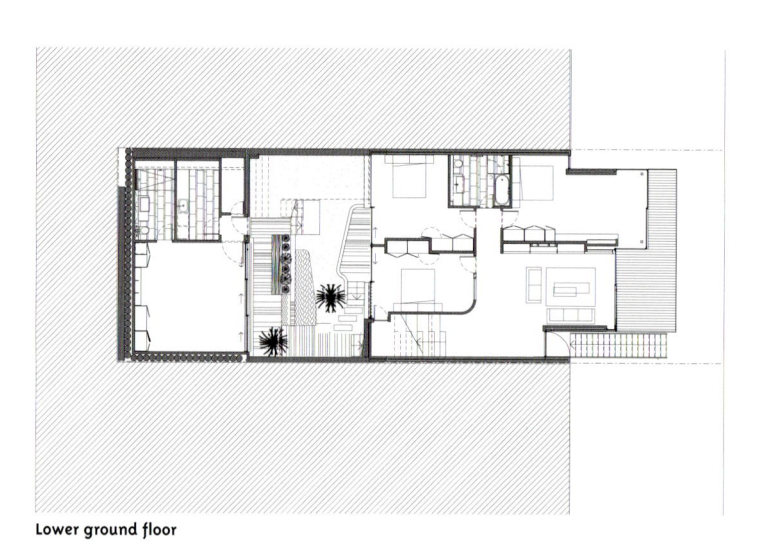

Lower ground floor

Rubinsztein House

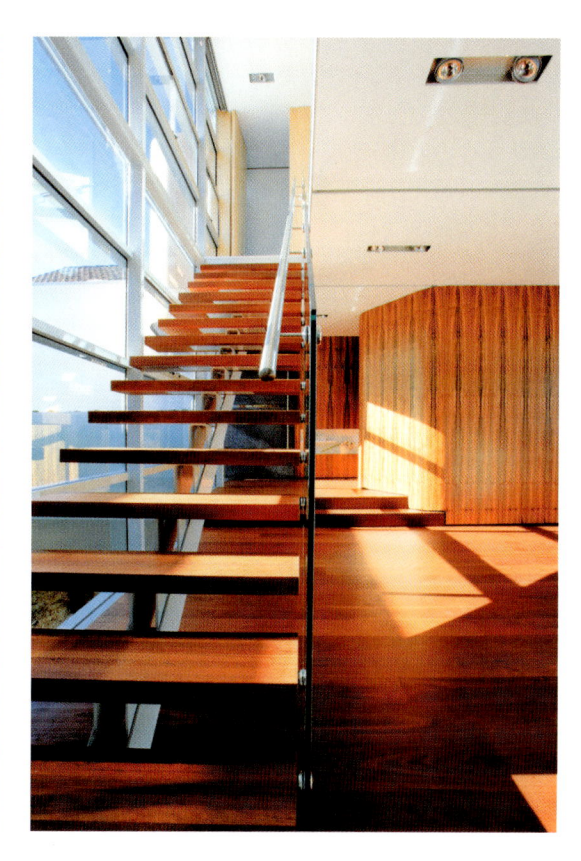

St George's Basin House

St George's Basin, New South Wales, Australia
Brian van der Plaat Design

This coastal house, located on a narrow, south-facing site, is designed as a casual and flexible series of spaces that encourages outdoor activities and entertaining. The house follows an informal structure in which all rooms are connected via an outdoor veranda. A central timber walkway connects the four separate pavilions—one for storage space, the second for guest accommodation, another for private accommodation, and the fourth comprises the main living spaces. The areas between these pavilions are used as private and communal courtyard spaces for relaxing and entertaining.

The main courtyard located between the accommodation and living pavilions constitutes the primary outdoor living space. The barbecue, bench, and fireplace elements help to contain this space while the main living pavilion, with its retractable glass walls to both front and back, frames the view looking over the water to the south. A steel frame and commercially glazed façade system is used to create a simple, open, and airy space with minimal detail; all other elements and details are pared back and well resolved so as not to detract from the view. The pavilions are constructed as simple lean-to structures with zincalume roofing and painted plywood cladding, and the timber walkway is built from locally sourced hardwood.

Photography by Sharrin Rees Photography

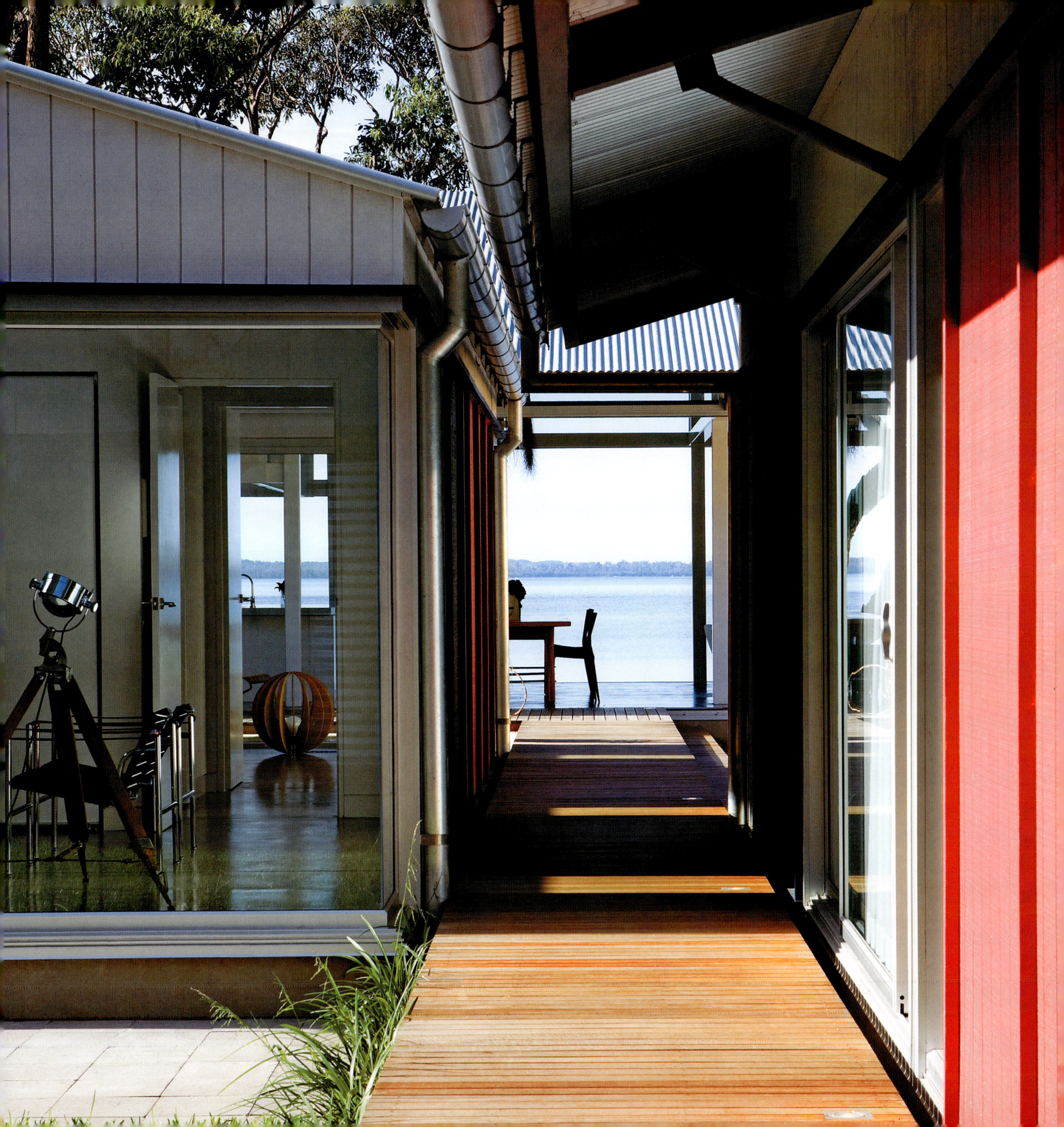

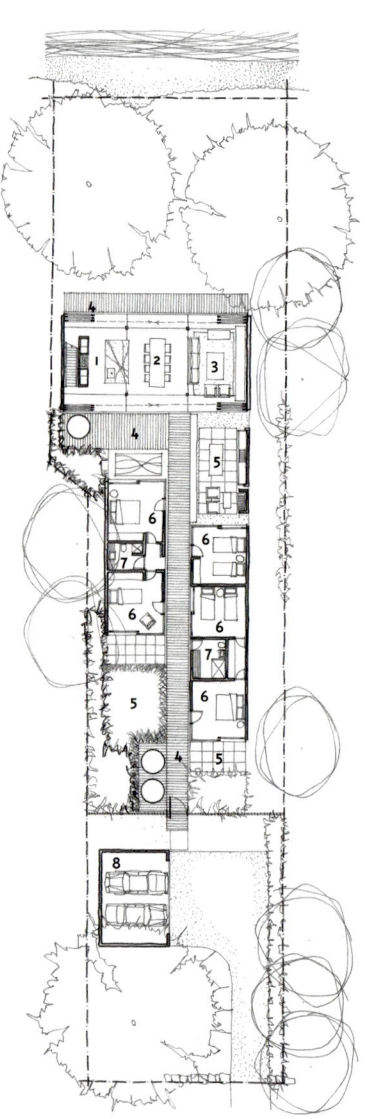

Ground floor

1	Kitchen	5	Courtyard
2	Dining	6	Bedroom
3	Living	7	Bathroom
4	Deck	8	Garage

0   10m

St George's Basin House

Sandhill House

Kangaroo Island, South Australia, Australia
Max Pritchard Architect

This vacation home, sited on a well-vegetated sandhill, comprises three pavilions linked by timber steps and a covered walkway. The multiple pavilion concept provides privacy and allows for economical, open, light-framed spaces. The pavilions were developed with a flexible building footprint that minimized land and vegetation disturbance. A relaxed, casual atmosphere was created by maximizing views of the sea and surrounding bushland. The highest pavilion is surrounded by external timber decking and has sea views through the coastal scrub.

The house is large enough to be shared by multiple families over extended periods, with the open internal and external living areas designed to facilitate a communal vacation environment. The kitchen, which features concealed amenities, is planned around an island bench that becomes the focal point for food preparation before firing the outdoor barbecue, the only cooking equipment in the house. Sustainability was an important concern for the owners and consequently the house includes green features such as solar hot water panels, double-glazed windows to the living area, and an efficient combustion heater. The open nature of the design allows for natural cooling and cross ventilation from sea breezes, which also encourages use of the outdoor terrace areas.

Photography by Sam Noonan

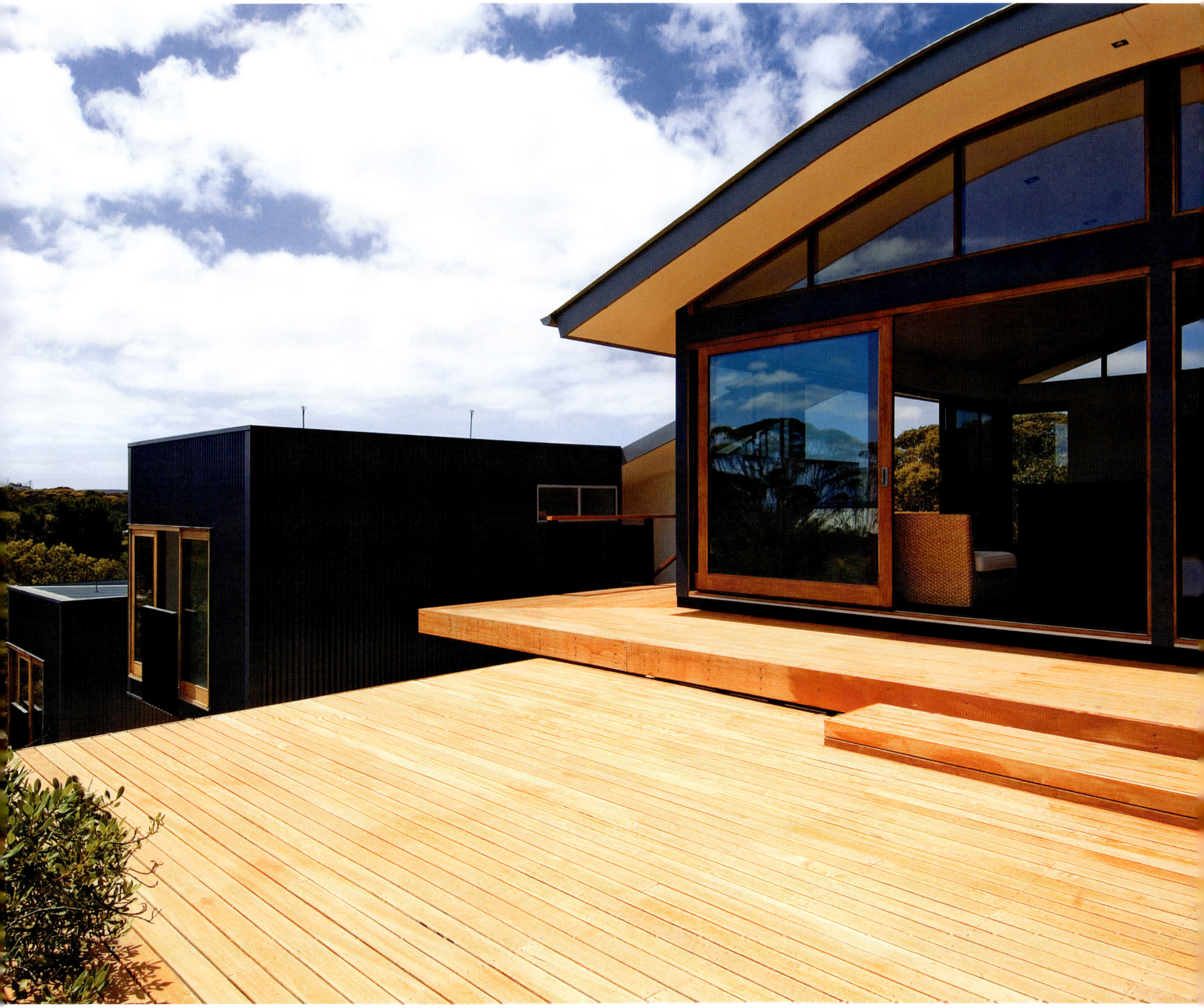

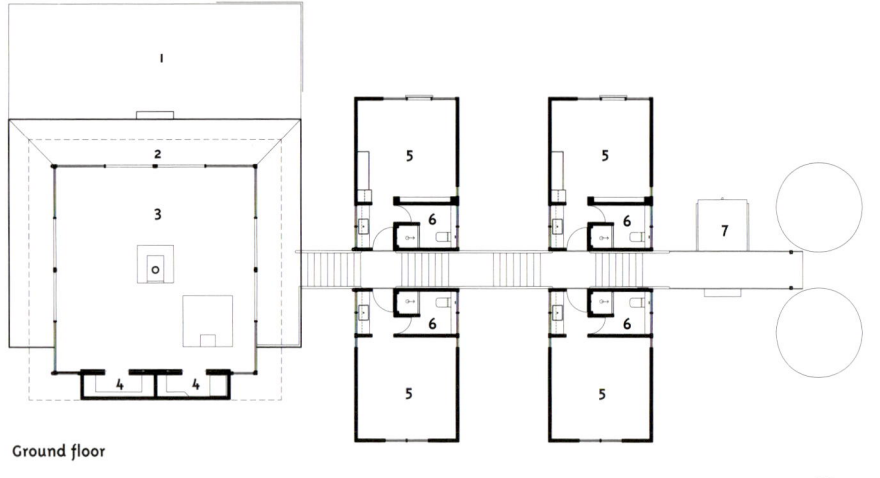

Ground floor

1. Lower deck
2. Upper deck
3. Kitchen, dining, lounge
4. Storeroom
5. Bedroom
6. Ensuite
7. Outdoor shower

Sandhill House

Seola Beach House

Burien, Washington, USA
Eggleston Farkas Architects

This 2,500-square-foot waterfront residence is located on a long and narrow site with views across Puget Sound. The house is set back from the water and elevated to protect the structure from storm-surge flooding. The topography of the site includes a steep slope, which although providing a pleasant buffering backdrop, is also a source for potential landslides. The existing house was replaced by a new building that establishes a simple, comfortable presence within this beach context.

The new residence was conceived as a mediating portal between hillside and waterfront. A massive, 10-foot-high concrete catchment wall was introduced near the bottom of the problematic slope to protect against landslides. The top of this wall serves as a starting point for a new steel-and-wood access bridge at the second-story main level. This elevated position serves to enhance views from the integrated entry, living, dining, kitchen, and deck spaces. The living area is a two-story volume with full-height window walls facing both the hill and water. Its transparency provides a dramatic view from the access road and allows views of both the hillside and the beach.

For privacy and optimal views, a master suite was placed on the top level, directly above the kitchen and dining areas. The beach-level plan comprises two rooms designed to be used as media, office, guest, and entertainment spaces. Cedar siding with exposed fasteners is used on the exterior walls and will weather to a silvery patina.

Photography by Jim Van Gundy and Alex Hayden

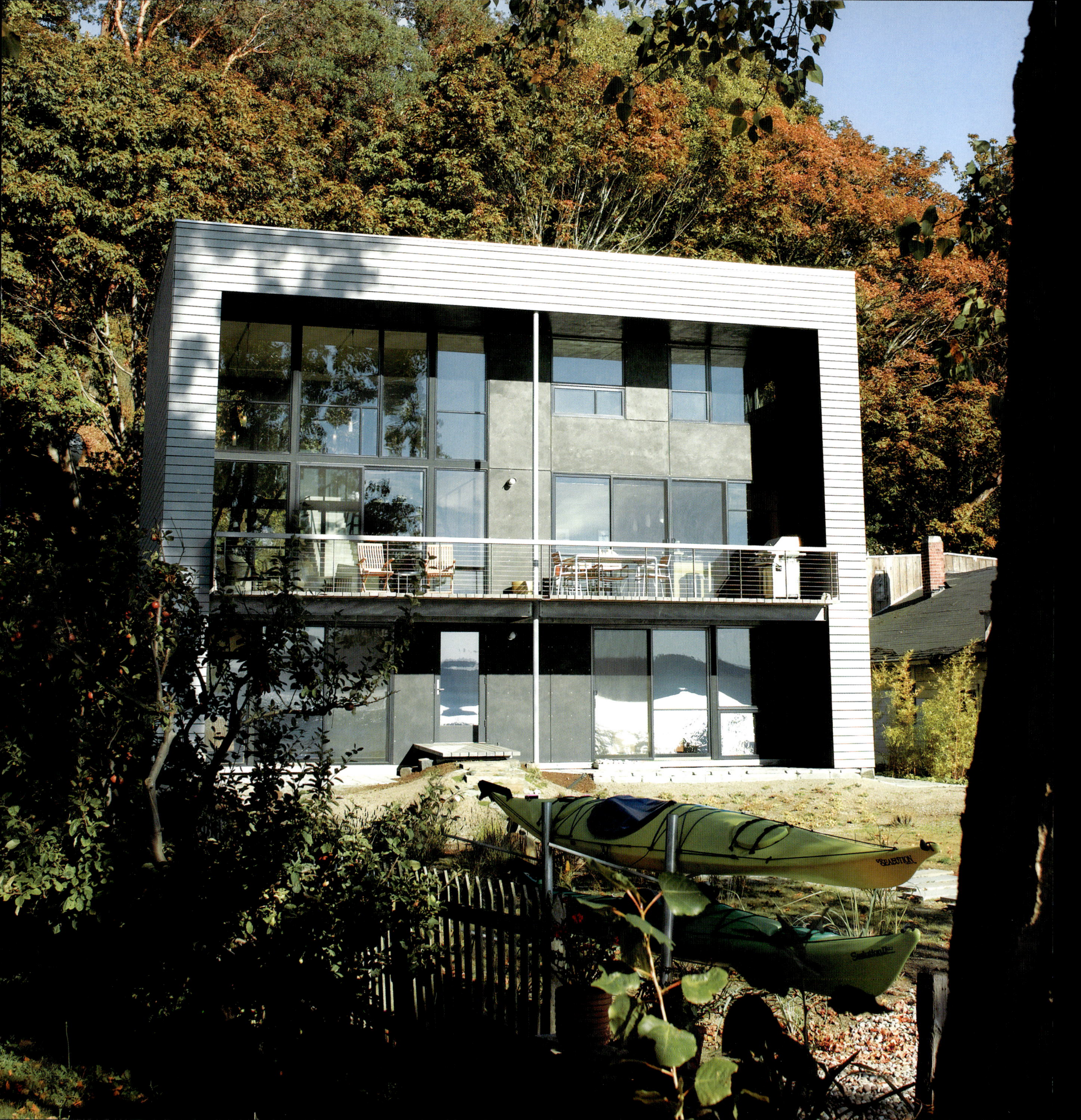

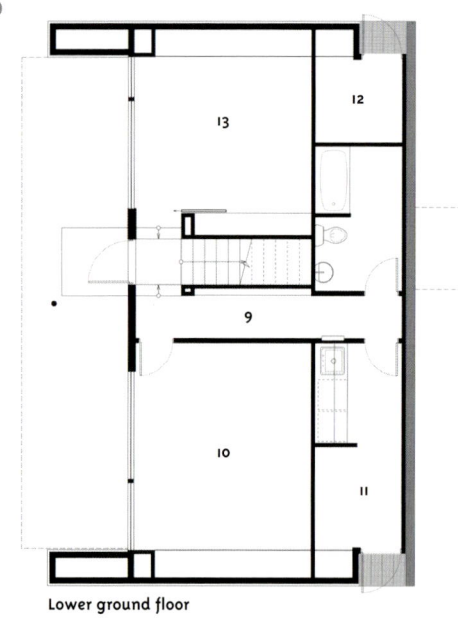

Lower ground floor

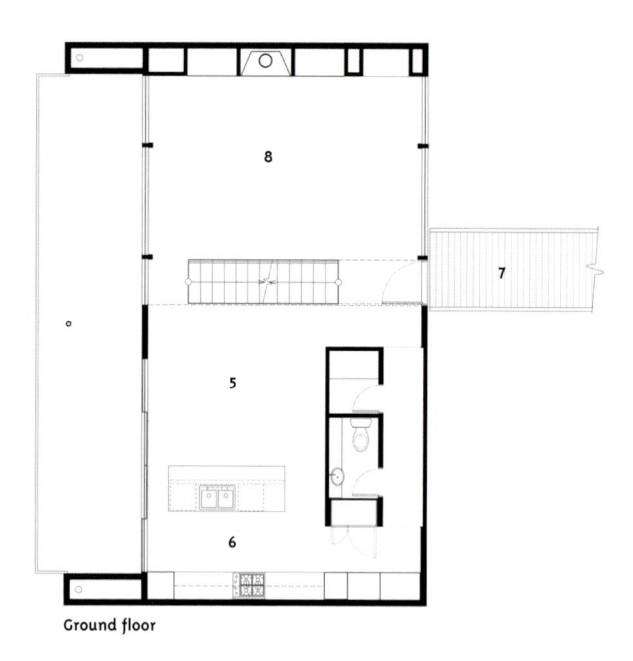

Ground floor

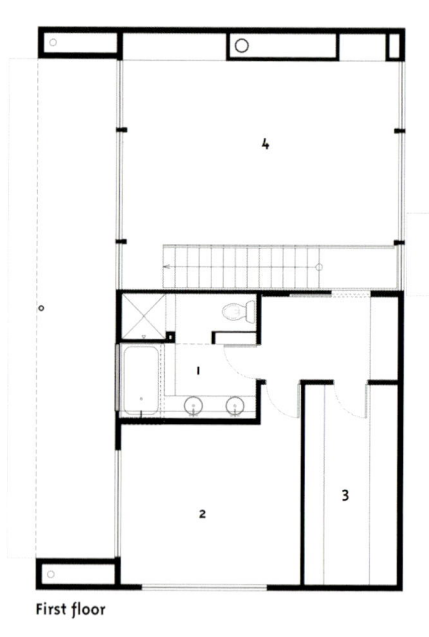

First floor

1 Bathroom	6 Kitchen	11 Mechanical room
2 Bedroom	7 Bridge	12 Storage
3 Closet	8 Living	13 Media room
4 Open to below	9 Hall	
5 Dining	10 Office	

0   8ft

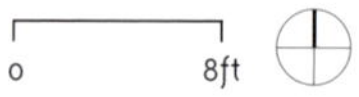

Seola Beach House

She Oak Beach House

Casuarina Beach, New South Wales, Australia
Base Architecture

The brief for this house on a beachfront lot specified spaces that were informal, casual, and welcoming. But most importantly, the building had to have adequate storage space for the owner's collection of long boards. It was also vital for the owner to have a building that was in tune with its surroundings and could withstand the harsh coastal conditions. The use of galvanized steel and stained ecoply gives the exterior skin a rawness that will age gracefully rather than deteriorate like most paint-type finishes. The exterior materials contrast with the refined and hard-wearing interior palette comprising polished concrete.

The double-height entry, with grass underfoot and natural landscaping, comprises a semi indoor–outdoor space constructed of clear weatherboards. This area allows for wetsuits to be abandoned in the concealed laundry, the surfboards to be "racked," and can be hosed out through the decking boards to flush away unwanted sand and salt. Once within this entry, large timber-clad sliding doors open into the house. On the ground level, a simple program of living spaces opens up to a courtyard off one side and a main outdoor room to the rear of the property that overlooks a pool and dunes. The first floor comprises simple bedroom and bathroom facilities that interact with the ground level and entry via a series of voids and openings.

Photography by Christopher Frederick Jones

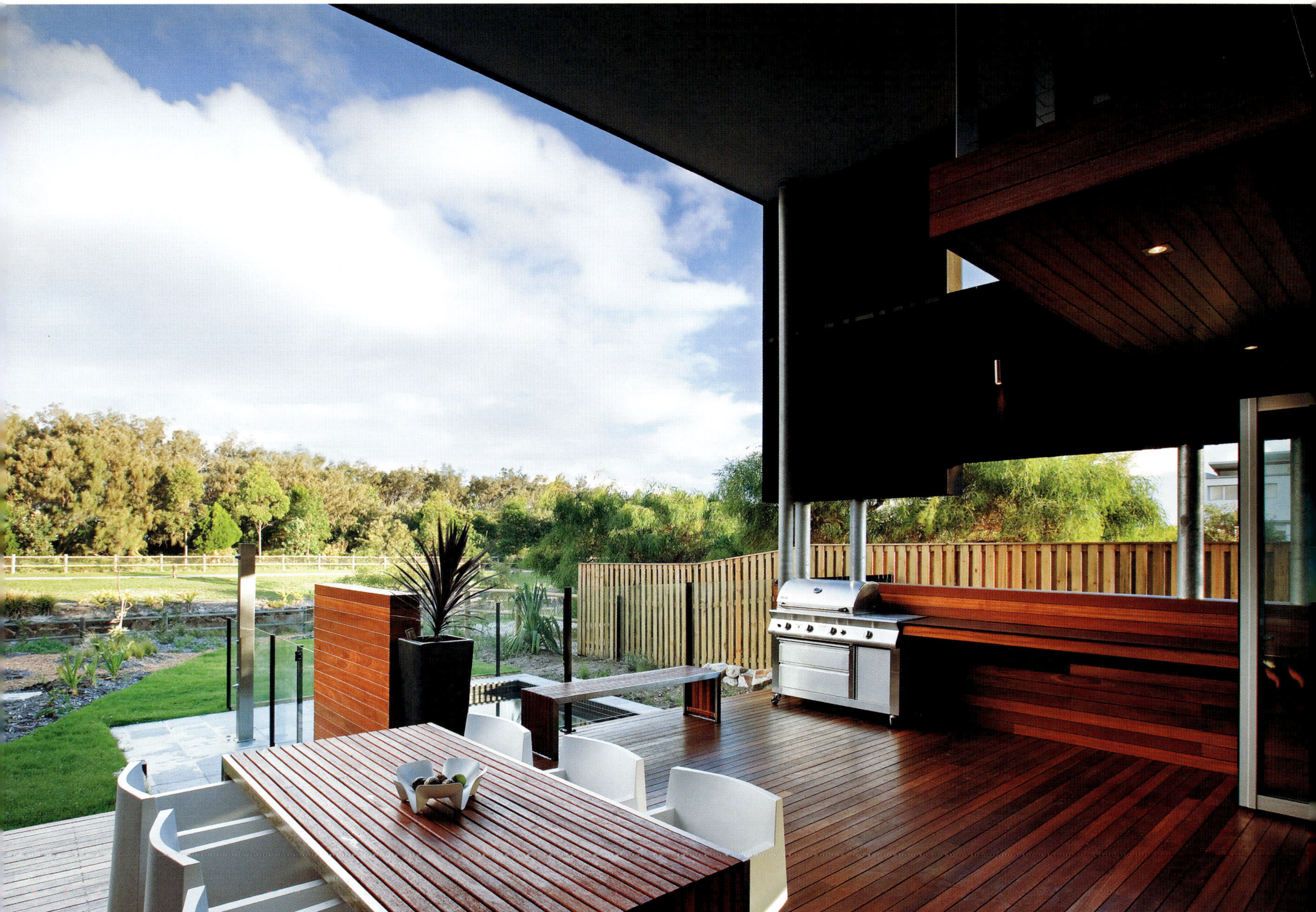

Ground floor

First floor

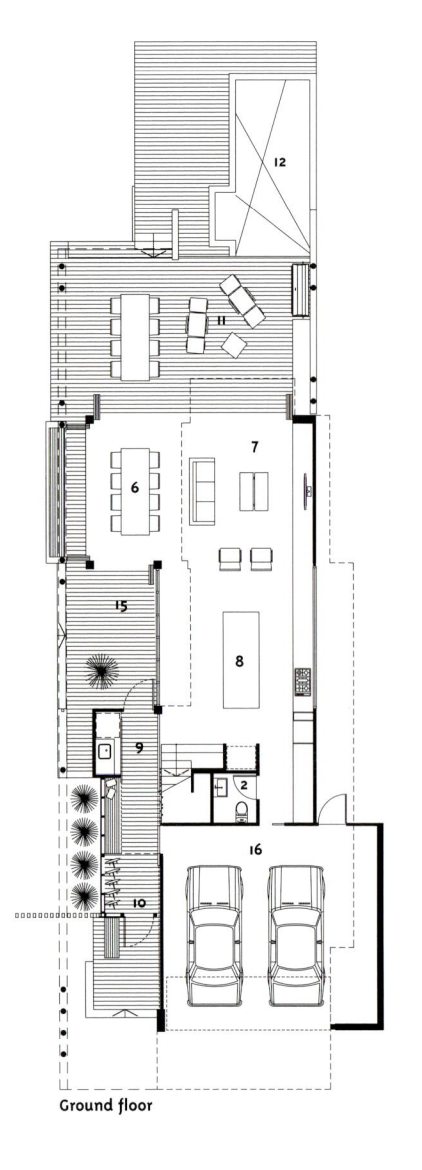

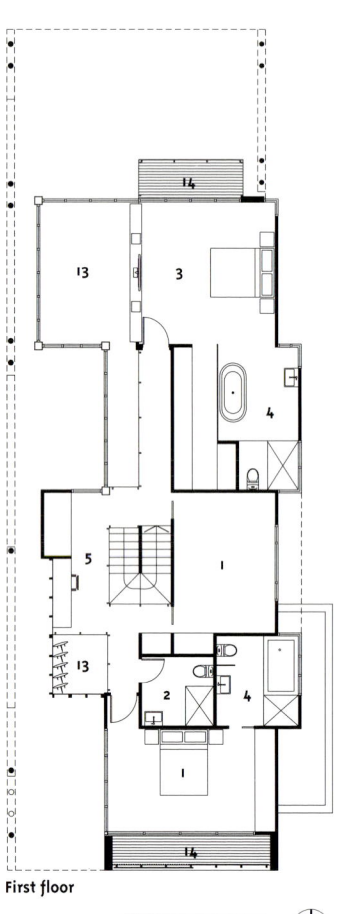

0 5m

1	Bedroom	9	Laundry
2	Bathroom	10	Entry
3	Master bedroom	11	Outdoor room
4	Ensuite	12	Pool
5	Study	13	Void
6	Dining	14	Balcony
7	Living	15	Courtyard
8	Kitchen	16	Garage

She Oak Beach House

Sorrento House

Sorrento, Victoria, Australia

F2 Architecture

This split-level home comprises a single-bedroom, self-contained residence on the uppermost level and expands to a five-bedroom house when the lower level is used. The extended family gathers for meals on the top level of the house, which provides access to an expansive deck and swimming pool, both with spectacular views of coastline. A number of indoor and outdoor living areas are accessible from the different levels, allowing the large family to disperse across the whole property.

The upper and lower levels of the home are both expressed as L-shaped forms, one sitting on top the other. The lower form is the more regular and encloses an entry forecourt. Its long side faces the ocean to provide all the bedrooms with a view of the bay and access to a private lawn. The upper form is more irregular and responds to the coastal height restrictions.

The cladding materials provide a different character to each of these two forms. The lower level features dark timber battens and the upper cladding is olive colored with vertically lapped aluminum panels. The external colors are based on the trunk and foliage of the indigenous moonah trees that have been retained and incorporated within the landscape around the residence.

The living areas of the house are oriented to maximize the available sun and opportunities for cross ventilation, and home automation is used to efficiently control lighting, window furnishings, and heating. All stormwater is collected in an underground tank and used to irrigate the extensive landscape environment around the home.

Photography by Derek Swalwell

0   5m

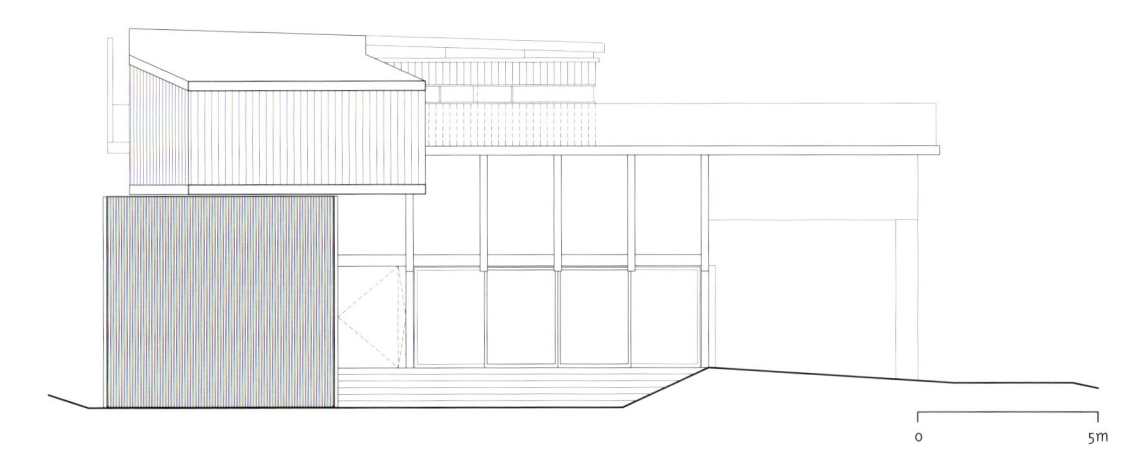

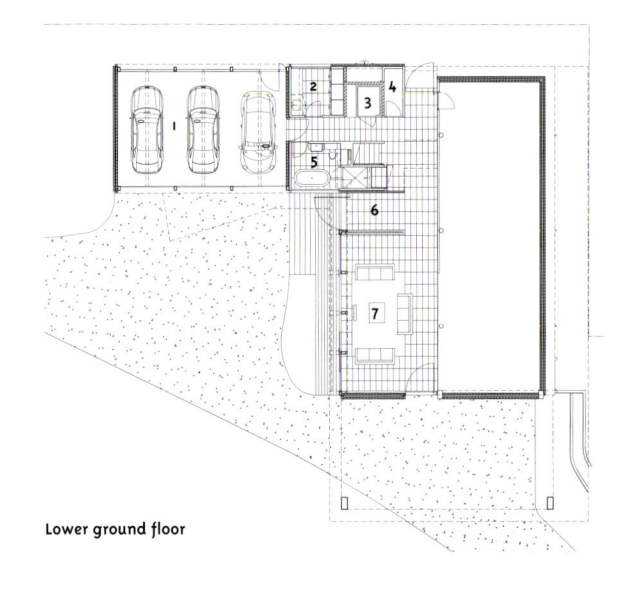

Lower ground floor　　　　Upper ground floor　　　　First floor

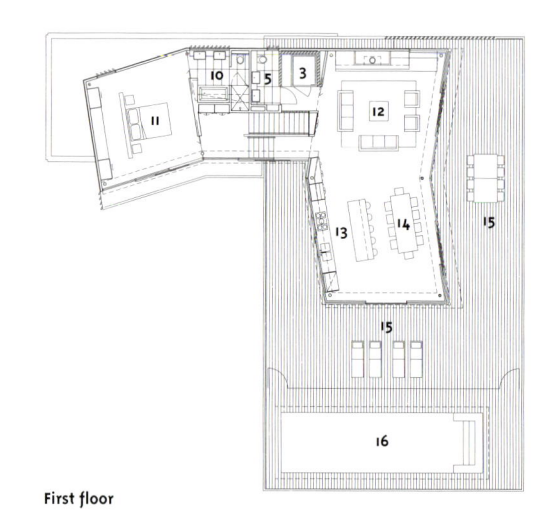

1	Garage	7	Theater/rumpus	13	Kitchen
2	Laundry	8	Void	14	Dining
3	Lift	9	Bedroom	15	Deck
4	Storeroom	10	Ensuite	16	Swimming pool
5	Powder room	11	Master bedroom		
6	Entry	12	Living		

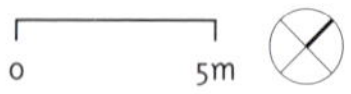

Sorrento House

Southampton Beach House

Southampton, New York, USA
Alexander Gorlin Architects

This striking, 12,000-square-foot modern summerhouse is set on a narrow spit of land between the ocean and the bay. While simple in form, the house is rich in texture, color, and detail, with African teak offsetting pale limestone. Created for a family of four, the house comprises three master bedrooms, three guest suites, staff quarters, and 6,000 square feet of living and entertaining areas.

At the entrance, the second floor cantilevers outward from the principal mass of the building in a bold formal gesture, creating a sheltered patio adjacent to the main entry. From here, an open staircase rises through a double-height glass atrium to the main level. Inside, the house is organized around a large, open living area. A central fireplace subtly partitions the space, creating an informal dining room to one side and a sitting area to the other. A light monitor in the ceiling above adds volume to the space and washes the room in a diffuse light.

The living room opens onto a terraced patio and pool beyond. Above, a great wing-like canopy extends from the building, shading the house. In marked contrast to the substantial mass of the limestone building, this finely tapered form floats above the patio. Clad in a soft gray metal, it seems almost to disappear against a pale sky. The pool looks out toward the ocean while a wooden boardwalk traces the gentle rise of the sand dunes, leading to a private beach below. A rooftop terrace offers spectacular views of the ocean and the sound. Bold sculptural elements clad in a pale metal punctuate the expanse. Their surfaces—gray and flat in the morning light—take on a warmer hue as the sun rises in the sky and at sunset they are set ablaze with color.

Photography by Michael Moran, ESTO

197

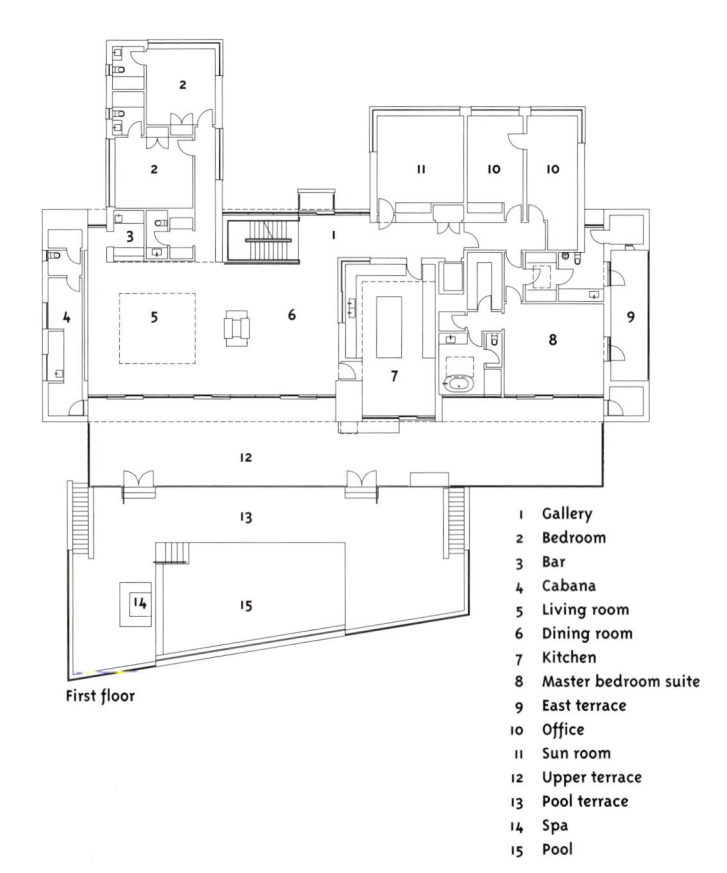

198

First floor

1. Gallery
2. Bedroom
3. Bar
4. Cabana
5. Living room
6. Dining room
7. Kitchen
8. Master bedroom suite
9. East terrace
10. Office
11. Sun room
12. Upper terrace
13. Pool terrace
14. Spa
15. Pool

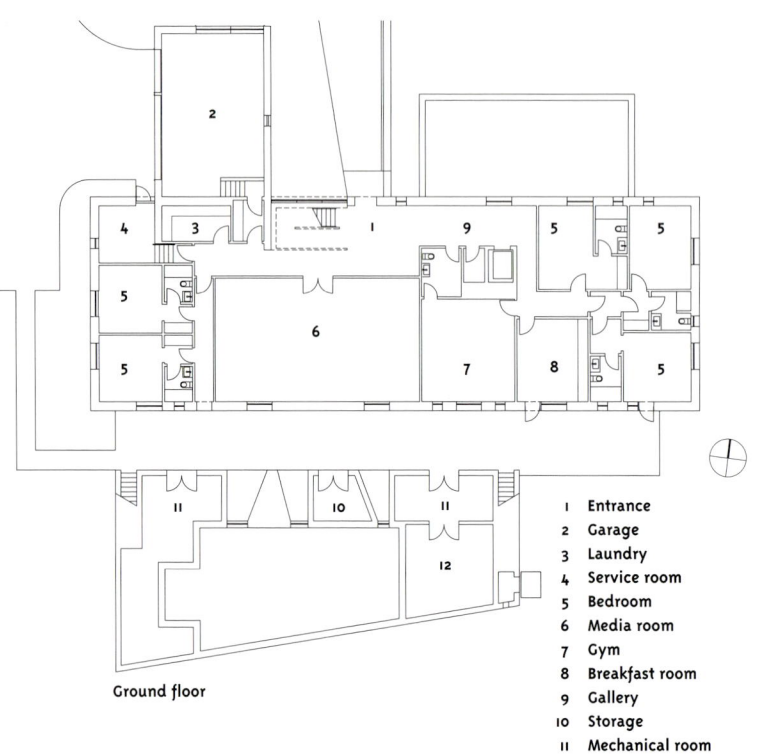

Ground floor

1. Entrance
2. Garage
3. Laundry
4. Service room
5. Bedroom
6. Media room
7. Gym
8. Breakfast room
9. Gallery
10. Storage
11. Mechanical room
12. Pool equipment

Southampton Beach House

Spotted Gum Beach House

Mornington Peninsula, Victoria, Australia
Jolson

This 6,000-square-foot residence is divided into two zones over two levels—one comprising the main elements and the other the guest facilities. Important elements of the design were to frame the uninterrupted coastal views and to maximize solar amenity and privacy. In response to these requirements, the house was positioned along the seaside cliff top, nestled low into the landscape to minimize the visual impact to the beach.

Designed as a place to retreat, entertain, and relax, the house features direct access to the beach. The coastal context is explored architecturally through form and material, including the use of spotted gum and other core materials that evoke a strong sense of place. Over time, the timber will gray through its exposure to the sun, connecting the structure to the surrounding bush landscape.

The range of local weather conditions influenced the design of the building. The house is positioned to optimize panoramic views, the terraces are sheltered from strong winds and direct sunlight, and cross breezes are encouraged through multiple opening windows and doors. Recycled timber posts are used to define the private garden and wet-edge pool, and natural, sustainable materials are used for all joinery.

Photography by Scott Newett Photography

201

1   Home theater
2   Kitchenette
3   Cellar
4   Laundry
5   Bedroom
6   Ensuite

Lower ground floor

1   Entry
2   Cloakroom
3   Garage
4   Powder room
5   Kitchen
6   Scullery
7   Sunroom
8   Dining
9   Lounge
10 Master bedroom
11 Master ensuite
12 Walk-in-robe
13 Pool

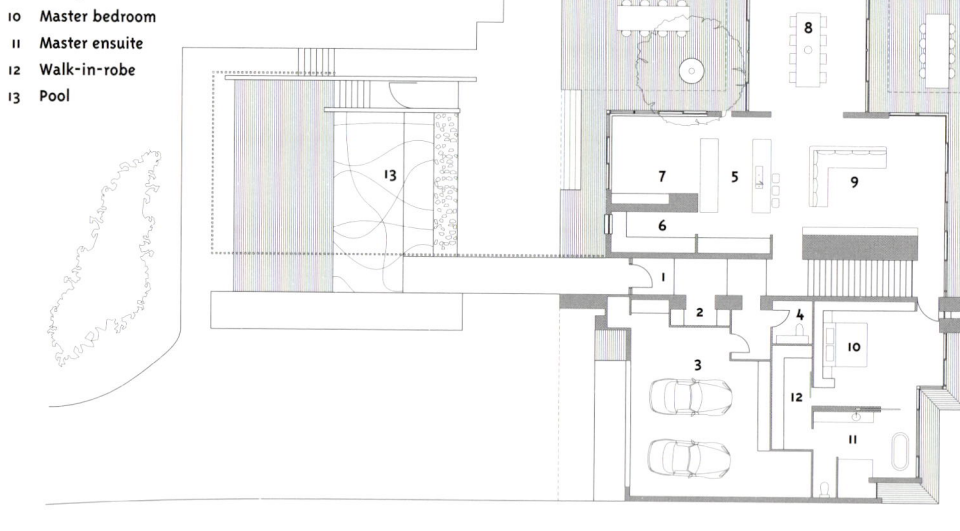

Ground floor

0   5m

Spotted Gum Beach House

Stonington House

Stonington, Connecticut, USA
Estes/Twombly Architects

The surrounding countryside of this waterfront location is classic New England, typified by bucolic open fields bordered by stonewalls. The program for this project included an open floor plan, private master and guest bedrooms, and space for a significant collection of paintings and ceramics. The outbuildings comprise a two-car garage, a barn for the owner's skiff, wood shop, and storage areas.

Only a small portion of this 7-acre site was suitable for building—a gentle knoll that constituted approximately six percent of the total area. However, this section of land also afforded panoramic views of the ocean and nearby protected wetlands. The architect used the knoll as a plinth for a cluster of small buildings—a living area, bedroom, garage, and barn. These buildings were pushed to the edge of the plinth and linked with a wall of local granite to help distinguish man-made and natural forms as well as manicured and un-manicured yards.

Durable metal roofing and deep overhangs protect the traditional cedar siding and painted trim. Large expanses of glass enclose the entry hall and wrap corners to capture sunlight and views. On the interior, detailing was kept simple and straightforward, with the palette of materials and subdued colors intended to serve as a backdrop for the owners' furniture and art.

Photography by Warren Jagger Photography Inc.

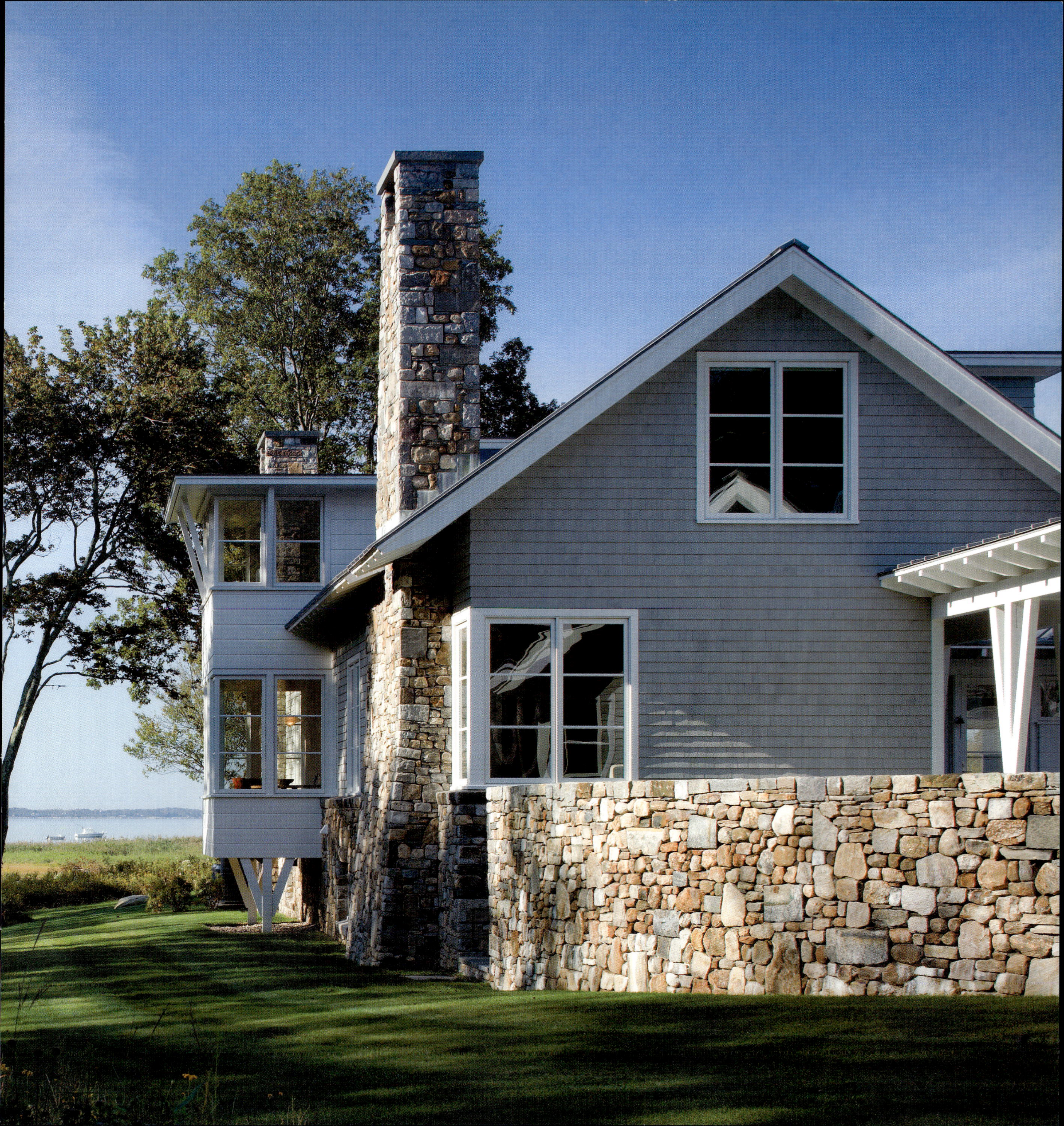

206

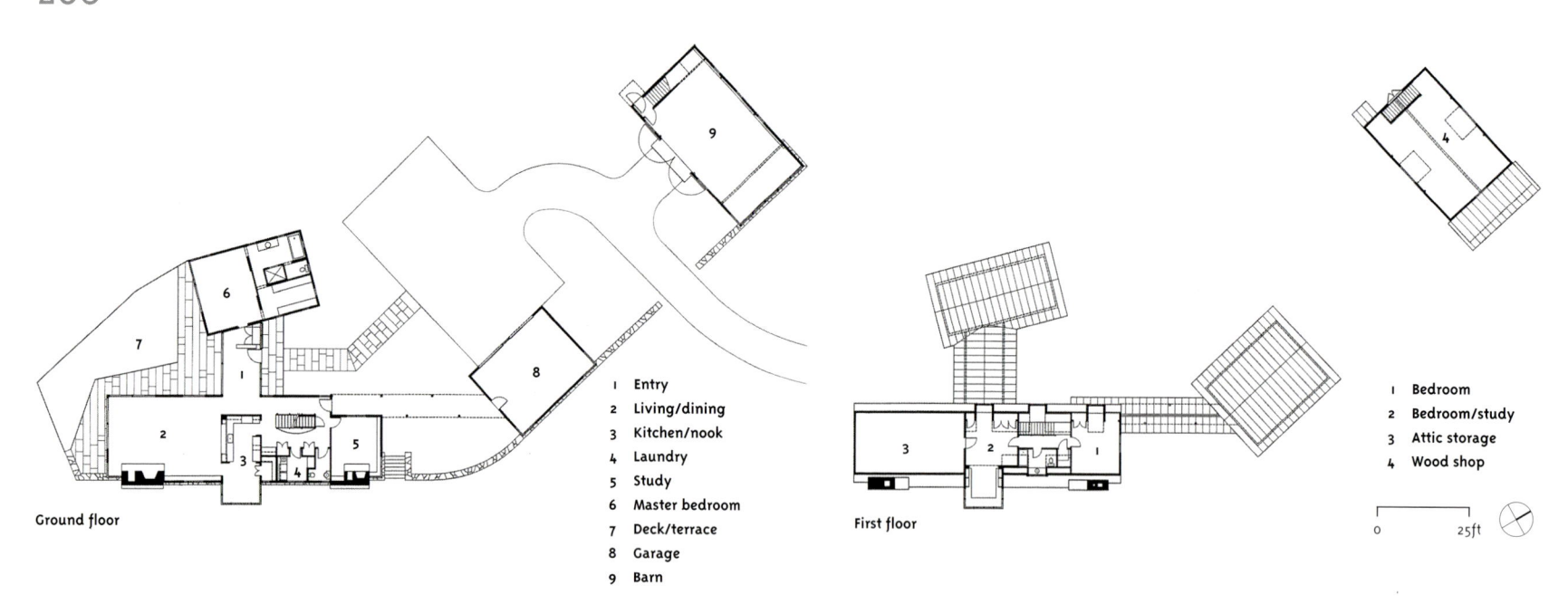

Ground floor

1	Entry
2	Living/dining
3	Kitchen/nook
4	Laundry
5	Study
6	Master bedroom
7	Deck/terrace
8	Garage
9	Barn

First floor

1	Bedroom
2	Bedroom/study
3	Attic storage
4	Wood shop

0   25ft

Stonington House

Sunrise Beach House

Sunrise Beach, Queensland, Australia
Wilson Architecture

Instead of hugging the site boundary to maximize sea views, this house is designed to capture a sequence of ocean vignettes that are playfully screened and framed against the house and landscape. The house is configured so that internal and external spaces are able to cope with the prevailing breezes under a variety of conditions. Subsequently, the interior and exterior spaces can be used in a number of ways, depending on the weather.

The immediate surrounding materials of caked sand, native pandanus, and water were the reference for a palette of raw concrete, glass, and zinc, offset with the warmth of timber and woven cane screens to create a casual, yet refined environment. The building primarily accommodates a family of five with room for another family. The plan includes a captured external space described by a series of landscaped courts and a lounge and study wing flanked by still water ponds, with an enclosed courtyard to the west and a loosely described court to the east.

The kitchen and dining wing pushes out toward the beach and can be opened directly to the ocean to the east and/or to the court to its north. In the children's wing above the lounge, the rooms are placed off a glazed corridor and on a raised platform so that the extent of view to the landscape, ocean, and sky can be expanded. Woven cane shoji screens conceal and reveal the extent of this prospect. The glazed parents' suite on the eastern wing is enclosed with articulated woven cane screens that modulate light views and privacy.

Photography by Scott Burrows

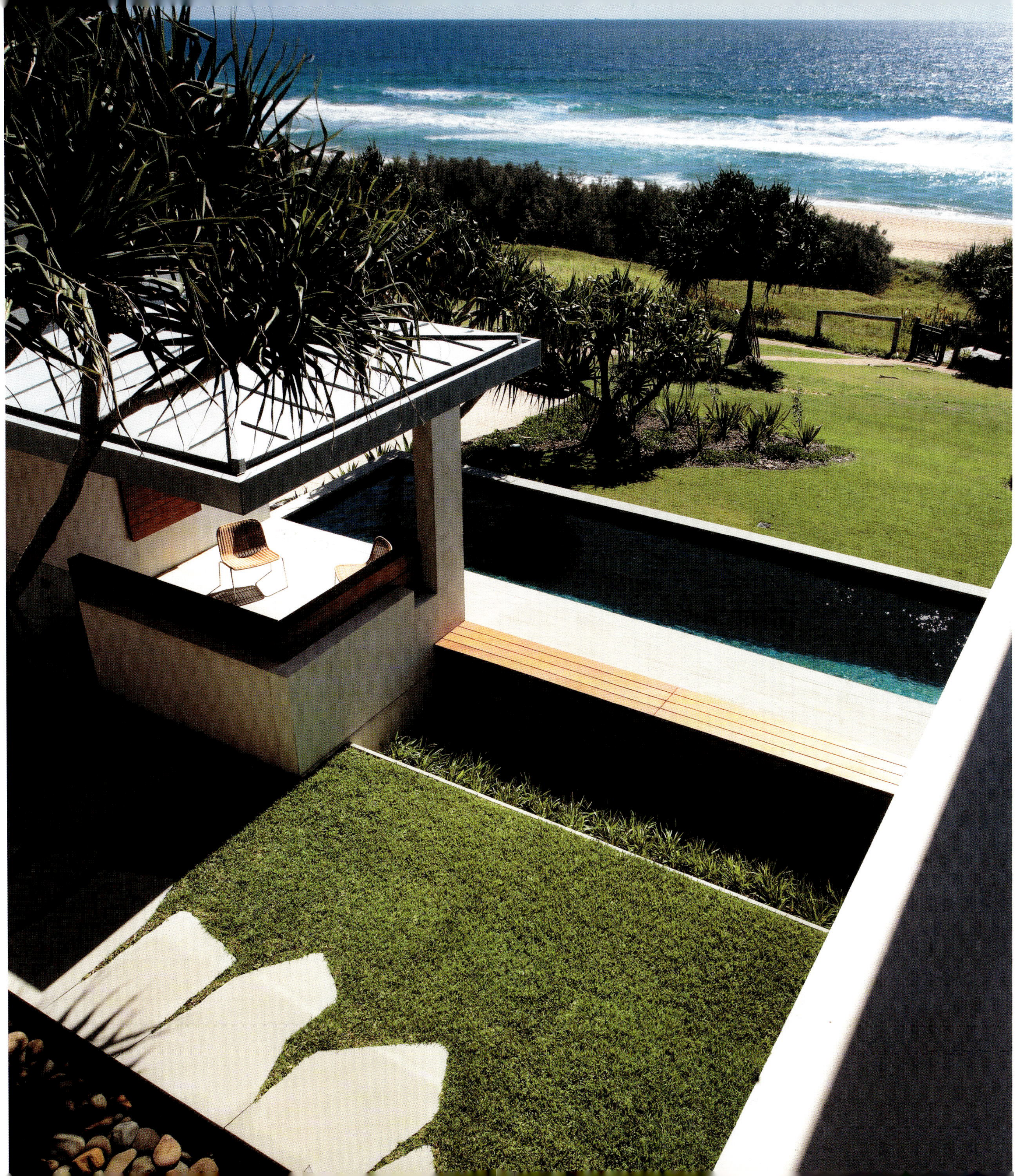

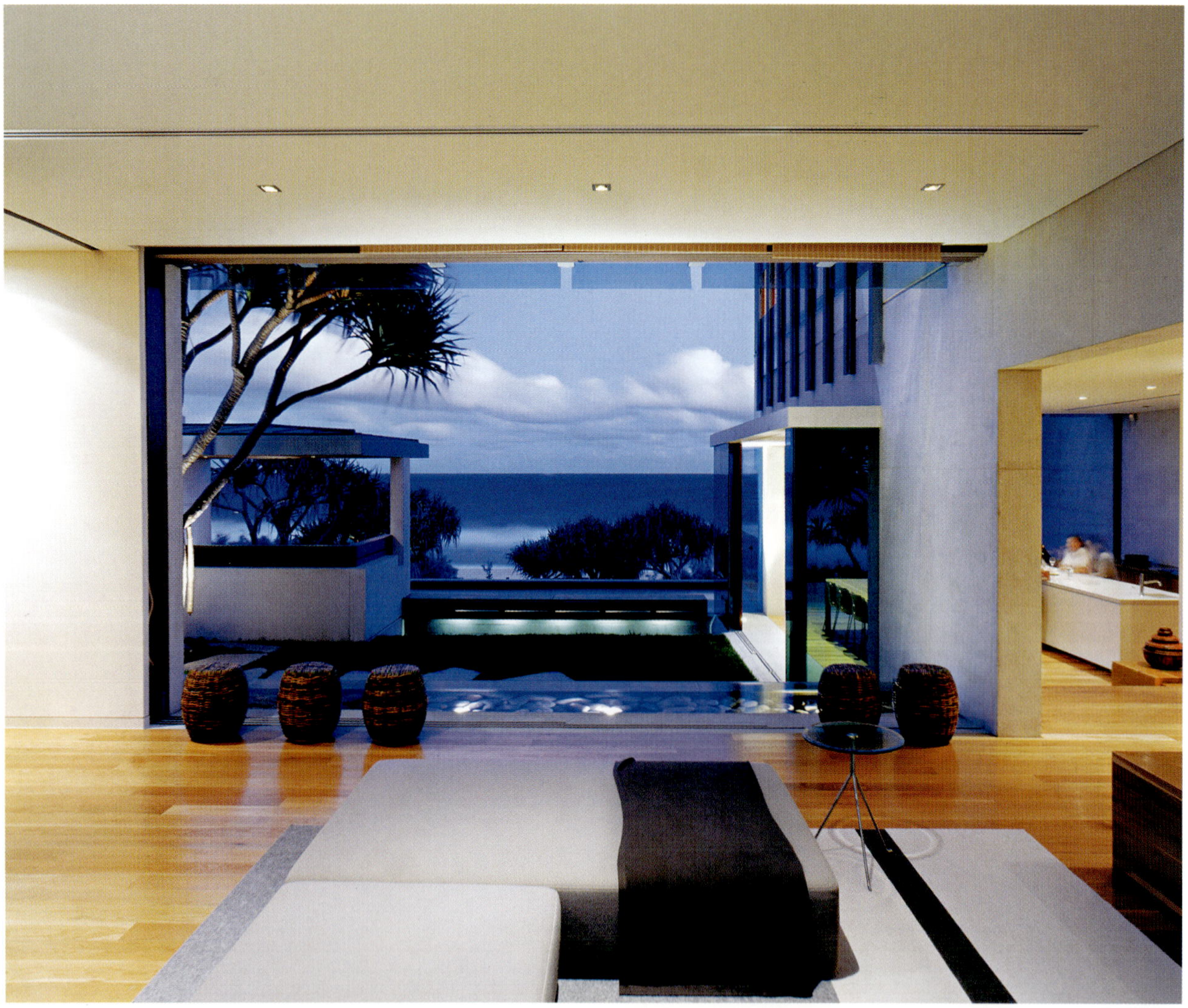
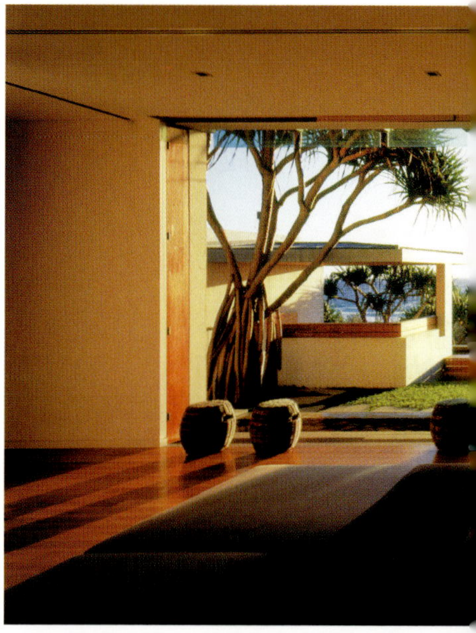

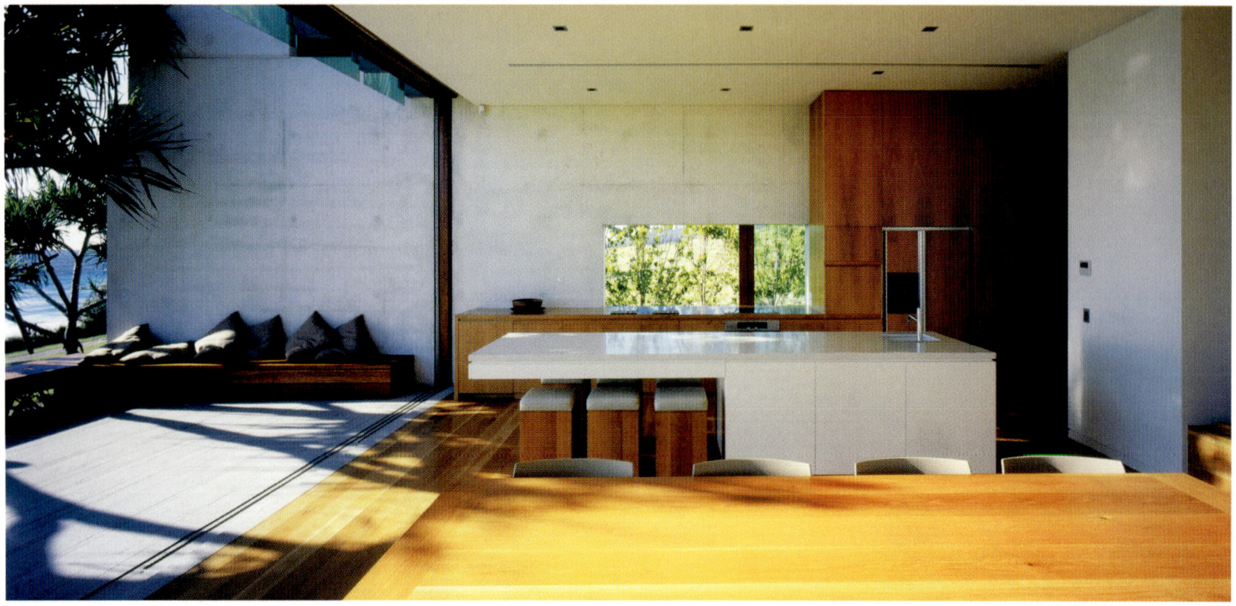
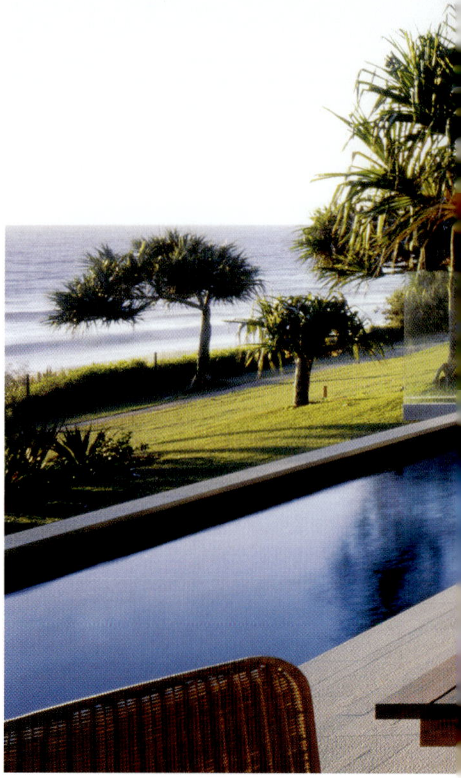

Sunrise Beach House

Sunshine Beach Residences

Sunshine Beach, Queensland, Australia
Bark Design Architects

These two adjoining double-story houses are designed with ambiguous boundaries between internal and external spaces. The structures celebrate outdoor living through generously proportioned screened outdoor rooms, and all spaces are characterized by a contemporary, coastal, and luxurious subtropical feel. Each house features its own private oasis, with the architecture promoting a casual, beach aesthetic. Oriented to the north, the outdoor living areas are maximized to the northern aspect while also framing ocean views to the south.

The palette comprises a subtle mix of natural white-on-white materials and textures, complemented by dark timber detailing. Tall stacking, sliding and bi-fold doors provide a seamless indoor–outdoor connection, and the galley kitchen opens out to a sun-drenched northern deck. The installation of sliding plantation shutters provides privacy and climate control, and high-levels of natural light and ventilation are achieved through carefully placed louvered clerestories. Each house has a private, landscaped northern courtyard that embraces a swimming pool. North-facing, open garden areas are planted with local subtropical vegetation, and the rooftop terraces allow for stunning views toward the Pacific Ocean.

Photography by Christopher Frederick Jones

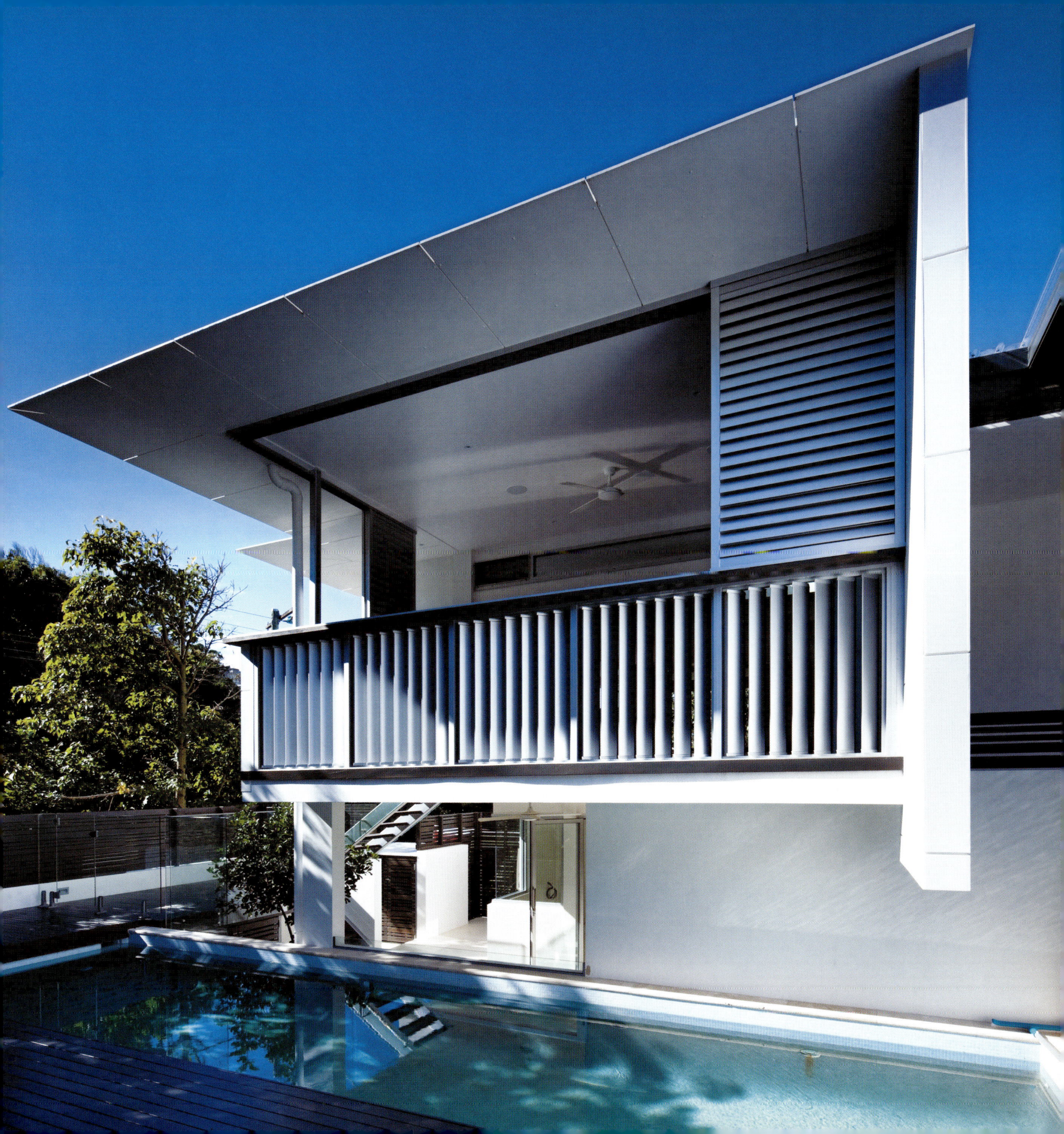

214

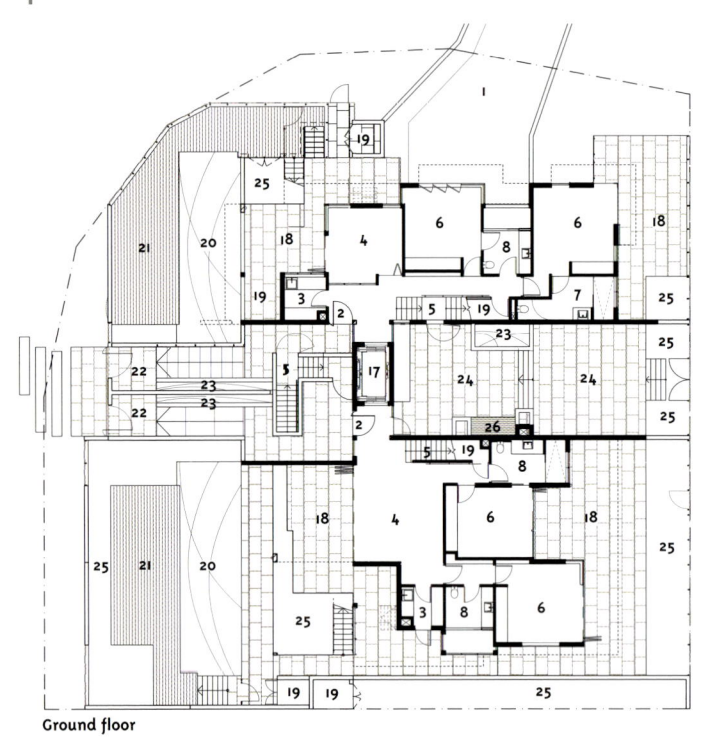

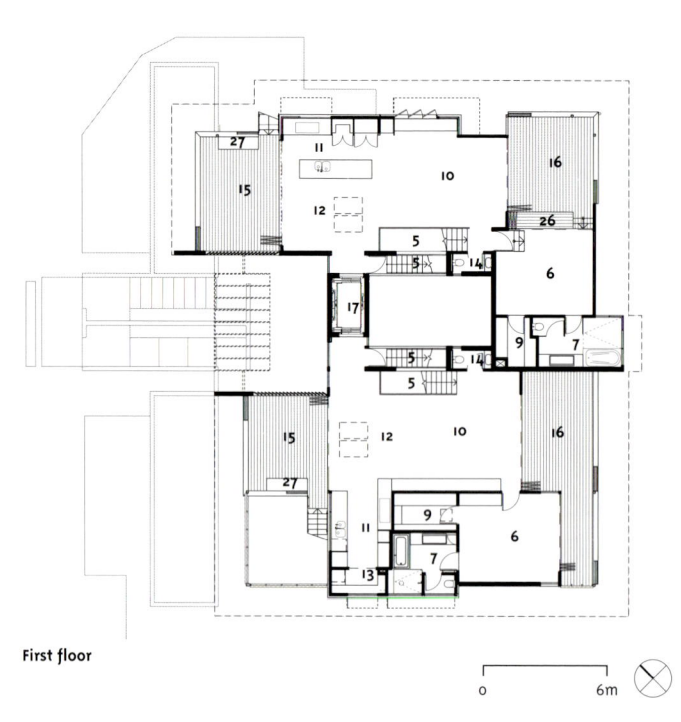

Ground floor

First floor

0　　6m

1	Driveway
2	Entry
3	Laundry
4	Media room
5	Stair
6	Bedroom
7	Ensuite
8	Bathroom
9	Walk-in closet
10	Living
11	Kitchen
12	Dining
13	Pantry
14	WC
15	Outdoor dining
16	Outdoor living
17	Elevator
18	Terrace
19	Storeroom
20	Pool
21	Pool deck
22	Entry path
23	Pond
24	Shared terrace
25	Garden
26	Seat
27	Barbecue

215

Sunshine Beach Residences

Tigh na Dobhran

Arduaine, Argyll, Scotland

studioKAP

The site of this single-family dwelling, a rural location on the west coast of Scotland, commands a wonderful aspect southwest across Loch Melfort to the Isle of Shuna, Croabh Haven and beyond. Seen from the water, the site is contained to the left by a small, tree-lined burn and to the right by the dirt road leading down to a massed concrete pier. Curving around the back of the site is the embanked coastal road.

As the location is highly exposed to the open sea-loch, the architect's primary considerations involved developing a strong link between building and landscape. With this in mind, a dialogue was established between house and pier in terms of opposition, orientation, and materials. The beach is a place where the natural and man-made meet—driftwood lodged amongst rock, pier cast over a rocky skerry—and the design of the house overtly recognizes this. Materials are self-finished and durable, responsive to changing light and landscape but also acknowledging local traditions from a non-traditional position, down on the shoreline

In the internal composition, the overriding theme was the resolution of exposure and shelter, namely how to provide the latter without diminishing the former. Both excitement and refuge are provided for and massively thick, creamy walls are played against cool gray windows. Through the plan and sectional composition—conceived as a held bunch of flowers—an inevitable journey toward the sea continues, passing by shady caves and through sunny volumes.

Photography by Keith Hunter

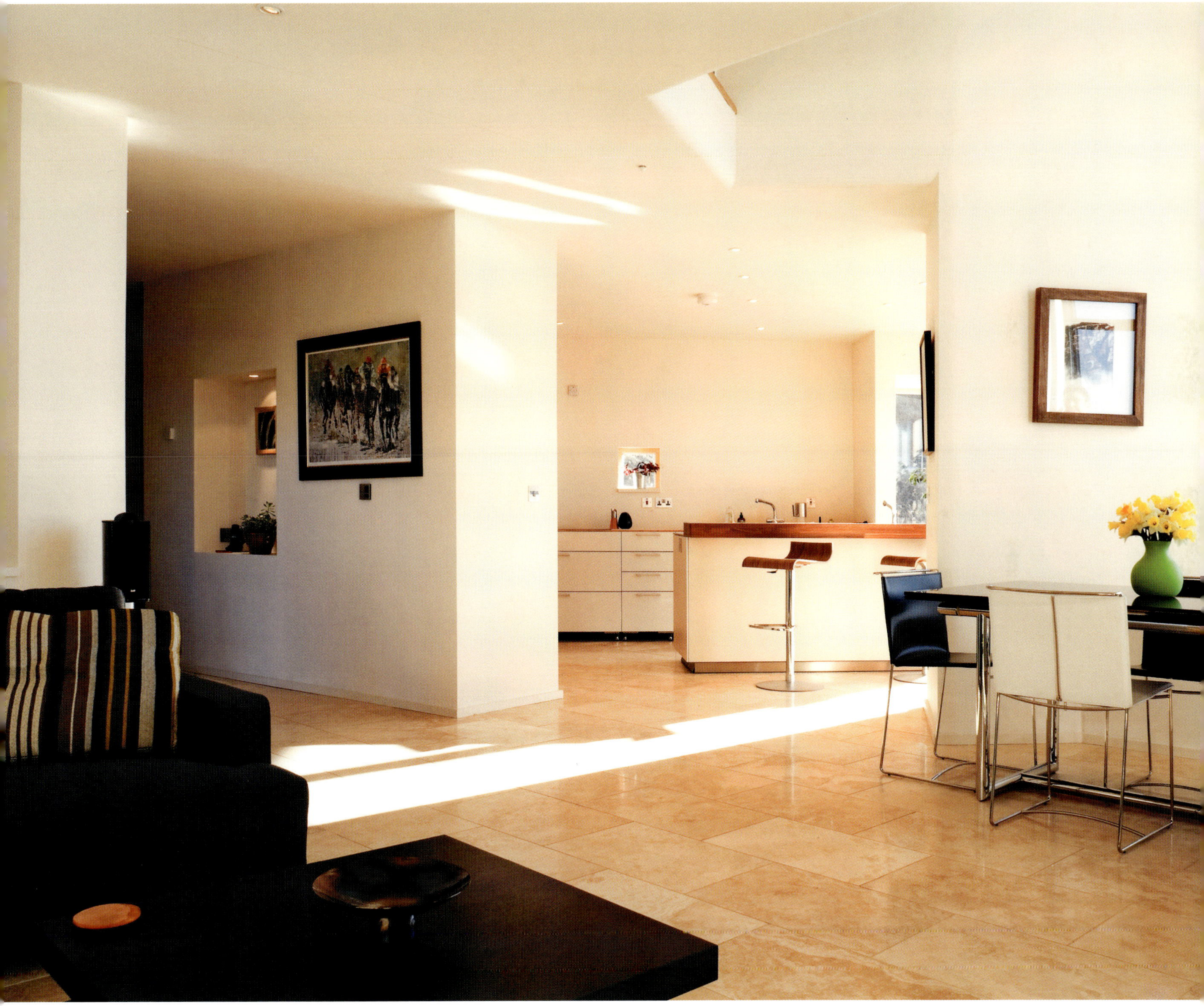

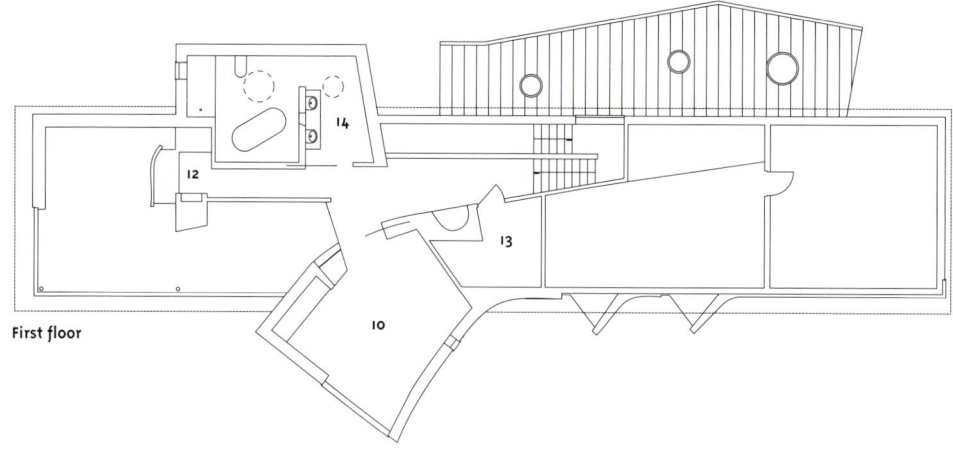

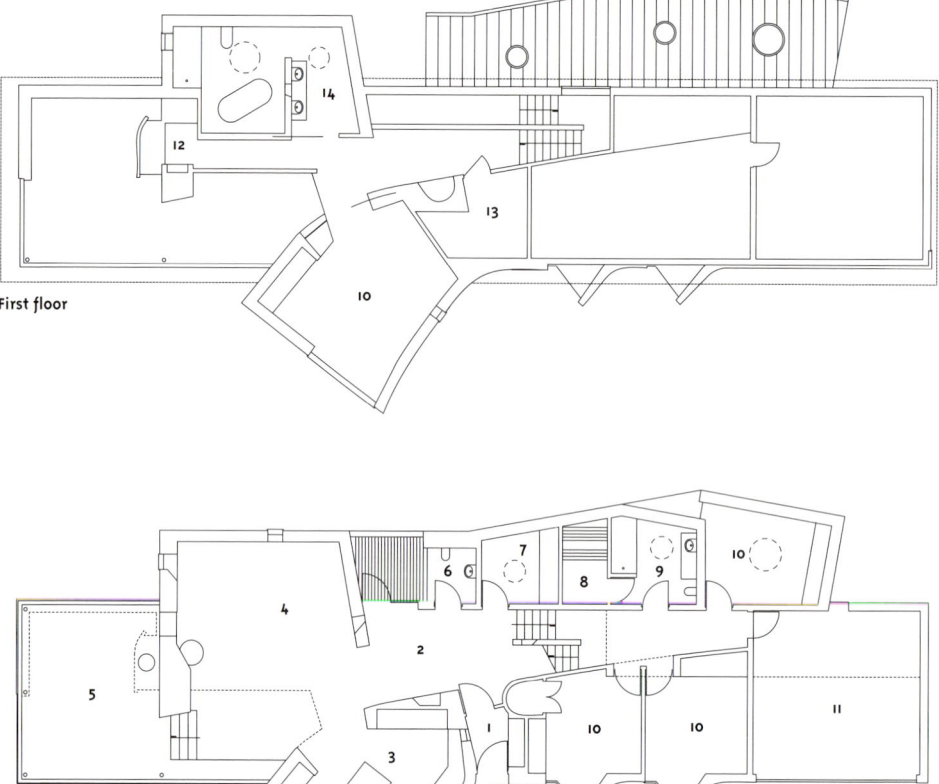

First floor

Ground floor

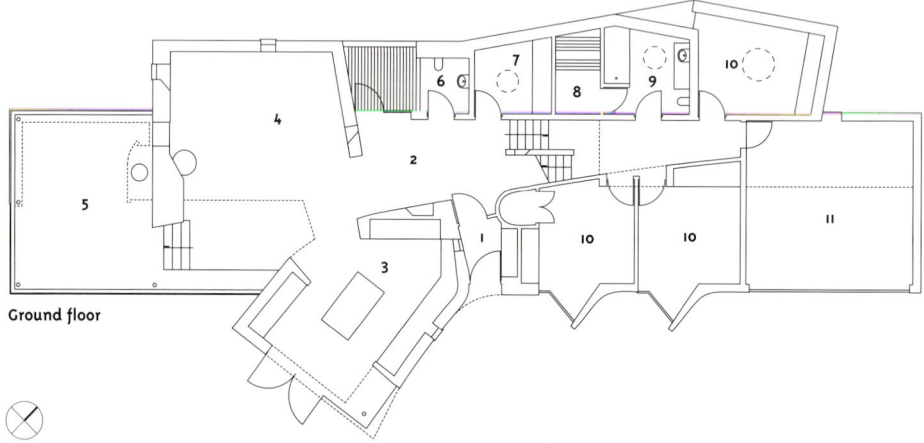

1 Entrance
2 Reception hall
3 Kitchen
4 Main living area
5 Sea room
6 WC
7 Utility
8 Sauna
9 Shower room
10 Bedroom
11 Garage
12 Study
13 Store
14 Bathroom

Tigh na Dobhran

Treehouse

Separation Creek, Victoria, Australia
Jackson Clements Burrows Pty Ltd Architects

This three-bedroom, 2,500-square-foot residence is sited on a steep, forested hillside that enjoys a combination of a bushland setting and intimate coastal views. The steepness of the site, landscape controls, and landslip potential resulted in a design that minimized its footprint by echoing a tree form, with rooms branching and cantilevering in all directions from a central "trunk." Upper-level projections include an entry branch with a study, a sunroom to the west, and a living area and deck that cantilevers 20 feet from the core structure. At a half-level lower, the master bedroom wing springs from the stair, landing into the bush to the east. A dining room and kitchen make up the upper-level core of the building, while two additional bedrooms, a bathroom, and a laundry complete the lower level.

In terms of materials, the house draws on a modest local vernacular of 1950s painted fibro shacks with cement sheet lining and expressed battens over joints. The cement sheet panels used on the house are painted green to help merge the building with the surrounding vegetation, reinforcing its relationship with the landscape. The two tones of green pick up on color variations and light and shade within the bush, and effectively reduce the mass of the object within the landscape. Varying light intensities across the course of the day further affect the colors and, consequently, the building's relationship with its environment in an engaging and dynamic manner. The vertical timber battens on the building are a naturally stained timber, which will gray over time like the branches and trunks of trees in the surrounding bushland.

Photography by John Gollings

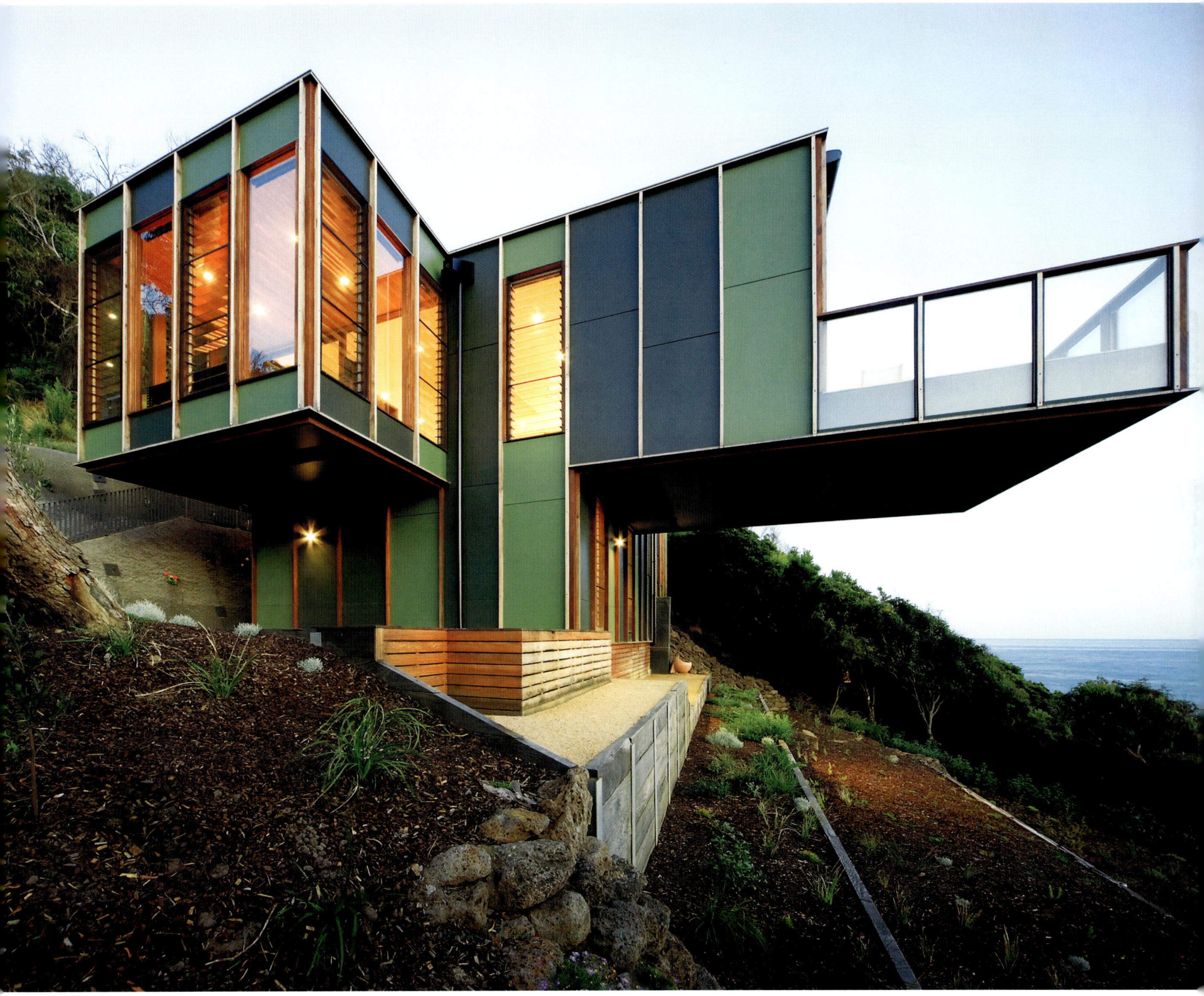

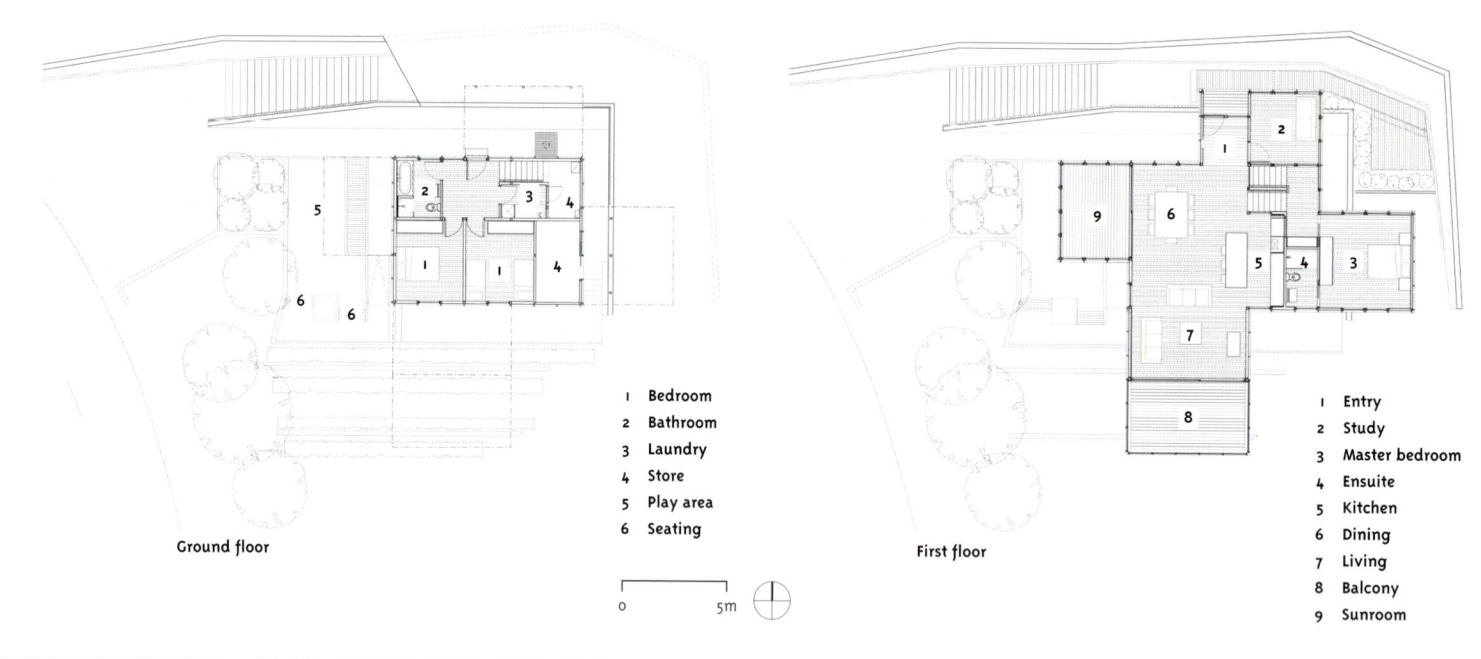

Ground floor

First floor

0   5m

1	Bedroom
2	Bathroom
3	Laundry
4	Store
5	Play area
6	Seating

1	Entry
2	Study
3	Master bedroom
4	Ensuite
5	Kitchen
6	Dining
7	Living
8	Balcony
9	Sunroom

Treehouse

Truro Residence

Cape Cod, Massachusetts, USA
ZeroEnergy Design

This modern, high-performance house, situated on a coastal bank 115 feet above the surrounding bay, was constructed using environmentally sound principles. The design conserves water use, features native landscaping, and sources nearly 75 percent of its energy from renewable sources, including a roof-mounted solar array.

The two shifting volumes of the house appear to drift within the coastal topography, each form expanding toward the ocean. The glazing asymmetrically wraps and exposes the corner of the interior living space, bringing in light and capturing the majestic ocean view. The tapered roof plane slopes up and out toward the view, drawing the eye outside while the glazing draws the horizon in, inviting the ocean to complete the dynamic fourth wall of the space.

These two primary volumes accommodate extreme fluctuations in seasonal occupancy. The living bar comprises the kitchen, living, and dining areas, a large outdoor decking area, and a guest suite—everything needed for a couple's weekend trips. The sleeping bar can accommodate up to 20 people and can be decommissioned to conserve energy when vacant, effectively halving the size of the house. The house features a super insulated building envelope, durable finishes inside and out, geothermal heating and cooling system, radiant heating, a solar electric system, and fresh air ventilation, which ensures healthy indoor air quality.

Photography by Eric Roth

225

Upper level

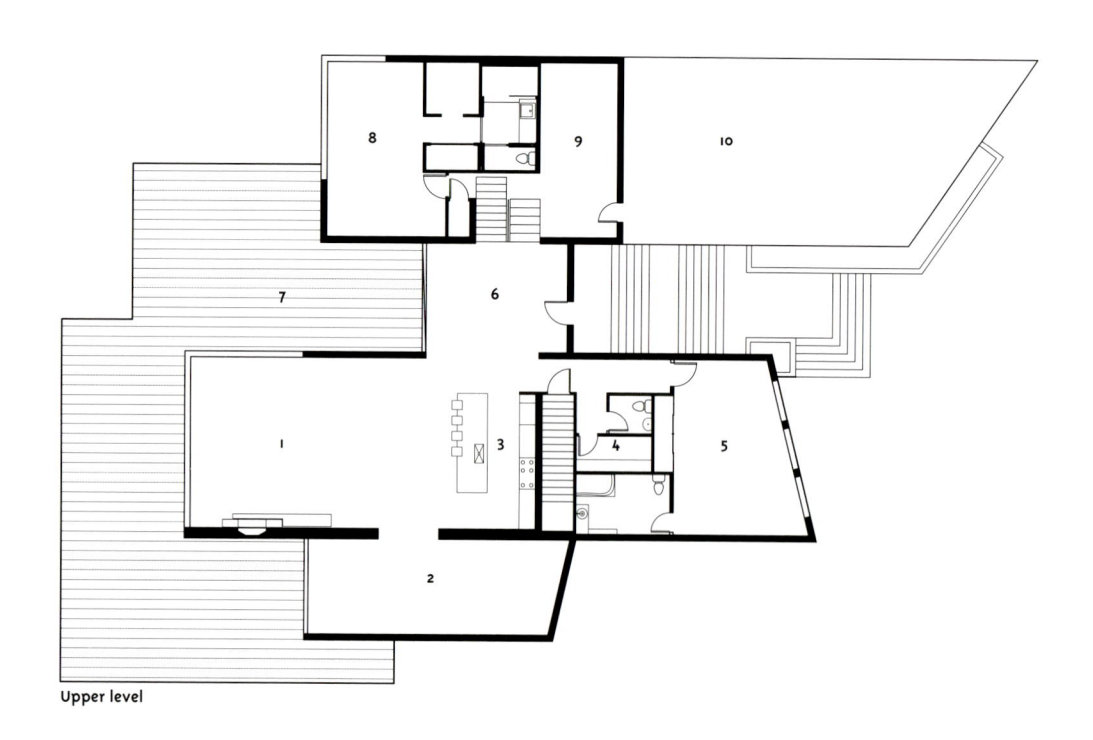

1 Living
2 Dining
3 Kitchen
4 Laundry
5 Guest suite
6 Foyer
7 Outdoor deck
8 Master suite
9 Study
10 Mechanical/attic
11 Bedroom
12 Mechanical room
13 Media room
14 Gym
15 Garage

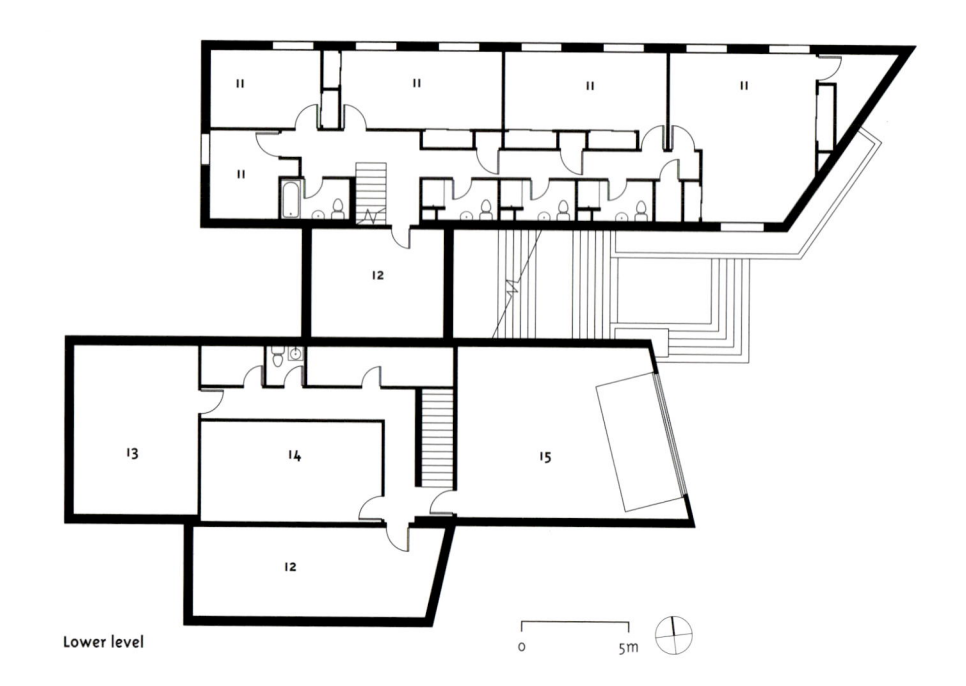

Lower level

0   5m

Truro Residence

Tuckeroo Residence

Byron Bay, New South Wales, Australia
Paul Uhlmann Architects

This beachfront project was designed as a holiday residence for five families. The structure operates on both private and communal levels to allow different families to use the residence at the same time. The scheme comprises a series of individual pavilions connected by a communal deck. The single-story beachfront pavilion contains the communal facilities, which open onto the adjacent pool and lawn areas. The street-front pavilions contain private sleeping and bathing spaces. Both pavilions were designed as double-story pods to facilitate views to the ocean and heighten a sense of privacy for individual families. The resort-like quality of the project is achieved through the pod-like building that requires circulation via the communal deck to access the living spaces and bedroom pavilions.

The scheme's formal approach led to a careful exploration of the spaces between the pavilions, which became decks, entry pathways, and private courtyards. The central communal deck links all pavilions and its fire-retardant screen doors can be closed down, resulting in a room protected from strong winds while remaining open to the sky above. These screen doors fully retract and disappear into the wall cavities, while a screen roof protects the house from embers in case of busfire.

Copper sheet external cladding, Australian hardwood timber, and cement sheet were selected to protect the house and its residents from potential bushfires. Spotted gum was used extensively, wrapping from exterior surfaces to the inside joinery details. Locally sourced basalt and marble helped to enrich the interior canvas, creating an earthy quality connecting the building to its surrounding environment.

Photography by David Sandison

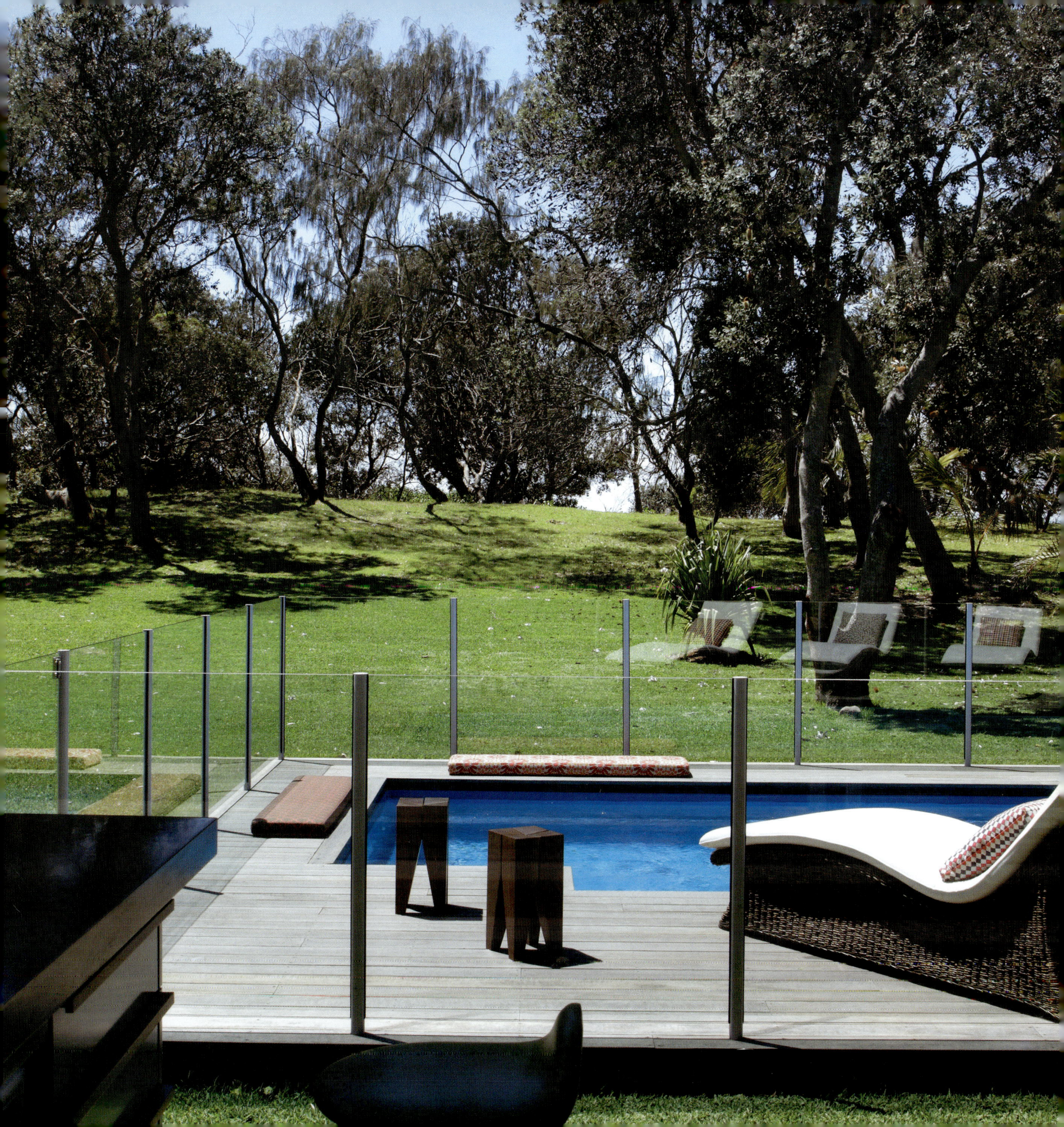

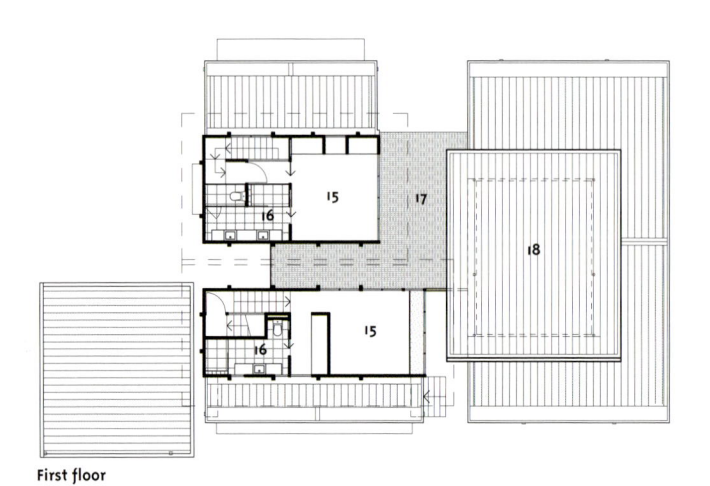

1 Entry
2 Deck
3 Communal deck
4 Living
5 Dining
6 Kitchen
7 Family room
8 Bathroom
9 Sauna
10 Laundry
11 Bunkroom
12 Bedroom
13 Courtyard
14 Pool
15 Master bedroom
16 Ensuite
17 Open pergola below
18 Living pavilion below
19 Carport

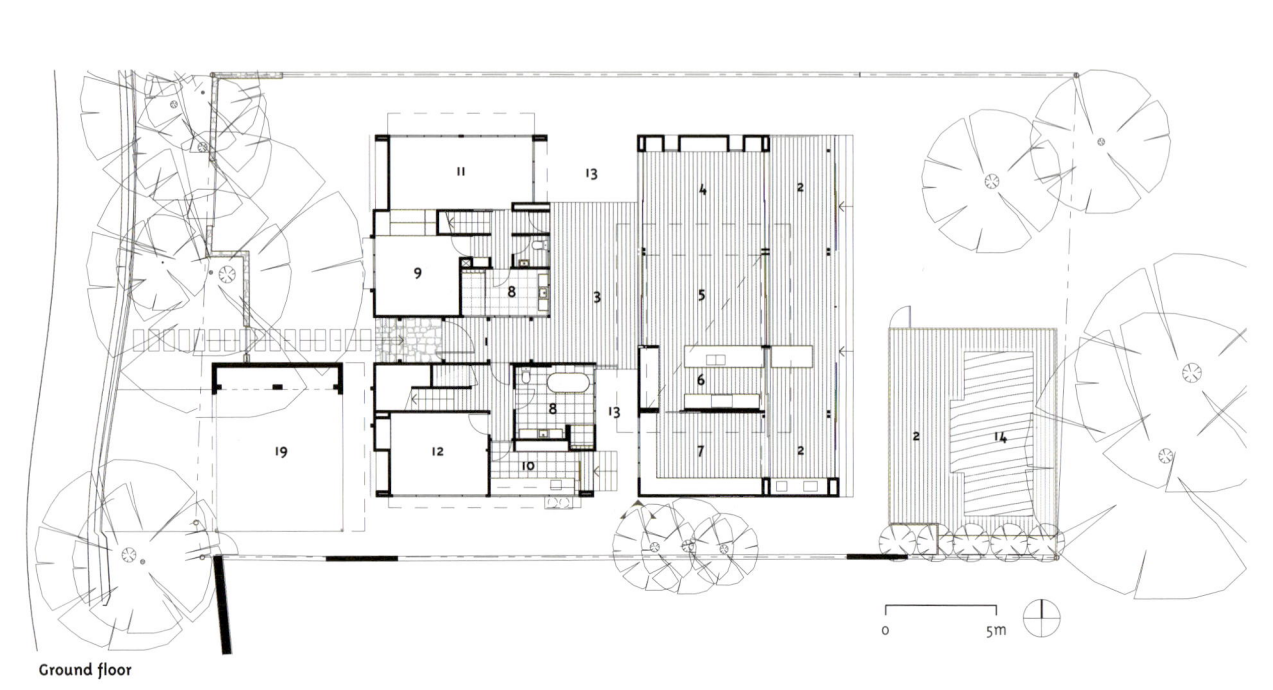

First floor

Ground floor

0 5m

Tuckeroo Residence

Villa Shambhala

Providenciales, Turks and Caicos Islands
RAD Architecture, Inc.

Located on the east coast of Providenciales, this 7,500-square-foot Barbadian-style beachfront vacation villa sits on a 2-acre beachfront lot. Interior and exterior spaces flow seamlessly into one another to create a magical indoor–outdoor beach living experience.

The architect's aim was to create a home where a couple, family, or group could be equally comfortable. The design includes large, open spaces for large groups to congregate, but equal attention was also given to smaller, more private areas for individuals or couples to enjoy solitude throughout the day. This was achieved by creating four separate pods of living areas, securely linked through open-air travertine galleries. These elegant covered halls feature traditional floor-to-ceiling aqua-colored wrought-iron gates and Tuscan columns entwined with night blooming jasmine and stephanotis from the bordering gardens.

Three of the four pods contain four bedrooms and the other central pod houses the kitchen, great room, and library on the upper level and an additional bedroom, games room, laundry, and cistern on the lower level. The main master bedroom pod sits atop the two-car garage and pool pump room. Each of the upper bedrooms overlooks the infinity-edge pool to the crystal clear azure waters of the Caicos Bank.

Photography by www.provopictures.com

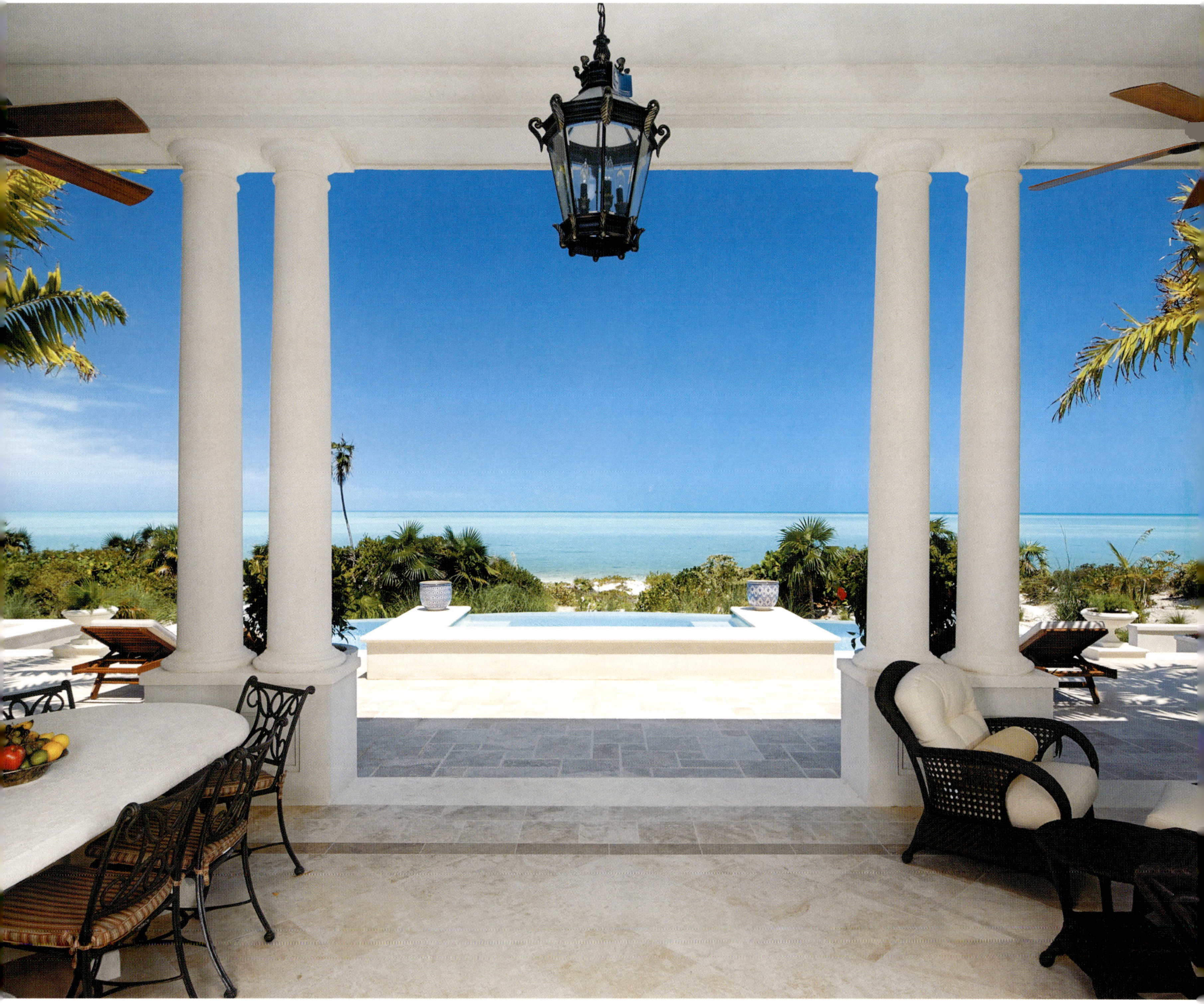

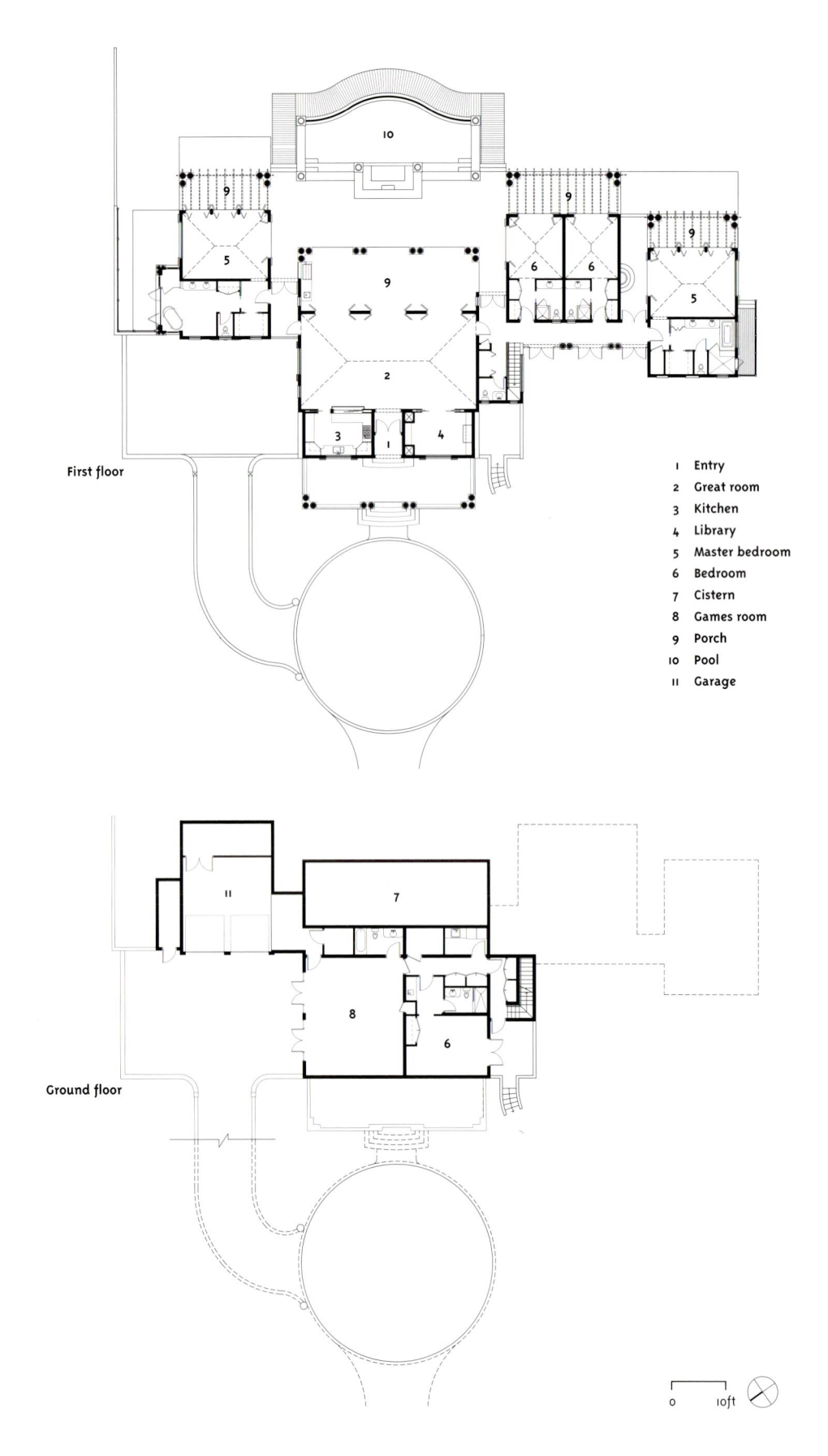

First floor

Ground floor

1 Entry
2 Great room
3 Kitchen
4 Library
5 Master bedroom
6 Bedroom
7 Cistern
8 Games room
9 Porch
10 Pool
11 Garage

0 10ft

Villa Shambhala

Villa Surgawi

Candi Dasa, Bali, Indonesia

Graham Jones Design/Manguning Architects

A 10-foot-high stone wall is all that separates the stunning Villa Surgawi from the ocean on Bali's central east coast. Located at the end of a beach shared by local fishermen and holidaymakers, this minimalist contemporary villa is a structure at one with the sea. The magnificent coastal scenery of islands, palm trees, and beaches seems almost to envelop the home. This connection is particularly evident in the large timber deck straddling the swimming pool that cantilevers out over the sea wall beyond the boundary of the property.

This private residence comprises two separate pavilions, staff quarters, and a guest cottage. A master suite and home office are positioned in a gabled roof pavilion on a flat section of the site, excavated for the pool and outdoor entertaining area. An internal stair provides access up into the main pavilion, which houses the kitchen, dining, and living areas. On the upper floor the pavilion opens out to a balcony overlooking the ocean to the west, and timber decks at ground level open to the south. The building protects these decks from the occasionally harsh coastal climate, yet the transparent design ensures the views are uncompromised. A tropical garden at the front of the villa leads via white palimanan stone steps to a solid timber gate at the street-level property entry.

Photography by Gali Gali

237

Bedroom pavilion

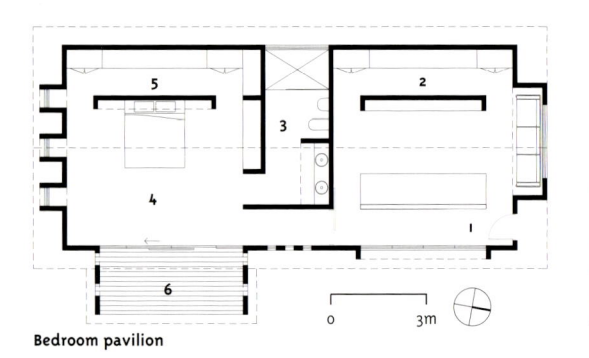

1. Entry
2. Office
3. Ensuite
4. Master bedroom
5. Walk-in-robe
6. Deck

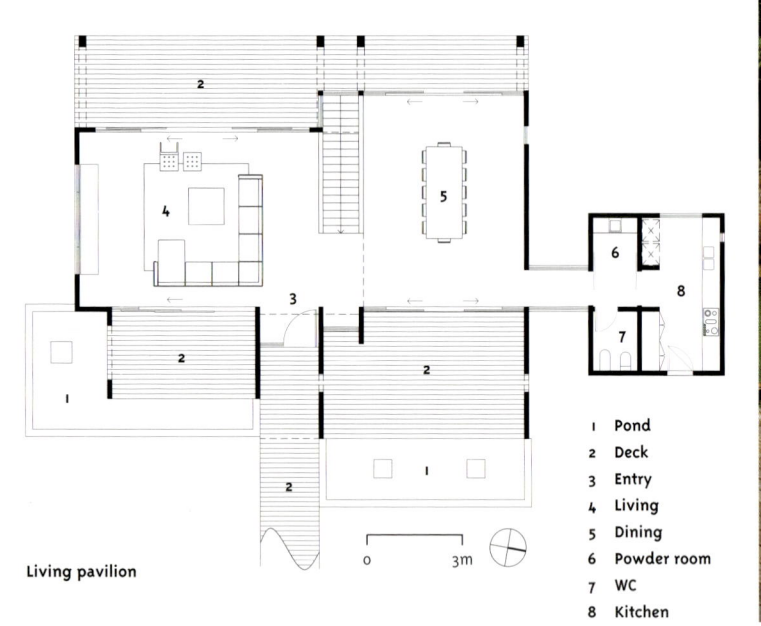

Living pavilion

1. Pond
2. Deck
3. Entry
4. Living
5. Dining
6. Powder room
7. WC
8. Kitchen

239

Villa Surgawi

Waimarama House

Waimarama, Hawke's Bay, New Zealand
Herriot + Melhuish: Architecture Ltd

Positioned on a narrow site overlooking the beach and fronting the Waimarama domain, this four-bedroom family residence is designed to be relocated if the need arises. The house is a simple composition of two interlocking volumes: a white single-story bedroom wing, loosely derived from the planning of shearers' quarters, inserted obliquely into a double-story "timber crate." The architect extended, layered, and truncated these two forms in response to the site, views, sun, and program. The resultant north-facing courtyard not only leads to the front door but also provides outdoor family space strongly connected to the house and sheltered from the afternoon sea breezes.

Visual connection right through the house, linking the beach to the courtyard, was a key element of the design. In the main bedroom upstairs, the architect ensured that the full drama of sunrise and the expansive views from Cape Kidnappers to Bare Island would be captured. On the exterior, the composition of oiled cedar weatherboards, painted plywood, and weathered zinc sheet clearly sets the house apart from its neighbors, but also connects the house to the rugged Hawke's Bay landscape.

Photography by Richard Brimer, Simon Devitt

241

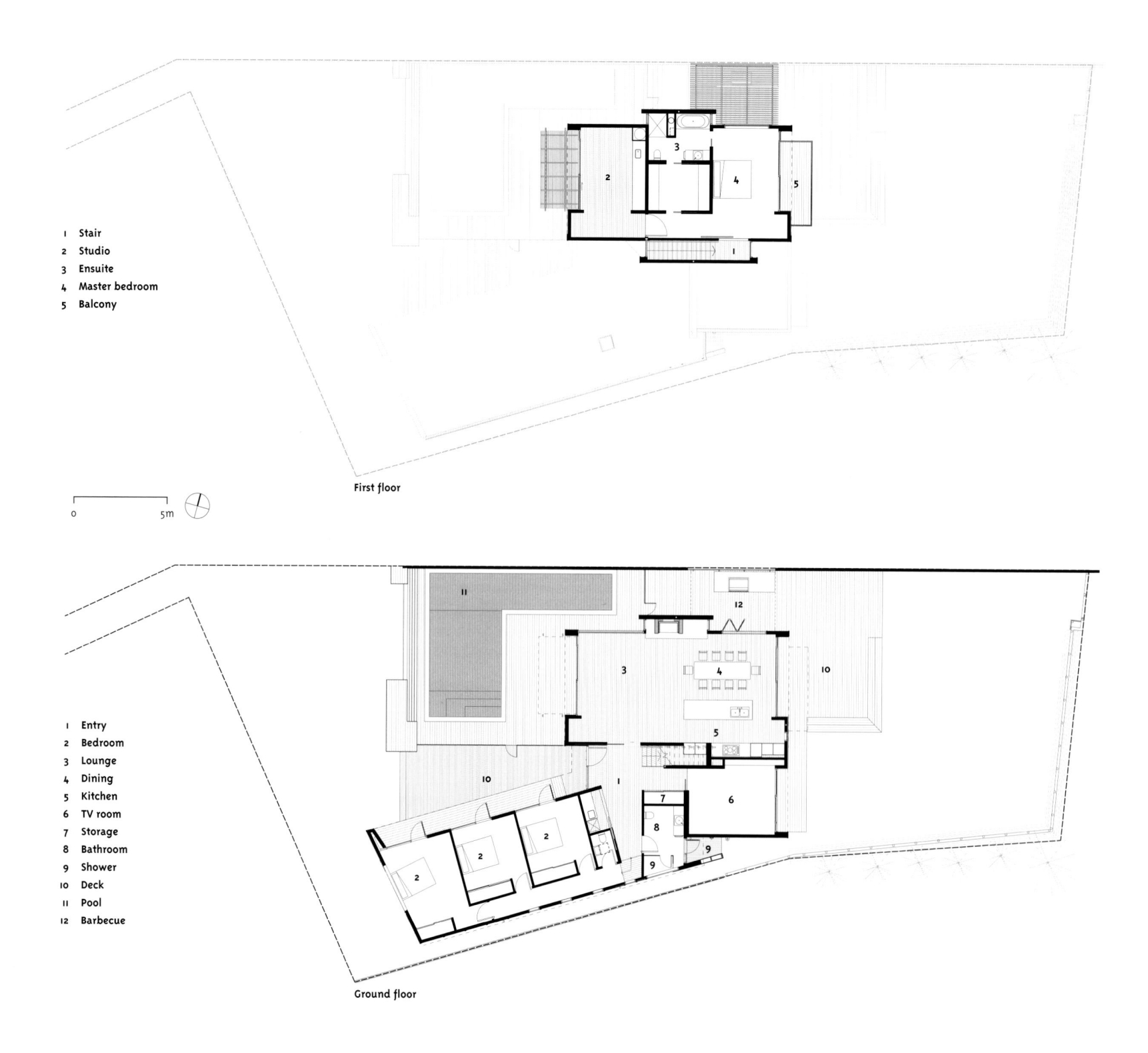

1 Stair
2 Studio
3 Ensuite
4 Master bedroom
5 Balcony

First floor

0 5m

1 Entry
2 Bedroom
3 Lounge
4 Dining
5 Kitchen
6 TV room
7 Storage
8 Bathroom
9 Shower
10 Deck
11 Pool
12 Barbecue

Ground floor

Waimarama House

Wallace Marshall House

Tahunanui Beach, Nelson, New Zealand
Arthouse Architecture Ltd.

This house encourages a casual, beach lifestyle and was built to allow a relaxed holiday style of living to permeate day-to-day domestic functions. Sited on the hillside, directly across the road from the beach and only ten minutes from the center of town, the house comprises three separate elements—a lower level space for older children and guests, a main living area that opens on to a large deck above the lower level, and a bedroom wing.

Approaching from the beach, three flights of stairs lead up past the garage and outside shower to the bright green front door. The entry and stairs link the three structural elements and accentuate the kink in the plan at the top, where the dominant single-pitched living area twists to face north. The consequent off-square deck, providing generous outdoor living, is oriented toward the beach and across to the western ranges, offering magnificent views.

The low profile and dark-stained exterior of this house belies a spacious and comfortable interior. High windows allow light to flood deep inside the house, where white walls contrast with rich timber, tiles, and polished concrete floors. The house is designed to maximize solar gain in winter with high levels of insulation, while deep overhangs were incorporated to moderate the heat of the summer sun.

Photography by Simon Devitt

245

1 Kitchen
2 Dining room
3 Living room
4 Bedroom
5 Bathroom
6 Laundry
7 Deck
8 Garage
9 Entry below

Wallace Marshall House

Wamberal Beach House

Wamberal, New South Wales, Australia
Virginia Kerridge Architect

Designed as a series of pavilion-like roof forms, this three-level family residence steps down the hilly site and affords 180-degree views over the beach and adjacent lagoon. The design of the house is based on the spiral shape found in nature. The rooms are designed in a cluster that wraps around the garden area and uses the various garden areas as focal points. On the top level, a master bedroom opens out to a large deck offering stunning coastal views. The open-plan living, dining, and kitchen areas are located on the ground floor; the outdoor area comprises decking and a swimming pool. A second bedroom is situated at the western end of this level, with three additional bedrooms and a media room located on the lower ground floor.

Throughout the house, principles of open and closed space—notions of compression and expansion—are explored, with overlapping perspectives arising in different areas of the structure. The entry offers a sense of compression, which contrasts to open areas connected with an introspective garden and a more open area that connects with the overall sense of the place and the expansive nature of the beach. This design of the house integrates it with the neighboring buildings and also provided large indentations in the structure that are used as garden spaces.

Sustainable design features of the house include the use of large, shaded areas of north-facing glass and natural ventilation. The house "breathes" through the use of large sliding doors that can be open and closed, and there is also a large, glass-louvered wall adjacent to the stairs that assists with ventilation on all three levels.

Photography by Brett Boardman

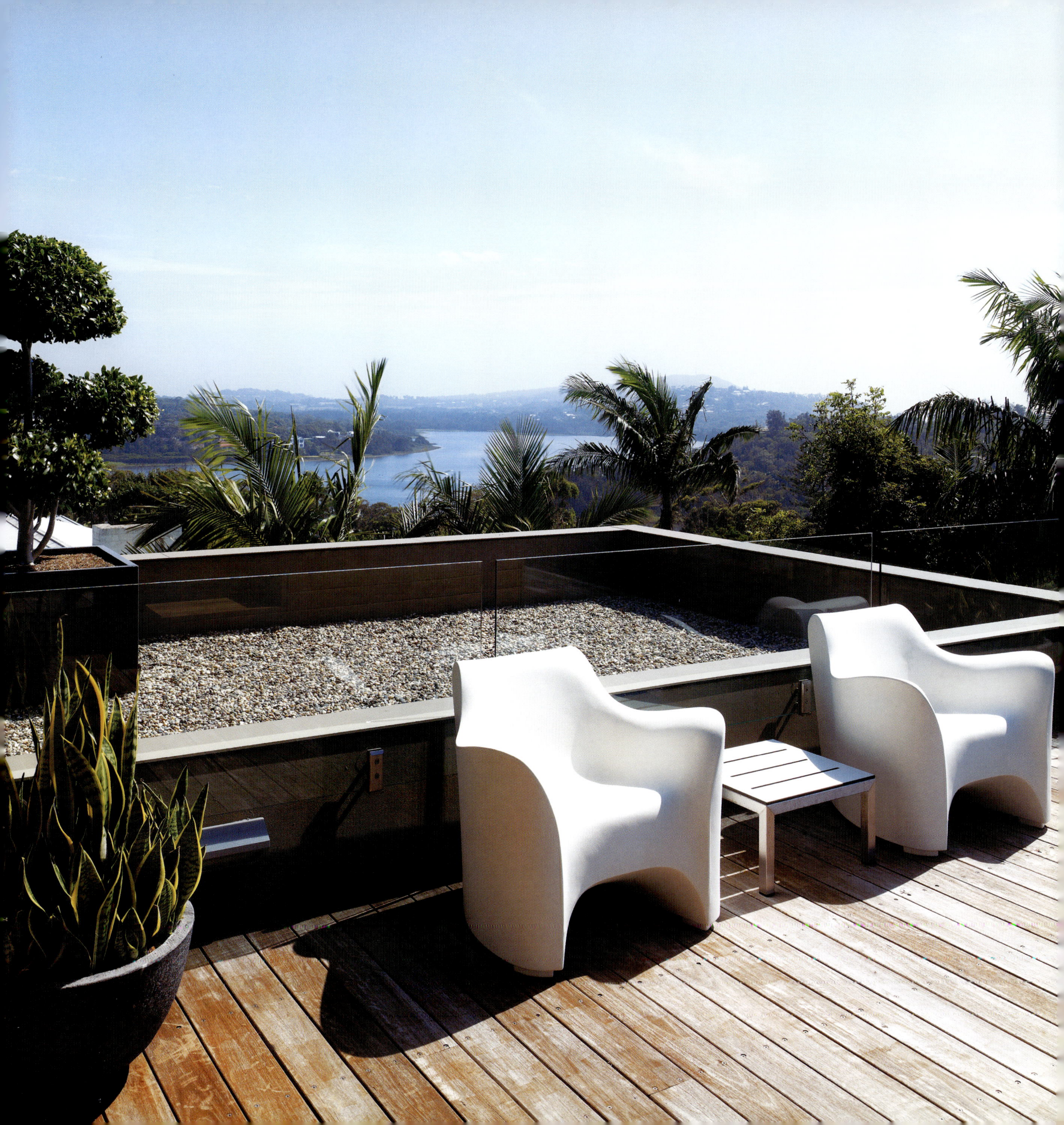

250

First floor

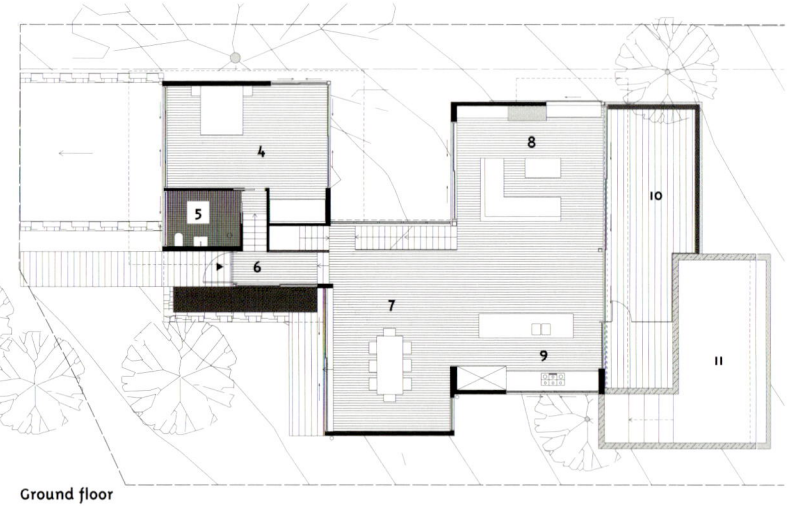

Ground floor

Lower ground floor

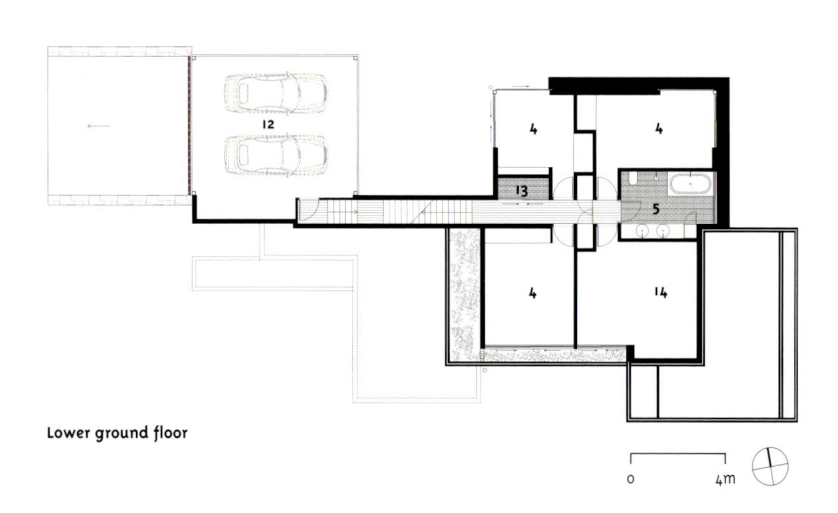

0   4m

1	Ensuite	8	Living
2	Master bedroom	9	Kitchen
3	Deck	10	Deck
4	Bedroom	11	Pool
5	Bathroom	12	Garage
6	Entry	13	Laundry
7	Dining	14	Media room

Wamberal Beach House

Whale Beach House

Sydney, New South Wales, Australia
Cullen Feng

This three-level residence was designed for a retired couple who needed to accommodate their extended family while also providing for their future accessibility requirements. The trapezoidal site is accessed from a private road at the rear and descends 36 feet on the north elevation.

Situated at the top of the southern hill overlooking Whale Beach, the design consists of three overlapping, offset rectangular volumes linked via a wide travertine staircase. The entry vestibule has a frameless glass skylight that floods the stair below with natural light. The magnificent view is anticipated via a horizontal slot in the vestibule and the compression of the walled staircase.

Each level of the house opens up to a northern terrace. The upper level consists of a master suite that can be secured independently from the rest of the house; the middle level comprises the living, dining, and kitchen areas, plus ancillary spaces; and the lower level incorporates bedrooms, a media room, and bathrooms. This lower level opens to a deck that features an offset, cantilevered lap pool with a dramatic glass end that juts out over the bouldered landscape.

Photography by Eric Sierins

253

1 Atrium/entry
2 Living
3 Kitchenette
4 Study
5 Master bedroom
6 Japanese bath
7 Robe
8 Ensuite
9 Stair
10 Deck
11 Garage
12 Porte cochère

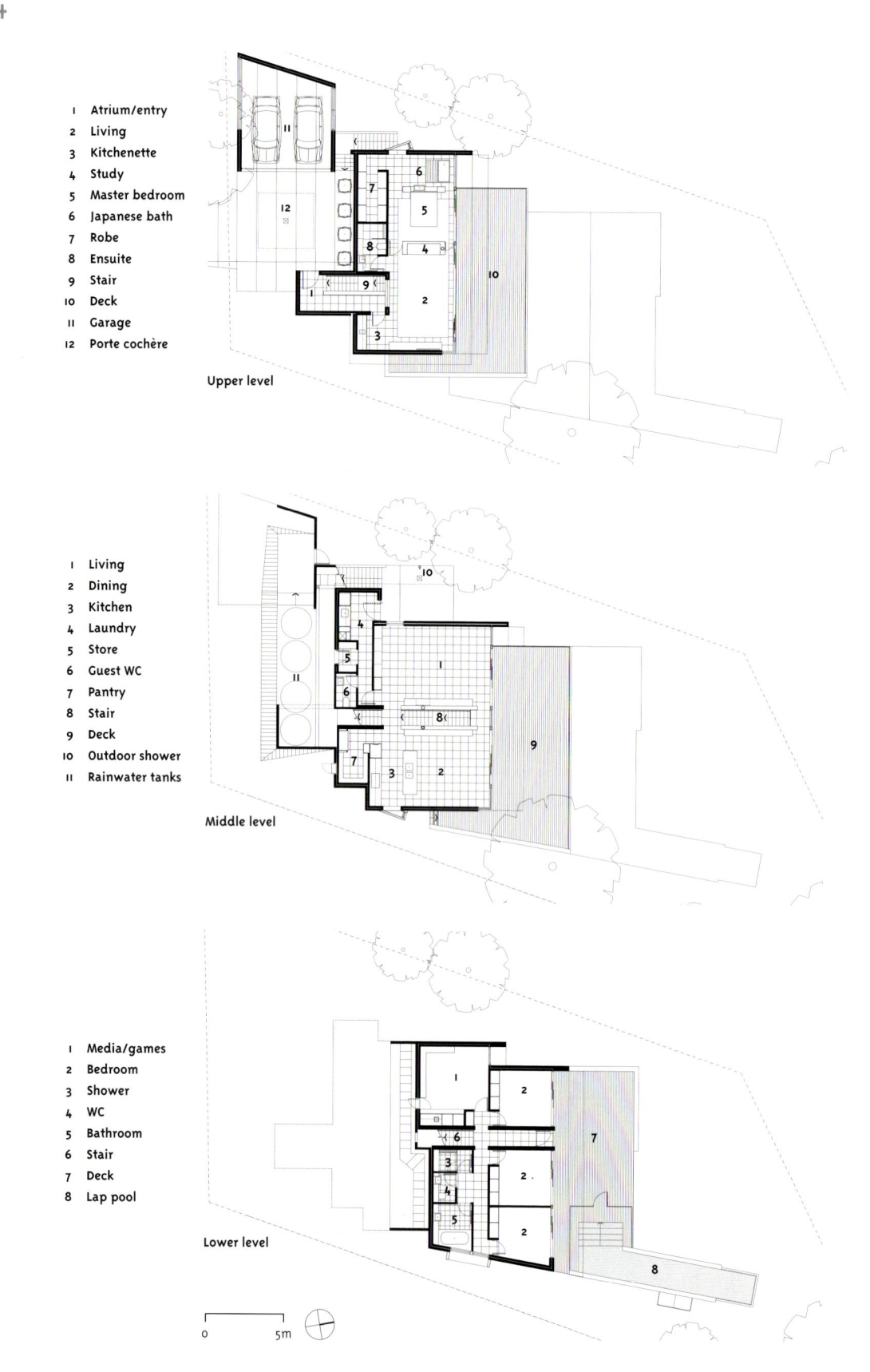

Upper level

1 Living
2 Dining
3 Kitchen
4 Laundry
5 Store
6 Guest WC
7 Pantry
8 Stair
9 Deck
10 Outdoor shower
11 Rainwater tanks

Middle level

1 Media/games
2 Bedroom
3 Shower
4 WC
5 Bathroom
6 Stair
7 Deck
8 Lap pool

Lower level

0   5m

Whale Beach House

Zeidler House

Aptos, California, USA
Ehrlich Architects

Located on the bluffs overlooking the Pacific Ocean, this 3,500-square-foot beach house arranges interior and exterior living spaces to maximize views, natural light, and ocean breezes within a subtle, sophisticated material palette. Designed for a retired couple with grown children, the house sits on a relatively flat corner lot with expansive views of the ocean and a vegetated cliff that leads from the site down to the beach.

The parti divides the program into two main structures connected by a sheltered courtyard. On the ocean side, the two-and-a-half-story main house features a double-height living space, with full-height glass doors that open the interior onto the exterior spaces. A mezzanine is oriented toward the view. At the end of the stair tower, a roof deck accommodates various entertaining configurations and provides strong connections to the landscape and views beyond. The front yard incorporates an area in which to play pétanque, a favorite pastime of the client.

The rear structure accommodates separate living quarters for friends and family in three oversized bedrooms. The second-level studio has a full kitchen and expansive deck with views toward the ocean. The two primary structures frame a landscaped courtyard with a lap pool and built-in barbecue that, when opened to the elements, form a complex of open-air pavilions connected through the landscape. A trellis with overhead panels covers a walkway from the main house to the guesthouse. A minimal palette ties the entire composition together and includes steel-troweled stucco, exposed concrete block, and Rheinzink.

Photography by Matthew Millman

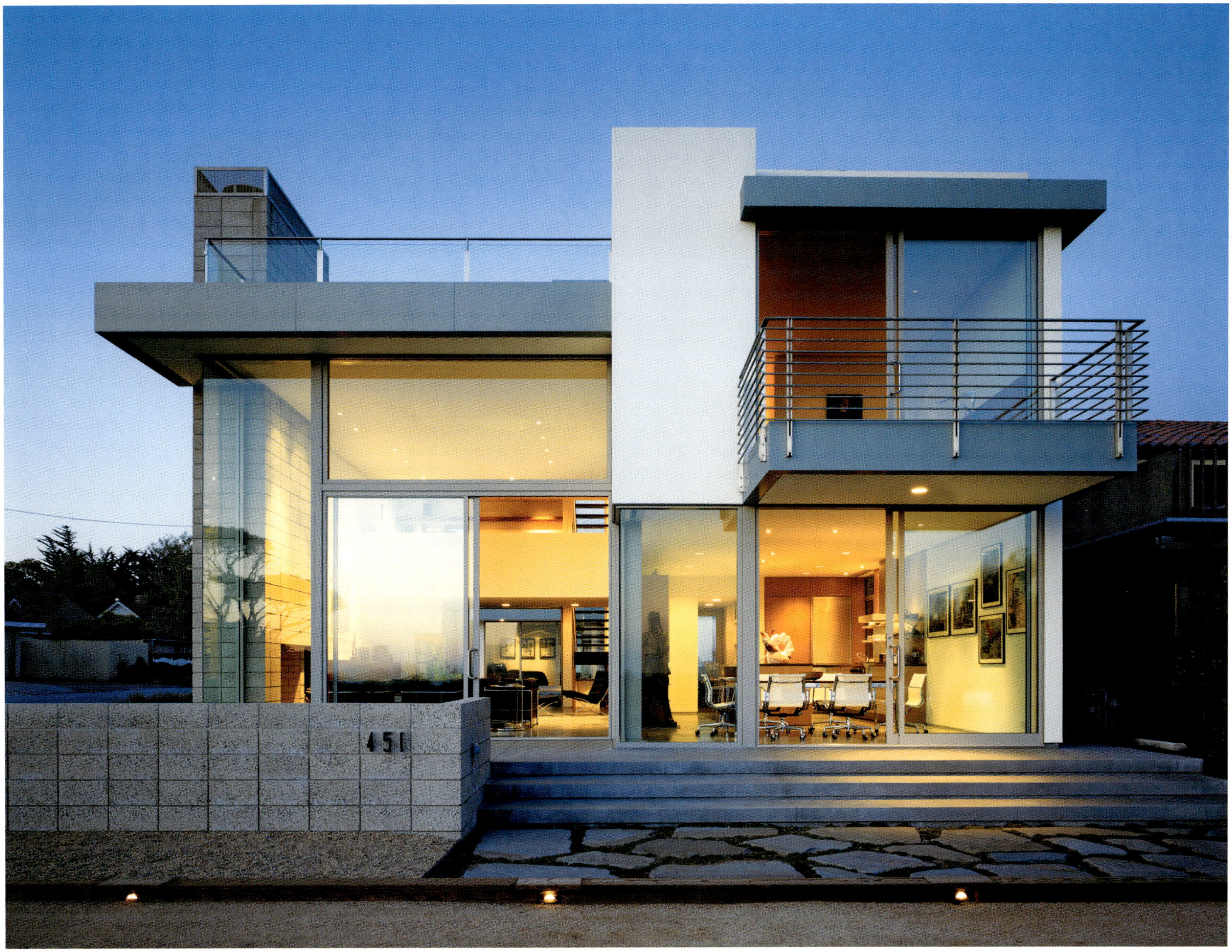
451

258

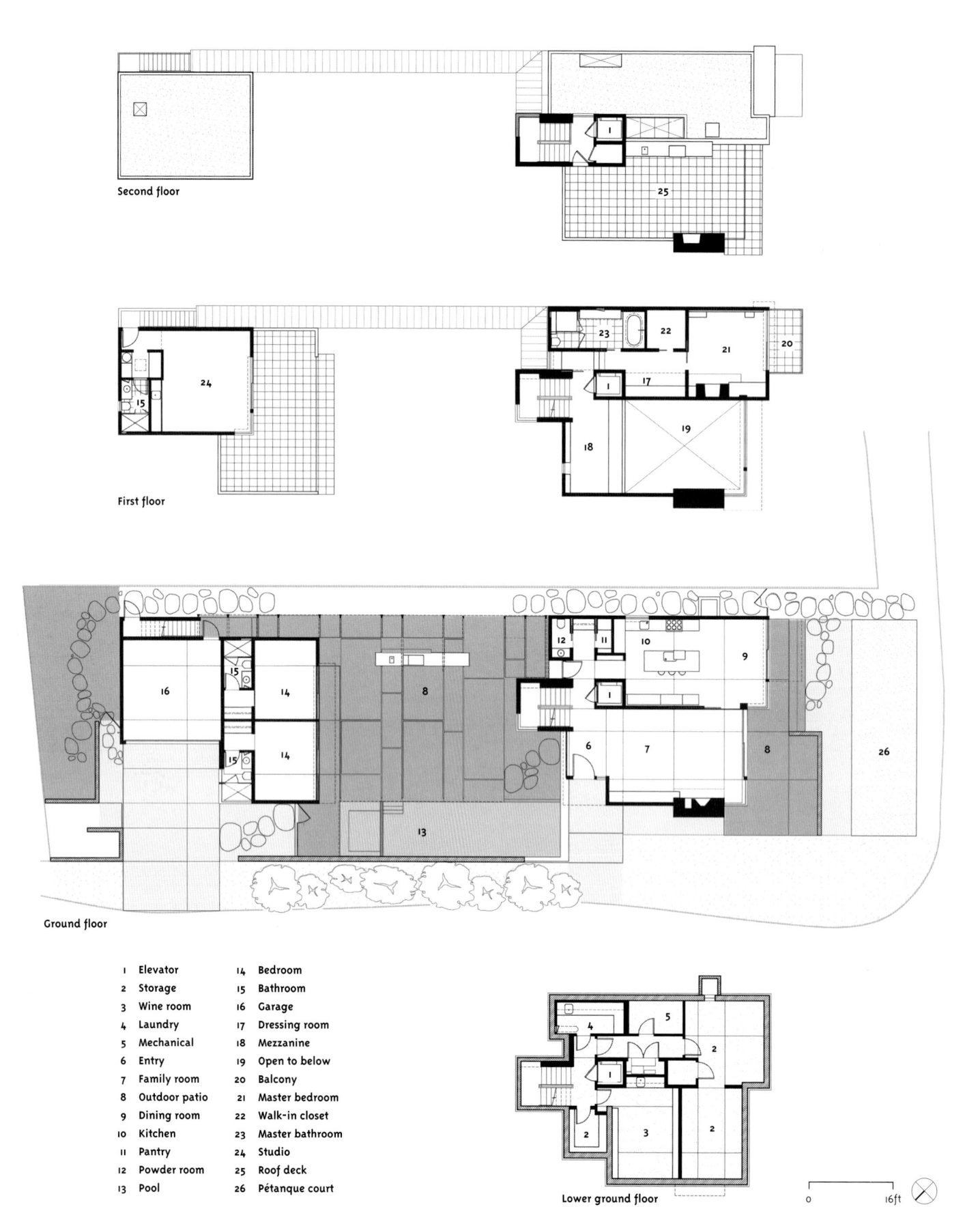

Second floor

First floor

Ground floor

1	Elevator	14	Bedroom
2	Storage	15	Bathroom
3	Wine room	16	Garage
4	Laundry	17	Dressing room
5	Mechanical	18	Mezzanine
6	Entry	19	Open to below
7	Family room	20	Balcony
8	Outdoor patio	21	Master bedroom
9	Dining room	22	Walk-in closet
10	Kitchen	23	Master bathroom
11	Pantry	24	Studio
12	Powder room	25	Roof deck
13	Pool	26	Pétanque court

Lower ground floor

0 — 16ft

Zeidler House

Index

1 + 2 Architecture, 56
1plus2architecture.com

Alexander Gorlin Architects, 196
gorlinarchitects.com

Alexandros N. Tombazis and Associates Architects Ltd, 148
meletitiki.gr

Andrew Maynard Architects, 24
maynardarchitects.com

Architects Ink, 92
architectsink.com.au

Arthouse Architecture Ltd., 244
arthousearchitecture.co.nz

Bark Design Architects, 212
barkdesign.com.au

Base Architecture, 188
basearchitecture.com.au

Bernades Jacobsen Arquitetura, 96
bjaweb.com.br

BGD Architects, 20
bgdarchitects.com

Brian van der Plaat Design, 176
bvdp.com.au

Bromley Caldari Architects, 128
bromleycaldari.com

Chenchow Little Pty Ltd, 76
chenchowlittle.com

Cullen Feng, 252
cullenfeng.com.au

Cullinan Ivanov Partnership, 120
cipartnership.com

Damien Murtagh Architects, 160
dmurtagh.com

Eggleston Farkas Architects, 184
eggfarkarch.com

Ehrlich Architects, 256
s-ehrlich.com

Emma Mitchell Architects, 28
emmamitchell.com.au

Estes/Twombly Architects, 204
estestwombly.com

F2 Architecture, 192
f2architecture.com.au

Gabbiani & Associati, 16
gabbianieassociati.it

Girvin Associates and Manolo Mestre, 140
girvinassoc.net

Godward Guthrie Architecture, 100
gga.co.nz

Graham Jones Design, 116, 132, 236
grahamjonesdesign.com.au

Griffin Enright Architects, 164
griffinenrightarchitects.com

Hammer Architects, 40
hammerarchitects.com

Helliwell + Smith: Blue Sky Architecture, 68
blueskyarchitecture.com

Herriot + Melhuish: Architecture Ltd, 168, 240
hma.net.nz

Jackson Clements Burrows Pty Ltd Architects, 220
jcba.com.au

Jolson, 200
jolson.com.au

KAA Design Group, 84
kaadesigngroup.com

Leon Meyer Architects, 44
leonmeyer.com.au

Longhi Architects, 104
longhiarchitect.com

Manguning Architects, 236
manguning.com

Max Pritchard Architect, 72, 180
maxpritchardarchitect.com.au

Middap Ditchfield Architects, 12, 80, 152
madarc.com.au

Obie G. Bowman, 60
obiebowman.com

Olson Kundig Architects, 124
oskaarchitects.com

Paul Uhlmann Architects, 64, 144, 228
pua.com.au

Pleysier Perkins, 156
pleysierperkins.com

R&D Architects, 8
rd-arch.net

RAD Architecture, Inc., 232
radmiami.com

Rolf Ockert Design, 172
rodesign.com.au

Seeley Architects, 88
seeleyarchitects.com.au

SJB Architects, 48
sjb.com.au

Stelle Architects, 36
stelleco.com

Stevens Lawson Architects Ltd, 136
stevenslawson.co.nz

studioKAP, 216
studiokap.com

Techne Architects, 108
ateliertechne.com.au

Ulloa Davet + Ding, 112
ulloadavet@yahoo.com

Virginia Kerridge Architect, 248
vk.com.au

watson architecture + design, 32
watsonarchitecture.com

Wilson Architecture, 208
wilsonarchitects.com.au

Wolveridge Architects, 52
wolveridge.com.au

ZeroEnergy Design, 224
ZeroEnergy.com

Every effort has been made to trace the original source of copyright material contained in this book. The publishers would be pleased to hear from copyright holders to rectify any errors or omissions. The information and illustrations in this publication have been prepared and supplied by the contributors. While all reasonable efforts have been made to ensure accuracy, the publishers do not, under any circumstances, accept responsibility for errors, omissions and representations express or implied.